David Dickson

The Psalms of David in Metre

With the Annotations of the Rev. David Dickson ..

David Dickson

The Psalms of David in Metre
With the Annotations of the Rev. David Dickson ..

ISBN/EAN: 9783744784948

Printed in Europe, USA, Canada, Australia, Japan

Cover: Foto ©Lupo / pixelio.de

More available books at **www.hansebooks.com**

PSALMS OF DAVID

In METR

WITH THE

ANNOTATIONS

OF

The Rev. DAVID DICKSON,
PROFESSOR of DIVINITY
In the College of EDINBURGH.

GLASGOW:

PRINTED BY J. AND J. DUNCAN, 1788.

THE PSALMS OF DAVID.

PSALM I.

This Psalm teacheth, That no ungodly man is blessed, but the godly man only, ver. 1, 2. which is proved by three reasons: The first, because God doth bless the godly even in this life with grace to bring forth good works profitable to themselves and others, in every state of life, ver. 3. But all that the wicked do for making themselves happy, shall be blasted, and found to be mere vanity, ver. 4. Another reason is, because after this life the wicked shall be secluded from the presence of God, and society of the godly at the Day of Judgment, ver. 5. The third reason, confirming both the former, is, because God approveth the way of the godly, and will make the end of the way of the ungodly, destruction, ver. 6.

1 THAT man hath perfect blessedness,
   who walketh not astray
In counsel of ungodly men,
   nor stands in sinners' way,
Nor sitteh in the scorner's chair:
2   But placeth his delight
Upon God's law, and meditates
   on his law day and night.

A

3 He shall be like a tree that grows,
    near planted by a river,
  Which in his season yields his fruit,
    and his leaf fadeth never:
  And all he doth shall prosper well.
4   The wicked are not so:
  But like they are unto the chaff,
    which wind drives to and fro.
5 In judgment therefore shall not stand
    such as ungodly are,
  Nor in th' assembly of the just
    shall wicked men appear.
6 For why? the way of godly men
    unto the Lord is known:
  Whereas the way of wicked men
    shall quite be overthrown.

PSALM II.

That this Psalm doth mainly, if not only, concern Christ, appeareth by this, That it hath not so much as David's name in the inscription, albeit he did write it, and by Acts iv. 25, 26. where it is appropriate to Christ. This Psalm hath two parts; in the former is set down the stability of Christ's kingdom, against all the enemies thereof, ver. 1, 2, 3. First, Because God the Father taketh part with his Son, against all his enemies, and will establish Christ's kingdom, maugre them all, ver. 4, 5, 6. Secondly, Because in the Covenant of Redemption the Father hath promised to the Son, enlargement of his kingdom and victory over all his enemies, ver 7, 8, 9. In the latter part of the Psalm, the Prophet delivereth the use of this doctrine in an exhortation to great and small, to repent of their sins, and to believe in Christ, ver. 10, 11, 12.

1 WHY rage the heathen? and vain things
    why do the people mind?
2 Kings of the earth do set themselves,
    and princes are combin'd,

To plot against the Lord, and his
   anointed, saying thus,
3 Let us asunder break their bands,
   and cast their cords from us.
4 He that in Heaven sits, shall laugh:
   the Lord shall scorn them all.
5 Then shall he speak to them in wrath,
   in rage he vex them shall.
6 Yet notwithstanding I have him
   to be my King appointed:
   And o'er Zion my holy hill,
   I have him King anointed.
7 The sure decree I will declare:
   the Lord hath said to me,
   Thou art mine only Son, this day
   I have begotten thee.
8 Ask of me, and for heritage
   the heathen I'll make thine:
   And, for possession, I to thee
   will give earth's utmost line.
9 Thou shalt, as with a weighty rod
   of iron, break them all;
   And, as a potter's sherd, thou shalt
   them dash in pieces small.
10 Now therefore, kings, be wise, be taught,
   ye judges of the earth:
11 Serve God in fear, and see that ye
   join trembling with your mirth.
12 Kiss ye the Son, lest in his ire
   ye perish from the way,
   If once his wrath begin to burn:
   blest all that on him stay.

A 2

PSALM III.

A Psalm of David, when he fled from Absalom his Son.

This Psalm holdeth forth a notable proof and benefit of Faith in David's experience; who when his own son Absalom rebelled against him, and forced him to flee for fear of his life; did, First, Lay before the Lord his pitiful condition, ver. 1, 2. Secondly, He settled his faith on God, prayed and obtained a comfortable answer, was quiet and refreshed in soul and body, and made confident against all fears possible, ver. 3, 4, 5, 6. Thirdly, He continueth in Prayer, confirming his faith from former experience, ver. 7. And, Lastly, He giveth forth the use of his experience to the Church's edification in a general doctrine, ver. 8.

1 O Lord, how are my foes increas'd?
    against me many rise.
2 Many say of my soul, For him
    in God no succour lies.
3 Yet thou my shield, and glory art,
    th' uplifter of mine head.
4 I cry'd, and from his holy hill
    the Lord me answer made.
5 I laid me down, and slept; I wak'd,
    for God sustained me.
6 I will not fear, tho' thousands ten
    set round against me be.
7 Arise, O Lord, save me, my God;
    for thou my foes hast stroke
All on the cheek-bone; and the teeth
    of wicked men hast broke.
8 Salvation doth appertain
    unto the Lord alone:
Thy blessing, Lord, for evermore
    thy people is upon.

PSALM IV.

To the chief Musician, on Niginoth, a Psalm of David.

Another experience of David, as an example of a Christian sufferer, unjustly persecuted and scorned for his piety by his profane enemies, such as Saul, and his courtiers were: Wherein, First, He setteth down his prayer, ver. 1. Secondly, Then being comforted in God, he insulteth over his enemies, and glorieth in God's favour, ver. 2, 3. Thirdly, He exhorteth his enemies to repentance, and faith in God, ver. 4, 5. Fourthly, He preferreth the blessedness of his estate above whatsoever the worldly man can enjoy, ver. 6, 7, 8.

1 GIVE ear unto me when I call,
    God of my righteousness:
Have mercy, hear my pray'r, thou hast
    enlarg'd me in distress.
2 O ye the sons of men, how long
    will ye love vanities?
How long my glory turn to shame,
    and will ye follow lies?
3 But know, that for himself the Lord
    the godly man doth chuse:
The Lord, when I on him do call,
    to hear will not refuse.
4 Fear, and sin not: talk with your heart:
    on bed, and silent be.
5 Off'rings present of righteousness,
    and in the Lord trust ye.
6 O who will shew us any good?
    is that which many say:
But of thy countenance the light
    Lord, lift on us alway.

7 Upon my heart, bestow'd by thee,
    more gladness I have found,
  Than they, ev'n then, when corn and wine
    did most with them abound.
8 I will both lay me down in peace,
    and quiet sleep will take:
  Because thou only me to dwell
    in safety, Lord, dost make.

PSALM V.

To the chief Musician, upon Nehiloth, a Psalm of David.

David, as a type of Christ, and one of the number of his afflicted followers, set forth in his affliction, as an example of exercise to others in after ages, doth pray for himself, and against his enemies, using sundry arguments to strengthen himself in his hope to be heard: First, From the grace of God bestowed on himself to use the means, ver. 1, 2, 3. Secondly, from the justice of God against his wicked enemies, ver 4, 5, 6. Thirdly, from his own stedfast purpose and desire to continue in God's service, and to walk so uprightly, as the enemy shall not have advantage of him by his miscarriage, ver. 7, 8. Fourthly, From the ripeness of sin in his adversaries, which did prepare them for sudden destruction, ver. 9, 10. Fifthly, From the certain hope of joy, and defence, and spiritual blessing to be bestowed on himself and all believers, out of the free love and favour of God toward them, ver. 11, 12.

1 GIVE ear unto my words, O Lord,
    my meditation weigh.
2 Hear my loud cry, my King, my God;
    for I to thee will pray.
3 Lord, thou shalt early hear my voice,
    I early will direct
  My pray'r to thee, and looking up
    an answer will expect.

4 For thou art not a God that doth
    in wickedness delight:
  Neither shall evil dwell with thee:
5   nor fools stand in thy sight:
  All that ill-doers are thou hat'st,
6   cutt'st off that liars be:
  The bloody and deceitful man
    abhorred is by thee.
7 But I into thy house will come
    in thine abundant grace:
  And I will worship, in thy fear,
    towards thy holy place.
8 Because of those mine enemies,
    Lord, in thy righteousness,
  Do thou me lead: do thou thy way
    make straight before my face.
9 For in their mouth there is no truth,
    their inward part is ill;
  Their throat's an open sepulchre,
    their tongue doth flatter still.
10 O God, destroy them, let them be,
    by their own counsel, quell'd:
  Them, for their many sins, cast out,
    for they 'gainst thee rebell'd.
11 But let all joy that trust in thee;
    and still make shouting noise:
  For them thou sav'st; let all that love
    thy name, in thee rejoice.
12 For, Lord, unto the righteous man
    thou wilt thy blessing yield;
  With favour thou wilt compass him
    about, as with a shield.

PSALM VI.

To the chief Musician on Neginoth, upon Sheminoth, a Psalm of David.

Another experience of David, useful to be known by all the children of God, who are subject to the like exercise; wherein David, being under the sense of the Lord's heavy hand, upon his body and spirit, prayeth for the removal of felt wrath, ver. 1, 2, 3. Next prayeth for the renewed feeling and experience of God's mercy towards him, laying forth his lamentable condition before the pitiful eye of God, ver. 4, 5, 6, 7. After which, being heard and comforted, in the third place, he defieth and triumpheth over all his enemies, ver. 8, 9.

1 LORD, in thy wrath, rebuke me not,
   Nor in thy hot rage chasten me.
2 Lord, pity me, for I am weak:
   Heal me, for my bones vexed be.
3 My soul is also vexed sore,
   But, Lord, how long stay wilt thou make?
4 Return, O Lord, my soul set free:
   O save me for thy mercies' sake.
5 Because those that deceased are,
   Of thee shall no remembrance have:
   And who is he that will to thee
   Give praises, lying in the grave?
6 I with my groaning weary am,
   I also, all the night my bed
   Have caused for to swim: and I
   With tears my couch have watered.
7 Mine eye, consum'd with grief, grows old,
   Because of all mine enemies.
8 Hence from me, wicked workers all;
   For God hath heard my weeping cries.
9 God hath my supplication heard;
   My pray'r received graciously.
10 Sham'd and sore vex'd be all my foes,
   Sham'd and back-turned suddenly.

Another of the same.

1 IN thy great indignation,
O Lord rebuke me not;
Nor on me lay thy chast'ning hand,
in thy displeasure hot.
2 Lord, I am weak, therefore on me
have mercy, and me spare:
Heal me, O Lord, because thou know'st
my bones much vexed are.
3 My soul is vexed sore, but, Lord,
how long stay wilt thou make?
4 Return, Lord, free my soul; and save
me, for thy mercies' sake.
5 Because of thee in death there shall
no more remembrance be:
Of those that in the grave do ly,
who shall give thanks to thee?
6 I with my groaning weary am,
and all the night my bed
I caused for to swim: with tears
my couch I watered.
7 By reason of my vexing grief,
mine eye consumed is:
It waxeth old, because of all
that be mine enemies.
8 But now depart from me, all ye
that work iniquity;
For why, the Lord hath heard my voice,
when I did mourn and cry.
9 Unto my supplication,
the Lord did hearing give;
When I to him my prayer make,
the Lord will it receive.

10 Let all be sham'd and troubled sore,
    that en'mies are to me;
Let them turn back, and suddenly
    ashamed let them be.

PSALM VII.

Shiggaion of David, which he sung unto the Lord, concerning the Words of Cush the Benjaminite.

The Prophet as a type of Christ mystical, and an example of Christians suffering, being slandered of treason against his Prince, by one of the courtiers; First, Flieth to God for delivery, ver. 1, 2. Secondly, Cleareth his innocence, ver. 3, 4, 5. Thirdly, Requesteth the Lord to judge between him and his enemies, ver. 6, 7, 8, 9. And, Fourthly, In prayer is made confident that the Lord will plead for him against his enemies, ver. 10, 11, 12, 13, and will return their devised mischief against him, upon their own head, ver. 14, 15, 16. Whereupon, in the last place, he promiseth praise to God for his righteous Judgment, ver. 17.

1 O Lord, my God, in thee do I
    my confidence repose;
Save and deliver me from all
    my persecuting foes.
2 Lest that the enemy my soul
    should like a lion tear,
In pieces renting it, while there
    is no deliverer.
3 O Lord my God, if it be so,
    that I committed this;
If it be so that in my hands
    iniquity there is;
4 If I rewarded ill to him
    that was at peace with me:
(Yea, ev'n the man that without cause
    my foe was, I did free).

5 Then let the foe purfue, and take
    my foul, and my life thruft
  Down to the earth, and let him lay
    mine honour in the duft.
6 Rife, in thy wrath, Lord, raife thyfelf,
    for my foes raging be:
  And to the judgment which thou haft
    commanded, wake for me.
7 So fhall th' affembly of thy folk
    about encompafs thee:
  Thou, therefore, for their fakes, return
    unto thy place on high.
8 The Lord, he fhall the people judge;
    my Judge, JEHOVAH, be,
  After my righteoufnefs, and mine
    integrity in me.
9 O let the wicked's malice end,
    but 'ftablifh ftedfaftly
  The righteous; for the righteous God
    the hearts and reins doth try.
10 In God, who faves the upright in heart,
    is my defence and ftay:
11 God juft men judgeth; God is wroth
    with ill men ev'ry day.
12 If he do not return again,
    then he his fword will whet;
  His bow he hath already bent,
    and hath it ready fet.
13 He alfo hath for him prepar'd
    the inftruments of death:
  Againft the perfecutors he
    his fhafts ordained hath.

14 Behold, he with iniquity
  doth travail as in birth;
 A mischief he conceived hath,
  and falshood shall bring forth.
15 He made a pit, and digg'd it deep,
  another there to take,
 But he is fall'n into the ditch
  which he himself did make.
16 Upon his own head his mischief
  shall be returned home;
 His vi'lent dealing also down
  on his own pate shall come.
17 According to his righteousness
  the Lord I'll magnify;
 And will sing praise unto the name
  of God that is most high.

PSALM VIII.

To the chief Musician upon Gittith, a Psalm of David.

To the end the Prophet may commend the glory of God's grace towards man: He first admireth his glory in the works of Creation and Providence, which are able to stop the mouth of all blasphemous Atheists, ver. 1, 2. In the second place, he admireth the Lord's love to man above all other, even the most glorious creatures, ver. 3, 4. Thirdly, he setteth out this grace of God to man, in the incarnation, humiliation, and exhaltation of Christ for man's cause, and for restoring of redeemed man in Christ, to their right unto, and over the visible creatures, ver. 5, 6, 7, 8. and closeth the Psalm with the admiration of God's glory in all the earth, ver. 9.

1 HOW excellent in all the earth,
  Lord, our Lord, is thy name!
 Who hast thy glory far advanc'd
  above the starry frame.

2 From infants and from fucklings mouth
    thou dideſt ſtrength ordain,
  For thy foes cauſe, that ſo thou might'ſt
    th' avenging foe reſtrain. .
3 When I look up unto the Heav'ns,
    which thine own fingers fram'd,
  Unto the moon, and to the ſtars,
    which were by thee ordain'd:
4 Then ſay I, What is Man, that he
    remembred is by thee?
  Or what the ſon of man, that thou
    ſo kind to him ſhould'ſt be?
5 For thou a little lower haſt
    him than the Angels made,
  With glory and with dignity,
    thou crowned haſt his head.
6 Of thy hand-works thou mad'ſt him lord,
    all under's feet didſt lay;
7 All ſheep and oxen, yea, and beaſts
    that in the field do ſtray;
8 Fowls of the air, fiſh of the ſea,
    all that paſs through the ſame.
9 How excellent in all the earth,
    Lord, our Lord, is thy name!

PSALM IX.

To the chief Muſician upon Muth Labben,
    a Pſalm of David.

Here is David's Song of Praiſe to God; firſt, for his own
experience of God's goodneſs towards himſelf, and God's

1 LORD, thee I'll praife with all my heart,
    thy wonders all proclaim.
2 In thee, moſt high, I'll greatly joy,
    and ſing unto thy name.
3 When back my foes were turn'd, they fell
    and periſh'd at thy ſight.
4 For thou maintain'dſt my right and cauſe;
    on throne ſatt'ſt judging right.
5 The heathen thou rebuked haſt,
    the wicked overthrown;
  Thou haſt put out their names, that they
    may never more be known.
6 O en'my! now deſtructions have
    an end perpetual:
  Thou cities raz'd, periſh'd with them
    is their memorial.
7 God ſhall endure for ay: he doth
    for judgment ſet his throne;
8 In righteouſneſs to judge the world,
    juſtice to give each one.
9 God alſo will a refuge be
    for thoſe that are oppreſt;
  A refuge will he be, in times
    of trouble, to diſtreſt.
10 And they that know thy name, in thee
    their confidence will place;
  For thou haſt not forſaken them
    that truly ſeek thy face.
11 O ſing ye praiſes to the Lord,
    that dwells in Zion hill,
  And all the nations among
    his deeds record ye ſtill.

12 When he enquireth after blood,
    he then remembreth them:
  The humble folk he not forgets,
    that call upon his name.
13 Lord, pity me, behold the grief
    which I from foes suftain,
  Ev'n thou who from the gates of death
    doth raife me up again:
14 That I, in Zion's daughters' gates,
    may all thy praife advance:
  And that I may rejoice always
    in thy deliverance.
15 The heathen are funk in the pit,
    which they themfelves prepar'd:
  And in the net which they have hid,
    their own feet faft are fnar'd.
16 The Lord is by the judgment known
    which he himfelf hath wrought:
  The finners' hands do make the fnares
    wherewith themfelves are caught.
17 They, who are wicked, into hell
    each one fhall turned be;
  And all the nations that forget
    to feek the Lord moft high.
18 For they that needy are, fhall not
    forgotten be alway:
  The expectation of the poor
    fhall not be loft for ay.
19 Arife, Lord, let not man prevail;
    judge heathens in thy fight.
20 That they may know themfelves but men,
    the nations, Lord, affright.

PSALM X.

This Psalm wanteth an inscription, and that in God's wisdom, that being less restricted to a particular man's case, it may be of more general use, whensoever the godly find themselves in a condition whereunto this Prayer may be suitable and especially in time of general persecution. The Prophet here complaineth to God, and craveth justice against the persecutors of his people, because of the intolerable wickedness of the oppressor, ver. 1, 2, 3, 4, 5, 6, 7, 8, 9, 10, 11. Secondly, He prayeth for hastening of the delivery of the Lord's people, and for hastning of judgment upon the persecutors, for vindication of the glory of God's justice against his enemies, and of his mercy to his people, ver. 12, 13, 14, 15. Thirdly, He professeth his confidence that he shall be heard, and so glorifieth God, ver. 16, 17, 18.

1 WHerefore is it, that thou, O Lord,
    dost stand from us afar?
And wherefore hidest thou thyself,
    when times so troublous are?
2 The wicked, in his loftiness,
    doth persecute the poor:
In these devices they have fram'd,
    let them be taken sure.
3 The wicked of his heart's desire
    doth talk with boasting great;
He blesseth him that's covetous,
    whom yet the Lord doth hate.
4 The wicked, through his pride of face,
    on God he doth not call:
And in the counsels of his heart
    the Lord is not at all.
5 His ways they always grievous are;
    thy judgments from his sight
Removed are: at all his foes
    he puffeth with despite.
6 With'n his heart he thus hath said,
    I shall not moved be:

And no adverfity at all
　　　　fhall ever come to me.
　7 His mouth with curfing, fraud, deceit,
　　　　is fill'd abundantly:
　　　And underneath his tongue there is
　　　　mifchief and vanity.
　8 He clofely fits in villages:
　　　　he flays the innocent;.
　　　Againft the poor that pafs him by,
　　　　his cruel eyes are bent.
　9 He, lion-like, lurks in his den:
　　　　he waits the poor to take;
　　　And when he draws him in his net,
　　　　his prey he doth him make.
10 Himfelf he humbleth very low,
　　　　he croucheth down withal,
　　　That fo a multitude of poor
　　　　may by his ftrong ones fall.
11 He thus hath faid, within his heart,
　　　　the Lord hath quite forgot;
　　　He hides his countenance, and he
　　　　for ever fees it not.
12 O Lord, do thou arife; O God,
　　　　lift up thine hand on high:
　　　Put not the meek afflicted ones
　　　　out of thy memory.
13 Why is it that the wicked man
　　　　thus doth the Lord defpife?
　　　Becaufe, that God will it require,
　　　　he in his heart denies
14 Thou haft it feen, for their mifchief
　　　　and fpite thou wilt repay:

The poor commits himſelf to thee,
    thou art the orphan's ſtay.
15 The arm break of the wicked man,
    and of the evil one:
  Do thou ſeek out his wickedneſs,
    until thou findeſt none.
16 The Lord is King thro' ages all,
    ev'n to eternity:
  The heathen people from his land
    are periſh'd utterly.
17 O Lord, of thoſe that humble are
    thou the deſire didſt hear:
  Thou wilt prepare their heart, and thou
    to hear wilt bend thine ear:
18 To judge the fatherleſs, and thoſe
    that are oppreſſed ſore,
  That man, that is but ſprung of earth,
    may them oppreſs no more.

PSALM XI.

To the chief Muſician, a Pſalm of David.

David, as an example of a Chriſtian under the trial of his faith in time of trouble, and tempted to deſperation, reſiſted the temptaion how deſperate ſoever his condition ſeemed, ver. 1, 2. And diſputeth for the confirmation of his own faith, ver. 3, 4, 5, 6, 7.

1 In the Lord do put my truſt;
    how is it then that ye
  Say to my ſoul, Flee as a bird
    unto your mountain high?
2 For lo, the wicked bend their bow,
    their ſhafts on ſtrings they fit:
  That thoſe who upright are in heart
    they privily may hit.

3 If the foundations be destroy'd,
 what hath the righteous done?
4 God in his holy temple is,
 in Heaven is his throne:
His eyes do see, his eye-lids try
5 men's sons. The just he proves:
But his soul hates the wicked man,
 and him that vi'lence loves.
6 Snares, fire and brimstone, furious storms
 on sinners he shall rain:
This, as the portion of their cup,
 doth unto them pertain.
7 Because the Lord most righteous doth
 in righteousness delight:
And with a pleasant countenance
 beholdeth the upright.

PSALM XII.

To the chief Musician upon Sheminith, a Psalm of David.

The Prophet having observed, as is set down, ver. 8. how wickedness lifteth up the head in all the land, when the places of power and trust do come into the hands of naughty and vile men, doth give direction by his own example unto the godly, first, To have their recourse to God by prayer, while they are borne down by the wicked in such an ill time, ver. 1, 2. And next how to comfort themselves by the word of God, pronouncing the sentence of justice upon all loose-tongued men, ver. 3, 4. And promising delivery to the oppressed godly, and preservation of the Church in all generations, ver 5, 6, 7. Howsoever he suffer wicked men to bear rule sometimes, and wickedness to abound by that mean, ver. 8.

1 HELP, Lord, because the godly man
 doth daily fade away;
And from among the sons of men
 the faithful do decay.

2 Unto his neighbour ev'ry one
    doth utter vanity:
  They with a double heart do speak,
    and lips of flattery.
3 God shall cut off all flatt'ring lips,
    tongues that speak proudly, thus:
4 We'll with our tongue prevail, our lips
    are ours: who's Lord o'er us?
5 For poor opprest, and for the sighs
    of needy, rise will I,
  Saith God, and him in safety set
    from such as him defy.
6 The words of God, are words most pure,
    they be like silver try'd
  In earthen furnace, seven times
    that hath been purify'd.
7 Lord, thou shalt them preserve and keep
    for ever from this race.
8 On each side walk the wicked, when
    vile men are high in place.

PSALM XIII.

To the chief Musician, a Psalm of David.

Another Christian experience, wherein David under the sense of desertion, layeth forth his lamentable case before the Lord, ver. 1, 2. Prayeth for relief, ver. 3, 4. And by faith is refreshed and comforted, ver. 5, 6.

1 HOW long wilt thou forget me, Lord,
    shall it for ever be?
  O how long shall it be, that thou
    wilt hide thy face from me?
2 How long take counsel in my soul,
    still sad in heart, shall I?
  How long exalted over me,
    shall be mine enemy?

3 O Lord my God, confider well,
  and anfwer to me make:
Mine eyes enlighten, left the fleep
  of death me overtake;
4 Left that mine enemy fhould fay,
  againft him I prevail'd:
And thofe that trouble me, rejoice
  when I am mov'd and fail'd.
5 But I have all my confidence
  thy mercy fet upon:
My heart within me fhall rejoice
  in thy falvation.
6 I will unto the Lord my God
  fing praifes chearfully,
Becaufe he hath his bounty fhown
  to me abundantly.

PSALM XIV.

To the chief Mufician, a Pfalm of David.

David looking on the Conftitution of the vifible Church, and feeing the great body of the people lying in their natural ftate, working iniquity, and hating the truly godly amongft them, even to the death, ver. 1, 2, 3. Comforteth the godly, firft, by the care the Lord hath of them, in pleading their caufe againft the ungodly, ver. 4, 5, 6. And next, by giving hope of better days for the godly, when after fore plagues come on that people, Chrift fhould manifeft himfelf to them, ver. 7.

1 THAT there is not a God, the fool
  doth in his heart conclude;
They are corrupt, their works are vile,
  not one of them doth good.
2 Upon mens' fons the Lord from heav'n
  did caft his eyes abroad;
To fee if any underftood
  and did feek after God.

3 They altogether filthy are,
   they all afide are gone:
And there is none that doeth good,
   yea, fure there is not one.
4 Thefe workers of iniquity,
   do they not know at all,
That they my people eat as bread
   and on God do not call?
5 There fear'd they much: for God is with
   the whole race of the juft.
6 You fhame the counfel of the poor;
   becaufe God is his truft.
7 Let Ifra'l's help from Zion come:
   when back the Lord fhall bring
His captives, Jacob fhall rejoice,
   and Ifrael fhall fing.

PSALM XV.
A Pfalm of David.

The Prophet for diftinguifhing of the true Members of the Church, from thofe who were only outwardly Profeffors, afketh of the Lord how the one may be known from the other? ver. 1. And receiveth anfwer to the queftion, ver. 2, 3, 4, 5.

1 WITHIN thy tabernacle, Lord,
   who fhall abide with thee?
And in thy high and holy hill
   who fhall a dweller be?
2 The man that walketh uprightly,
   and worketh righteoufnefs;
And, as he thinketh in his heart,
   fo doth he truth exprefs.
3 Who doth not flander with his tongue,
   nor to his friend doth hurt,

> Nor yet againſt his neighbour doth
> take up an ill report.
> 4 In whoſe eyes vile men are deſpis'd;
> but thoſe that God do fear
> He honoureth, and changeth not,
> though to his hurt he ſwear.
> 5 His coin puts not to uſury,
> nor take reward will he
> Againſt the guiltleſs. Who doth thus,
> ſhall never moved be.

PSALM XVI.

Michtam of David.

David, in this Pſalm, finding himſelf in the ſtate of grace, prayeth for preſervation in general, in relation unto all dangers and evils in body and ſoul, and whatſoever other evil, from which a godly man, with allowance of God's word might pray to be preſerved. His only reaſon to aſſure himſelf to be heard, is becauſe he had gotten grace to truſt in God. The ſincerity of which faith in God he proveth by ſundry evidences, ver. 1, 2, 3, 4. In the ſecond place, He climbeth up to the comfort and joy of believing; and all the grounds of joy whereupon he goeth, do ſerve both to confirm his faith, and to give him aſſurance of the granting of his prayer, ver. 5, 6, 7, 8, 9, 10, 11.

> 1 LORD, keep me: for I truſt in thee.
> 2 To God thus was my ſpeech:
> Thou art my Lord, and unto thee
> my goodneſs doth not reach.
> 3 To ſaints on earth, to th' excellent
> where my delight's all plac'd.
> 4 Their ſorrows ſhall be multiply'd
> to other gods that haſte:

Of their drink offerings of blood
 I will no off'ring make;
Yea, neither I their very names
 up in my lips will take.

5 God is of mine inheritance
 and cup the portion:
The lot that fallen is to me
 thou doſt maintain alone.

6 Unto me happily the lines
 in pleaſant places fell;
Yea, the inheritance I got,
 in beauty doth excel.

7 I bleſs the Lord, becauſe he doth
 by counſel me conduct:
And, in the ſeaſons of the night,
 my reins do me inſtruct.

8 Before me ſtill the Lord I ſet:
 ſith it is ſo that he
Doth ever ſtand at my right hand,
 I ſhall not moved be.

9 Becauſe of this my heart is glad,
 and joy ſhall be expreſt
Ev'n by my glory: and my fleſh
 in confidence ſhall reſt.

10 Becauſe my ſoul in grave to dwell
 ſhall not be left by thee;
Nor wilt thou give thine holy One
 corruption to ſee.

11 Thou wilt me ſhew the path of life:
 of joys there is full ſtore
Before thy face, at thy right hand
 are pleaſures evermore.

PSALM XVII.

A Prayer of David.

This Psalm, according to the inscription thereof, is a Prayer of David, mixed with sundry reasons for helping; wherein, first, He craveth in general justice in the controversy between him and his oppressors, ver. 1, 2, 3, 4. Secondly, More specially, he requesteth for a wise carriage of himself under his exercise, ver. 5, 6. Thirdly, Prayeth for protection and preservation from his enemies, ver. 7, 8, 9, 10, 11, 12. Fourthly, For disappointment to his enemies, and for delivery of himself from them, ver. 13, 14. And closeth comfortably in confidence of a good answer and hope of satisfactory happiness, ver. 15.

1 LORD, hear the right, attend my cry,
    unto my pray'r give heed,
That doth not, in hypocrisy,
    from feigned lips proceed.
2 And from before thy presence forth
    my sentence do thou send:
Toward these things that equal are
    do thou thine eyes intend.
3 Thou provd'st mine heart, thou visit'dst me
    by night, thou didst me try,
Yet nothing found'st: for that my mouth
    shall not sin, purpos'd I.
4 As for mens' works, I, by the word
    that from thy lips doth flow,
Did me preserve out of the paths
    wherein destroyers go.
5 Hold up my goings, Lord, me guide
    in those thy paths divine.
So that my footsteps may not slide
    out of these ways of thine.

B

6 I called have on thee, O God,
   becaufe thou wilt me hear:
  That thou may'ft hearken to my voice,
   to me incline thine ear.
7 Thy wond'rous loving-kindnefs fhow,
   thou that by thy right hand
  Sav'ft them that truft in thee, from thofe
   that up againft them ftand.
8 As th' apple of the eye, me keep;
   in thy wings fhade me clofe:
9 From lewd oppreffors, compaffing
   me round, as deadly foes.
10 In their own fat they are inclos'd;
   their mouth fpeaks loftily.
11 Our fteps they compaft; and to ground
   down bowing fet their eye.
12 He like unto a lion is
   that's greedy of his prey,
  Or lion young, which lurking doth
   in fecret places ftay.
13 Arife, and difappoint my foe,
   and caft him down, O Lord;
  My foul fave from the wicked man,
   the man which is thy fword.
14 From men which are thy hand, O Lord,
   from worldly men me fave,
  Which only in this prefent life
   their part and portion have:
  Whofe belly with thy treafure hid
   thou fill'ft: they children have
  In plenty, of their goods the reft
   they to their children leave.

15 But as for me, I thine own face
    in righteousness will see:
And with thy likeness, when I wake
    I satisfy'd shall be.

PSALM XVIII.

To the chief Musician, a Psalm of David the servant of the Lord, who spake unto the Lord the words of this Song, in the day that the Lord delivered him from the hand of all his enemies, and from the hand of Saul. And he said,

David in this Psalm as a Type of Christ, and fellow partaker of the sufferings of Christ in his mystical members, and of deliveries and victories over his and their enemies, being now settled in the kingdom, praiseth God for his marvellous mercies; and as a Type of Christ, he prophesieth of the enlargement and stability of his own kingdom, and of Christ's Kingdom, represented thereby; and first obligeth himself thankfully to depend upon God, whatsoever enemies he shall have to deal with, ver. 1, 2, 3. Secondly, He giveth a reason of his resolution, from the experience of the Lord's delivering of him out of his deepest distresses, ver. 4, 5. to ver. 19. Thirdly, He amplifieth this mercy, acknowledging than this was a fruit of his faith, and righteous dealing with his party-adversary; the like whereof every Believer might expect, as well as he for time coming, by reason of this his by-gone large experience, from ver. 20, to ver. 30. Fourthly, He praiseth God in particular, for the experience he hath had in time by-gone in warfare, and victories in battle, to ver. 43. Fifthly, As a Type of Christ he promiseth to himself the enlargement of his own kingdom, and prophesieth of the enlargement of Christ's kingdom among the Gentiles, for which he praiseth God unto the end of the Psalm, ver. 43, 44, 45, 46, 47, 48, 49, 50.

1 THee will I love, O Lord, my strength.
2   My fortress is the Lord,
   My rock, and he that doth to me
    deliverance afford:

My God. my ſtrength, whom I will truſt,
  a buckler unto me,
The horn of my ſalvation,
  and my high tow'r is he.
3 Upon the Lord, who worthy is
  of praiſes, will I cry:
And then ſhall I preſerved be
  ſafe from mine enemy.
4 Floods of ill men affrighted me,
  death's pangs about me went.
5 Hell's ſorrows me invironed;
  death's ſnares did me prevent.
6 In my diſtreſs I call'd on God,
  cry to my God did I:
He from his temple heard my voice,
  to his ears came my cry.
7 Th' earth, as affrighted, then did ſhake,
  trembling upon it ſeiz'd:
The hills' foundations moved were,
  becauſe he was diſpleas'd.
8 Up from his noſtrils came a ſmoke,
  and from his mouth there came
Devouring fire: and coals by it
  were turned into flame.
9 He alſo bowed down the heav'ns,
  and thence he did deſcend:
And thickeſt clouds of darkneſs did
  under his feet attend.
10 And he upon a cherub rode,
  and thereon he did fly:
Yea, on the ſwift wings of the wind,
  his flight was from on high.

11 He darkness made his secret place:
    about him for his tent
  Dark waters were, and thickest clouds
    of th' airy firmament.
12 And at the brightness of that light
    which was before his eye,
  His thick clouds past away, hail stones
    and coals of fire did fly.
13 The Lord God also in the heav'ns
    did thunder in his ire,
  And there the Highest gave his voice,
    hail-stones and coals of fire.
14 Yea, he his arrows sent abroad,
    and them he scattered:
  His light'nings also he shot out,
    and them discomfited.
15 The water's channels then were seen;
    the world's foundations vast
  At thy rebuke discover'd were,
    and at thy nostrils' blast.
16 And from above the Lord sent down,
    and took me from below,
  From many waters he me drew,
    which would me overflow.
17 He me reliev'd from my strong foes,
    and such as did me hate:
  Because he saw that they for me
    too strong were and too great.
18 They me prevented in the day
    of my calamity:
  But, even then, the Lord himself,
    a stay was unto me.

19 He to a place where liberty
   and room was, hath me brought:
 Becaufe he took delight in me,
   he my deliv'rance wrought.
20 According to my righteoufnefs
   he did me recompenfe,
 He me repaid according to
   my hands' pure innocence.
21 For I God's ways kept, from my God
   did not turn wickedly.
22 His judgments were before me, I
   his laws put not from me.
23 Sincere before him was my heart,
   with him upright was I;
 And watchfully I kept myfelf
   from mine iniquity.
24 After my righteoufnefs the Lord
   hath recompenfed me,
 After the cleannefs of my hands
   appearing in his eye.
25 Thou gracious to the gracious art,
   to upright men upright.
26 Pure to the pure, froward thou kyth'ft
   unto the froward wight.
27 For thou wilt the afflicted fave,
   in grief that low do lie:
 But wilt bring down the countenance
   of them whofe looks are high.
28 The Lord will light my candle fo,
   that it fhall fhine full bright:
 The Lord my God will alfo make
   my darknefs to be light.

29 By thee thro' troops of men I break,
   and them discomfit all:
' And, by my God assisting me,
   I overleap a wall.
30 As for God, perfect is his way:
   the Lord his word is try'd:
He is a buckler to all those
   who do in him confide.
31 Who but the Lord is God? but he
   who is a rock and stay?
32 'Tis God that girdeth me with strength,
   and perfect makes my way.
33 He made my feet swift as the hinds,
   set me on my high places.
34 Mine hands to war he taught, mine arms
   brake bows of steel in pieces.
35 The shield of thy salvation
   thou didst on me bestow:
Thy right hand held me up, and great
   thy kindness made me grow.
36 And in my way, my steps thou hast
   enlarged under me:
That I go safely, and my feet
   are kept from sliding free.
37 Mine en'mies I pursued have,
   and did them overtake:
Nor did I turn again, till I
   an end of them did make.
38 I wounded them, they could not rise:
   they at my feet did fall.
39 Thou girdest me with strength for war,
   my foes thou brought'st down all.

40 And thou hast given to me the necks
  of all mine enemies,
 That I might them destroy and slay
  who did against me rise.
41 They cried out, but there was none
  that would or could them save:
 Yea, they did cry unto the Lord,
  but he no answer gave.
42 Then did I beat them small as dust
  before the wind that flies:
 And I did cast them out like dirt
  upon the street that lies.
43 Thou mad'st me free from people's strife,
  and heathen's head to be:
 A people whom I have not known,
  shall service do to me.
44 At hearing they shall me obey:
  to me they shall submit.
45 Strangers, for fear, shall fade away,
  who in close places sit.
46 God lives, blest be my rock: the God
  of my health praised be.
47 God doth avenge me, and subdues
  the people under me.
48 He saves me from mine enemies:
  yea, thou hast lifted me
 Above my foes: and from the man
  of vi'lence set me free.
49 Therefore, to thee will I give thanks
  the heathen folk among:
 And to thy name, O Lord, I will
  sing praises in a song.

50 He great deliv'rance gives his king;
    he mercy doth extend
To David, his anointed One,
    and his feed without end.

PSALM XIX.

To the chief Musician, a Psalm of David.

This Psalm is a sweet contemplation of the glory of God's wisdom, power and goodness, shining in the works of creation, ver. 1, 2, 3, 4, 5, 6. And of the glory of his holiness and rich grace, shining thro' his word and ordinances in his Church, ver. 7, 8, 9, 10. Whereof the Prophet having proof, prayeth to have the right use and benefit, ver. 11, 12, 13, 14.

1 THE Heav'ns God's glory do declare:
    the skies his hand-works preach.
2 Day utters speech to day, and night
    to night doth knowledge teach.
3 There is no speech, nor tongue to which
    their voice doth not extend.
4 Their line is gone thro' all the earth,
    their words to the world's end:
In them he set the sun a tent,
5   Who bridegroom-like forth goes,
From's chamber, as a strong man doth
    to run his race rejoice.
6 From heav'n's end is his going forth,
    circling to the end again:
And there is nothing from his heat
    that hidden doth remain.
7 God's law is perfect, and converts
    the soul in sin that lies:
God's testimony is most sure,
    and makes the simple wise.

8 The ſtatutes of the Lord are right,
 and do rejoice the heart:
 The Lord's command is pure, and doth
 light to the eyes impart.
9 Unſpotted is the fear of God,
 and doth endure for ever:
 The judgements of the Lord are true,
 and righteous altogether.
10 They more than gold, yea, much fine gold,
 to be deſired are:
 Than honey, from the honey-comb
 that droppeth, ſweeter far.
11 Moreover they thy ſervant warn
 how he his life ſhould frame:
 A great reward provided is
 for them that keep the ſame.
12 Who can his errors underſtand?
 O cleanſe thou me within
13 From ſecret faults. Thy ſervant keep
 From all preſumptuous ſin.
 And do not ſuffer them to have
 dominion over me:
 Then righteous and innocent
 I from much ſin ſhall be.
14 The words which from my mouth proceed,
 the thoughts ſent from my heart,
 Accept, O Lord, for thou my ſtrength
 and my Redeemer art.

PSALM XX.

To the chief Muſician, a Pſalm of David.

This Pſalm was indited to the Church in the form of a Prayer for the Kings of Iſrael, but with a ſpecial eye upon, and relation unto Chriſt, the King of Iſrael; in reſpect of whom this Prayer is a Prophecy, and a form of bleſſing of Chriſt, and praying for his Kingdom, whereof the Kingdom of Iſrael was a Type, and the Kings thereof are Types of Chriſt. Not that the kingdom in every condition was figurative, or every King a Type of him; but as the Prieſts being taken not ſeverally, one by one, but together, ſhadowed forth in ſomething, Chriſt in the office of his Prieſthood: ſo the Kings, not every one, but taken together, ſhadowed forth in ſomething, Chriſt in his Royal office, and their kingdom reſembled his kingdom in his viſible Church in ſome things, and in his inviſible Church in other ſome things, leaving room to ſome perſons, both among the Prieſts and Kings, to be more ſpecially Types than any of the reſt in common, ver. 1, 2, 3, 4, 5. After which the Church's confidence to be heard is ſet down, and their gloriation in God over their enemies, with dependence on God for ſalvation in all difficulties and ſtraits, ver. 6, 7, 8, 9.

1 JEHOVAH hear thee in the day
    when trouble he doth ſend,
And let the name of Jacob's God
    thee from all ill defend.
2 O let him help ſend from above,
    out of his ſanctuary:
From Zion his own holy hill
    let him give ſtrength to thee.
3 Let him remember all thy gifts,
    accept thy ſacrifice:
4 Grant thee thine heart's wiſh, and fulfil
    thy thoughts and counſel wiſe.
5 In thy ſalvation we will joy,
    in our God's name we will
Diſplay our banners, and the Lord
    thy prayers all fulfil.
6 Now know I God his King doth ſave:
    he from his holy heav'n
Will hear him, with the ſaving ſtrength,
    by his own right hand giv'n.

7. In chariots some put confidence,
   some horses trust upon:
  But we remember will the name
   of our Lord God alone.
8. We rise, and upright stand, when they
   are bowed down and fall.
9. Deliver, Lord, and let the King
   us hear when we do call.

PSALM XXI.
To the chief Musician, a Psalm of David.

As the former Psalm was a Prayer for the preservation of the kingdom of Israel, in relation to the kingdom of Christ, represented by it: so this Psalm is a form of thanksgiving unto God by the Church, for blessing of the kingdom of Israel, representing the blessing and cause of thanksgiving, to be found in Christ, and his kingdom, wherein a number of good things are set forth, heaped upon the King, ver. 1, 2, 3, 4, 5, 6, 7. And a number of miseries set forth, heaped on the head of his enemies, ver. 8, 9, 10, 11, 12. For both which the Lord is glorified, ver. 13. The reason why the former Psalm and this are referred in so many particulars unto Christ, is, because the verity of these things here spoken of, is to be sought in Christ, and his Kingdom; for but in some few only of the Kings, and in some few times of the kingdom only, was the shadow of what is here spoken of to be found, when the whole history is consulted.

1. THE king in thy great strength, O Lord,
    shall very joyful be;
   In thy salvation rejoice
    how veh'mently shall he?
2. Thou hast bestowed upon him
    all that his heart would have;
   And thou from him didst not with-hold
    whate'er his lips did crave.
3. For thou with blessings him prevent'st
    of goodness manifold;
   And thou hast set upon his head
    a crown of purest gold.

4 When he defired life of thee,
    thou life to him didft give;
  Ev'n fuch a length of days, that he
    for evermore fhould live.
5 In that falvation wrought by thee,
    his glory is made great;
  Honour and comely majefty
    thou haft upon him fet.
6 Becaufe that thou for evermore
    moft bleffed haft him made;
  And thou haft with thy countenance
    made him exceeding glad.
7 Becaufe the king upon the Lord
    his confidence doth lay,
  And thro' the grace of the moft High
    fhall not be mov'd away.
8 Thine hand fhall all thofe men find out
    that en'mies are to thee,
  Ev'n thy right hand fhall find out thofe
    of thee that haters be.
9 Like firey ov'n thou fhalt them make,
    when kindled is thine ire;
  God fhall them fwallow in his wrath,
    devour them fhall the fire.
10 Their fruit from earth thou fhalt deftroy
    their feed men from among.
11 For they, beyond their might, 'gainft thee
    did plot mifchief and wrong.
12 Thou therefore fhalt make them turn back
    when thou thy fhafts fhalt place
  Upon thy ftrings, made ready all
    to fly againft their face.

13 In thy great pow'r and strength, O Lord,
    be thou exalted high;
So shall we sing with joyful hearts,
    thy power praise shall we.

PSALM XXII.

*To the chief Musician upon Aijeleth Shahar,
a Psalm of David.*

This Psalm is a propheey of Christ's deepest sufferings, whereof David's exercise is a Type. The agony of spirit in Christ, and wrestling, of David's faith as the Type, is set down to ver. 22. and the victory, and the outgate to the end of the Psalm. In the exercise there are three conflicts between sense and faith. The first conflict, wherein the sense of trouble is set down, ver. 1, 2. and faith's wrestling against it, ver. 3, 4, 5. The second conflict, wherein is the second assault of sense, ver. 6, 7, 8. And faith's wrestling against it, ver. 9, 10, 11. The third conflict, wherein the third assault of sense is ver. 12, 13, 14, 15, 16, 17, 18. and faith's wrestling with it, ver. 19, 20, 21. Then follows the victory, set forth first in a promise of praise, ver. 22. Secondly, In an exhortation to all the godly, to praise the Lord, with a reason from his experience, ver. 23, 24. Thirdly, In a renewed promise of praise and thanks to the edification of the Church, ver. 25. Fourthly, In a prophecy of the increase of God's glory in the earth, as a fruit of Christ's sufferings and victory, ver. 26, 27, 28, 29, 30, 31.

1 MY God, my God, why hast thou me
    forsaken? why so far.
Art thou from helping me, and from
    my words that roaring are?
2 All day, my God, to thee I cry,
    yet am not heard by thee;
And in the season of the night
    I cannot silent be.
3 But thou art holy, thou that dost
    inhabit Isra'l's praise.
4 Our fathers hop'd in thee, they hop'd,
    and thou didst them release.

5 When unto thee they sent their cry,
    to them deliv'rance came:
Because they put their trust in thee,
    they were not put to shame.
6 But as for me, a worm I am,
    and as no man am priz'd:
Reproach of men I am, and by
    the people am despis'd.
7 All that me see, laugh me to scorn:
    shoot out the lip do they,
They nod and shake their heads at me,
    and mocking, thus do say,
8 This man did trust in God, that he
    would free him by his might:
Let him deliver him, sith he
    had in him such delight.
9 But thou art he out of the womb
    that didst me safely take;
When I was on my mother's breasts,
    thou me to hope didst make.
10 And I was cast upon thy care,
    ev'n from the womb till now:
And from my mother's belly, Lord,
    my God and guide art thou.
11 Be not far off, for grief is near;
    and none to help is found.
12 Bulls many compass me: strong bulls
    of Bashan me surround.
13 Their mouths they open'd wide on me,
    upon me gape did they,
Like to a lion ravening
    and roaring for his prey,

14 Like water I'm poured out, my bones
   all out of joint do part:
 Amidst my bowels as the wax,
   so melted is my heart.
15 My strength is like a potsherd dry'd:
   my tongue it cleaveth fast
 Unto my jaws; and to the dust
   of death thou brought me hast.
16 For dogs have compass'd me about;
   the wicked that did meet
 In their assembly, me enclos'd,
   they pierc'd my hands and feet.
17 I all my bones may tell: they do
   upon me look and stare.
18 Upon my vesture lots they cast,
   and clothes among them share.
19 But be not far, O Lord, my strength,
   haste to give help to me.
20 From sword my soul, from pow'r of dogs
   my darling set thou free.
21 Out of the roaring lion's mouth
   do thou me shield and save:
 For from the horns of unicorns
   an ear to me thou gave.
22 I will shew forth thy name unto
   those that my brethren are:
 Amidst the congregation
   thy praise I will declare.
23 Praise ye the Lord, who do him fear
   him glorify, all ye,
 The seed of Jacob; fear him all
   that Israel's children be.

24 For he defpis'd not, nor abhorr'd
    th' afflicted's mifery :
  Nor from him hid his face, but heard
    when he to him did cry.
25 Within the congregation great
    my praife fhall be of thee :
  My vows before them that him fear
    fhall be perform'd by me.
26 The meek fhall eat, and fhall be fill'd :
    they alfo praife fhall give
  Unto the Lord, that do him feek :
    your heart fhall ever live.
27 All ends of the earth remember fhall,
    and turn the Lord unto :
  All kindreds of the nations
    to him fhall homage do.
28 Becaufe the kingdom to the Lord
    doth appertain as his :
  Likewife among the nations
    the governor he is.
29 Earth's fat ones eat, and worfhip fhall :
    all who to duft defcend
  Shall bow to him : none of them can
    his foul from death defend.
30 A feed fhall fervice do to him ;
    unto the Lord it fhall
  Be for a generation
    reckon'd in ages all.
31 They fhall come, and they fhall declare
    his truth and righteoufnefs
  Unto a people yet unborn,
    and that he hath done this.

PSALM XXIII.

A Psalm of David.

This Psalm is the expression of the Prophet's confidence in God's grace, wherein from the settling himself in the belief of our covenanted relation, between God and him, he doth draw sundry comfortable conclusions and confirmations of faith from it, concerning the Lord's furnishing every necessary good thing to him, ver. 1, 2. For recovery of him from every evil condition, wherein he may fall, ver. 3. And for assisting and comforting him in the greatest danger he could fall into, ver. 4. And for making him blessed in despite of his enemies, ver. 5. And for continuing in God's grace and fellowship for ever, ver. 6.

1 THE Lord's my shepherd I'll not want.
2   He makes me down to lie
In pastures green; he leadeth me
    the quiet waters by.
3 My soul he doth restore again:
    and me to walk doth make
Within the paths of righteousness,
    ev'n for his own name's sake.
4 Yea, tho' I walk in death's dark vale,
    yet will I fear none ill:
For thou art with me, and thy rod
    and staff me comfort still.
5 My table thou hast furnished
    in presence of my foes:
My head thou dost with oil anoint,
    and my cup overflows.
6 Goodness and mercy all my life
    shall surely follow me:
And in God's house for evermore
    my dwelling-place shall be.

PSALM XXIV.

A Psalm of David.

The Psalmist having in the first place set down God's Lordship in the world, that he may thereby commend the special prerogative of the true Church, ver. 1, 2. Describeth in the next place the true citizens of this spiritual kingdom, ver. 3, 4, 5, 6. And exhorteth in the third place all incorporations, and in special the visible Church, to accept the offer of a more entire communication with God in Christ, that they may enjoy spiritual privileges of the subjects of the invisible and spiritual kingdom, ver. 7, 8, 9, 10.

1 THE earth belongs unto the Lord,
  and all that it contains:
The world, that is inhabited,
  and all that there remains.
2 For the foundations thereof
  he on the seas did lay,
And he hath it established
  upon the floods to stay.
3 Who is the man that shall ascend
  into the hill of God?
Or who within his holy place
  shall have a firm abode?
4 Whose hands are clean, whose heart is pure;
  and unto vanity
Who hath not lifted up his soul,
  nor sworn deceitfully.
5 He from th' eternal shall receive
  the blessing him upon,
And righteousness ev'n from the God
  of his salvation.
6 This is the generation
  that after him enquire,
O Jacob, who do seek thy face
  with their whole heart's desire.

7 Ye gates, lift up your heads on high,
     ye doors that laſt for ay,
  Be lifted up, that ſo the King
     of glory enter may.
8 But who of glory is the King?
     the mighty Lord is this,
  Ev'n that ſame Lord, that great in might
     and ſtrong in battle is.
9 Ye gates, lift up your heads, ye doors,
     doors that do laſt for ay,
  Be lifted up, that ſo the King
     of glory enter may.
10 But who is he that is the King
     of glory? who is this?
  The Lord of hoſts, and none but he,
     the King of glory is.

PSALM XXV.

A Pſalm of David.

In this Pſalm the Prophet being in danger of his life by his enemies without, and troubled with the ſenſe of ſin within, maketh his prayer for relief from both, mixing meditation with prayer along the Pſalm, for ſtrengthening of his faith: So, fiſt he prayeth from ver. 1, to ver. 8. Then meditateth, ver. 8, 9. 10. In the third room he prayeth again, ver. 11. In the fourth is a new meditation, ver. 12. 13, 14, 15. In the laſt room is a prayer from ver. 16. to the end.

1 TO thee I lift my ſoul.
2   O Lord, I truſt in thee:
  My God, let me not be aſham'd,
     nor foes triumph o'er me.
3 Let none that wait on thee
     Be put to ſhame at all;
  But thoſe that without cauſe tranſgreſs,
     let ſhame upon them fall.

4 Shew me thy ways, O Lord;
  thy paths, O teach thou me.
5 And do thou lead me in thy truth,
  therein my teacher be:
For thou art God that doſt
  to me ſalvation ſend,
And I upon thee all the day
  expecting, do attend.
6 Thy tender mercies, Lord,
  I pray thee to remember,
And loving-kindneſſes: for they
  have been of old for ever.
7 My ſins and faults of youth
  do thou, O Lord, forget;
After thy mercy think on me,
  and for thy goodneſs great.
8 God good and upright is:
  the way he'll ſinners ſhow.
9 The meek in judgment he will guide,
  and make his path to know.
10 The whole paths of the Lord,
  are truth and mercy ſure,
To thoſe that do his cov'nant keep,
  and teſtimonies pure.
11 Now for thine own name's ſake,
  O Lord, I thee intreat
To pardon mine iniquity:
  for it is very great.
12 What man is he that fears
  the Lord, and doth him ſerve?
Him ſhall he teach the way that he
  ſhall chooſe, and ſtill obſerve:

13 His soul shall dwell at ease;
    and his posterity
Shall flourish still, and of the earth
    inheritors shall be.
14 With those that fear him, is
    the secret of the Lord :
The knowledge of his covenant
    he will to them afford.
15 Mine eyes upon the Lord
    continually are set :
For he it is that shall bring forth
    my feet out of the net.
16 Turn unto me thy face,
    and to me mercy shew ;
Because that I am desolate,
    and am brought very low.
17 My heart's griefs are increas'd,
    me from distress relieve.
18 See mine affliction, and my pain,
    and all my sins forgive.
19 Consider thou my foes,
    because they many are,
And it a cruel hatred is
    which they against me bear.
20 O do thou keep my soul,
    do thou deliver me :
And let me never be asham'd,
    because I trust in thee.
21 Let uprightness and truth
    keep me, who thee attend
22 Redemption, Lord, to Israel
    from all his troubles send.

Another of the same.

1 TO thee I lift my soul, O Lord:
2 My God, I trust in thee:
 Let me not be asham'd; let not
  my foes triumph o'er me.
3 Yea, let thou none ashamed be,
  that do on thee attend;
 Ashamed let them be, O Lord,
  who without cause offend.
4 Thy ways, Lord, shew; teach me thy paths.
5 Lead me in truth, teach me:
 For of my safety thou art God,
  all day I wait on thee.
6 Thy mercies that most tender are,
  do thou, O Lord, remember,
 And loving kindnesses: for they
  have been of old for ever.
7 Let not the errors of my youth,
  nor sins remember'd be:
 In mercy, for thy goodness sake,
  O Lord, remember me:
8 The Lord is good and gracious,
  he upright is also:
 He therefore sinners will instruct
  in ways that they should go.
9 The meek and lowly he will guide
  in judgment just alway:
 To meek and poor afflicted ones
  he'll clearly teach his way.
10 The whole paths of the Lord our God
  are truth and mercy sure,
 To such as keep his covenant
  and testimonies pure.

11 Now for thine own name's sake, O Lord,
  I humbly thee intreat
 To pardon mine iniquity,
  for it is very great.
12 What man fears God? him shall he teach
  the way that he shall choose.
13 His soul shall dwell at ease: his seed
  the earth as heirs shall use.
14 The secret of the Lord is with
  such as do fear his name:
 And he his holy covenant
  will manifest to them.
15 Towards the Lord my waiting eyes
  continually are set:
 For he it is that shall bring forth
  my feet out of the net.
16 O turn thee unto me, O God,
  have mercy me upon:
 Because I solitary am,
  and in affliction.
17 Enlarg'd the griefs are of my heart:
  me from distress relieve.
18. See mine affliction, and my pain,
  and all my sins forgive.
19 Consider thou mine enemies,
  because they many are,
 And it a cruel hatred is,
  which they against me bear.
20 O do thou keep my soul, O God,
  do thou deliver me:
 Let me not be asham'd: for I
  do put my trust in thee.

21 O let integrity and truth
    keep me, who thee attend.
22 Redemption, Lord, to Israel
    from all his troubles send.

PSALM XXVI.
A Psalm of David.

David being oppressed by the Judges of the land, his powerful adversaries, and being exiled from the House of God, he appealeth to God, the supreme Judge in the testimony of a good conscience, bearing him witness, first of his endeavour to walk uprightly as became a believer, ver. 1, 2, 3. And, Secondly, Of his keeping himself from the contagion of evil counsel, sinful courses, and example of the wicked, ver. 4, 5. Thirdly, Of his purpose still to behave himself holily and righteously, out of love to be partaker of the public privileges of the Lord's people in the Congregation, ver. 6, 7, 8. Whereupon he prayeth to be free of the judgment coming on the wicked, ver. 9, 10. According as he was purposed to eschew their sins, ver. 11. And he closeth his prayer with comfort and assurance to be heard, ver. 12.

1 JUDGE me, O Lord, for I have walk'd
    in mine integrity:
  I trusted also in the Lord,
    slide therefore shall not I.
2 Examine me, and do me prove;
    try heart and reins, O God.
3 For thy love is before mine eyes,
    thy truth's paths I have trod.
4 With persons vain I have not sat,
    nor with dissemblers gone.
5 Th' assembly of ill men I hate:
    to sit with such I shun.
6 Mine hands in innocence, O Lord,
    I'll wash and purify;
  So to thine holy altar go,
    and compass well I.

7 That I with voice of thanksgiving
    may publish and declare,
And tell of all thy mighty works
    that great and wond'rous are.
8 The habitation of thy house,
    Lord, I have loved well;
Yea, in that place I do delight,
    where doth thine honour dwell.
9 With sinners gather not my soul,
    and such as blood would spill:
10 Whose hands mischievous plots, right
    corrupting bribes do fill.   [hand
11 But as for me, I will walk on
    in mine integrity:
Do thou redeem me, and, O Lord,
    be merciful to me.
12 My foot upon an even place
    doth stand with stedfastness:
Within the congregations
    th' Eternal I will bless.

PSALM XXVII.
A Psalm of David.

In this Psalm David setteth down what use he had of his faith in God, in the time of his trouble; and, first how he strengthened his faith ver. 1, 2, 3, 4, 5, 6. And next, how he prayed upon the aforesaid grounds, ver. 7, 8, 9, 10, 11, 12. And thirdly, what advantage he had by believing in God, in the time of his exercise, ver. 13. Whereupon he exhorts all the godly to follow his example, under hope to be helped, as he was helped, ver. 14.

1 THE Lord's my light and saving health
    who shall make me dismay'd?
My life's strength is the Lord, of whom
    then shall I be afraid?

2 When as mine enemies and foes,
    moſt wicked perſons all,
To eat my fleſh againſt me roſe,
    they ſtumbled and did fall.

3 Againſt me though an hoſt encamp,
    my heart yet fearleſs is:
Though war againſt me riſe, I will
    be confident in this.

4 One thing I of the Lord deſir'd,
    and will ſeek to obtain,
That all days of my life I may
    within God's houſe remain:
That I the beauty of the Lord
    behold may and admire,
And that I in his holy place
    may rev'rently enquire.

5 For he in his pavilion ſhall
    me hide in evil days:
In ſecret of his tent me hide,
    and on a rock me raiſe.

6 And now, ev'n at this preſent time,
    mine head ſhall lifted be
Above all thoſe that are my foes,
    and round encompaſs me:
Therefore unto his tabernacle
    I'll ſacrifices bring
Of joyfulneſs; I'll ſing, yea, I
    to God will praiſes ſing.

7 O Lord, give ear unto my voice,
    when I do cry to thee:
Upon me alſo mercy have,
    and do thou anſwer me.

8 When thou didst say, Seek ye my face;
   then unto thee reply
  Thus did my heart, above all things
   thy face, Lord, seek will I.
9 Far from me hide thou not thy face,
   put not away from thee
  Thy servant in thy wrath; thou hast
   an helper been to me;
  O God of my salvation,
   leave me not, nor forsake.
10 Tho' me my parents both should leave,
   the Lord will me up take.
11 O Lord, instruct me in thy way,
   to me a leader be
  In a plain path, because of those
   that hatred bear to me.
12 Give me not to mine en'mies will;
   for witnesses that lie,
  Against me risen are, and such
   as breathe out cruelty.
13 I fainted had, unless that I
   believed had, to see
  The Lord's own goodness in the land
   of them that living be.
14 Wait on the Lord, and be thou strong,
   and he shall strength afford
  Unto thine heart: yea, do thou wait,
   I say, upon the Lord.

PSALM XXVIII.
A Psalm of David.

In the first part of this Psalm, we have the Prophet's conflict against his enemies, such as in the former Psalm is to be seen, wherein he prayeth for audience, ver. 1, 2. and delivery to himself, ver. 3. and that God would vindicate his own justice against his disdainful enemies, ver. 4, 5. In the latter part, the Prophet having gotten comfort in his Prayer, doth glorify God, ver. 6. and strengthens his own and the rest of the Godlies' faith, ver. 7, 8. and prayeth for a blessing to the Church, ver 9.

1 TO thee I'll cry, O Lord my rock,
    hold not thy peace to me:
Lest, like those that to pit descend,
    I by thy silence be.
2 The voice hear of my humble pray'rs,
    when unto thee I cry:
When to thy holy oracle
    I lift my hands on high.
3 With ill men draw me not away,
    that work iniquity:
That speak peace to their friends, while in
    their hearts doth mischief lie.
4 Give them according to their deeds,
    and ills endeavoured:
And as their handy-works deserve,
    to them be rendered.
5 God shall not build, but them destroy,
    who would not understand,
The Lord's own works, nor did regard
    the doing of his hand.
6 For ever blessed be the Lord,
    for graciously he heard
The voice of my petitions,
    and prayers did regard.
7 The Lord's my strength and shield, my heart
    upon him did rely;
And I am helped; hence my heart
    doth joy exceedingly,

And with my song I will him praise.
8   Their strength is God alone,
He also is the saving strength
of his anointed One.

9 O thine own people do thou save,
bless thine inheritance:
Them also do thou feed, and them
for evermore advance.

PSALM XXIX.
A Psalm of David.

David exhorteth Princes and great men, to humble themselves before God, and to worship him (as he hath commanded) in his public ordinances, ver. 1, 2. First, Because he is infinitely higher than they, and more terrible to all men, than they can be to their subjects, or inferiors, as the uttering of his majesty and power by thunder doth make evident, ver. 3, 4, 5, 6, 7, 8, 9. Secondly, Because he offereth the means of saving knowledge, even all his ordinances, whereby men may heartily glorify him in their assemblies, ver. 9! Thirdly, Because he is an everlasting King and Ruler of all the creatures; ver. 10. And Fourthly, Because such as do humbly submit themselves to him, and worship him as his people should do, shall be furnished with abilities for every good work, and shall be abundantly blessed.

1 GIVE ye unto the Lord, ye sons
    that of the mighty be,
All strength and glory to the Lord
    with cheerfulness give ye.

2 Unto the Lord the glory give
    that to his name is due;
And in the beauty of holiness
    unto JEHOVAH bow.

3 The Lord's voice on the waters is:
    the God of Majesty
Doth thunder, and on multitudes
    of waters sitteth he.

4 A pow'rful voice it is that comes
    out from the Lord most high;
The voice of that great Lord is full
    of glorious majesty.
5 The voice of the Eternal doth
    asunder cedars tear:
Yea, God the Lord doth cedars break
    that Lebanon doth bear.
6 He makes them like a calf to skip:
    ev'n that great Lebanon,
And, like to a young unicorn,
    the mountain Sirion.
7 God's voice divides the flames of fire
8   The desart it doth shake:
The Lord doth make the wilderness
    of Kadesh all to quake.
9 God's voice doth make the hinds to calve,
    it makes the forest bare:
And in his temple ev'ry one
    his glory doth declare.
10 The Lord sits on the floods: the Lord
    sits King, and ever shall.
11 The Lord will give his people strength,
    and with peace bless them all.

PSALM XXX.

A Psalm and Song at the Dedication of the House of David.

David praiseth God for his late deliverance from the hand of Absalom, ver. 1, 2, 3. And, Secondly, He exhorteth others to praise God also for his mercies, ver. 4, 5. Thirdly, He confesseth his carnal security, and how he was corrected, ver. 6, 7. Fourthly, He sheweth how he prayed mercy, ver. 8, 9, 10. And fifthly, He praiseth the Lord for his gracious answer, ver. 11, 12.

1 LORD, I will thee extol, for thou
    haſt lifted me on high,
And over me thou to rejoice
    mad'ſt not mine enemy.
2 O thou who art the Lord my God,
    I in diſtreſs to thee
With loud cries lifted up my voice,
    and thou haſt healed me.
3 O Lord, my ſoul thou haſt brought up,
    and reſcued from the grave:
That I to pit ſhould not go down,
    alive thou didſt me ſave.
4 O ye that are his holy ones,
    ſing praiſe unto the Lord,
And give unto him thanks, when you
    his holineſs record.
5 For but a moment laſts his wrath;
    life in his favour lies:
Weeping may for a night endure,
    at morn doth joy ariſe.
6 In my proſperity, I ſaid,
    that nothing ſhall me move.
7 O Lord, thou haſt my mountain made
    to ſtand ſtrong by thy love:
But when that thou, O gracious God,
    didſt hide thy face from me,
Then quickly was my proſp'rous ſtate
    turn'd into miſery.
8 Wherefore unto the Lord my cry
    I cauſed to aſcend;
My humble ſupplication
    I to the Lord did ſend.

9 What profit is there in my blood,
    when I go down to pit?
Shall unto thee the duſt give praiſe?
    thy truth declare ſhall it?
10 Hear, Lord, have mercy, help me, Lord:
11   Thou turned haſt my ſadneſs
To dancing: yea, my ſackcloth loos'd,
    and girded me with gladneſs:
12 That ſing thy praiſe my glory may,
    and never ſilent be:
O Lord my God, for evermore
    I will give thanks to thee.

PSALM XXXI.

To the chief Muſician, a Pſalm of David.

Another exerciſe of David, wherein he being in great danger to be taken by his enemies, prayeth for delivery, ver. 1, 2, 3, 4, 5, 6. Secondly, He ſtrengtheneth his faith by his by-gone experience, ver. 7, 8. Thirdly, In prayer he layeth out his lamentable condition before God, ver. 9, 10, 11, 12, 13. Fourthly, He wreſtleth on in prayer for comfort and ſafety to himſelf, and confuſion to his enemies, ver. 14, 15, 16, 17, 18. Fifthly, Being delivered and comforted by a new experience of God's merciful preſervation of him, he maketh good uſe of it, by praiſing God for it, and exhorting the godly to love God and rely on him, ver. 19, 20, 21, 22, 23, 24.

1 IN thee, O Lord, I put my truſt,
    ſham'd let me never be:
According to thy righteouſneſs,
    do thou deliver me.
2 Bow down thine ear to me with ſpeed,
    ſend me deliverance:
To ſave me, my ſtrong rock be thou,
    and my houſe of defence.

3 Becauſe thou art my rock, and thee
　　I for my fortreſs take:
Therefore do thou me lead and guide,
　　ev'n for thine own name's ſake:
4 And ſith thou art my ſtrength, therefore,
　　pull me out of the net,
Which they in ſubtilty for me
　　ſo privily have ſet.
5 Into thine hands I do commit
　　my ſpirit; for thou art he,
O thou JEHOVAH, God of truth,
　　that haſt redeemed me.
6 Thoſe that do lying vanities
　　regard, I have abhorr'd:
But as for me, my confidence
　　is fixed on the Lord.
7 • I'll in thy mercy gladly joy:
　　for thou my miſeries
Conſider'd haſt; thou haſt my ſoul
　　known in adverſities;
8 And thou haſt not incloſed me
　　within the en'my's hand:
And by thee have my feet been made
　　in a large room to ſtand.
9 O Lord, upon me mercy have,
　　for trouble is on me;
Mine eye, my belly, and my ſoul
　　with grief conſumed be,
10 Becauſe my life with grief is ſpent,
　　my years with ſighs and groans:
My ſtrength doth fail, and for my ſin
　　conſumed are my bones.

11 I was a scorn to all my foes,
　　and to my friends a fear,
And specially reproach'd of those
　　that were my neighbours near:
When they me saw, they from me fled.
12　　Ev'n so I am forgot,
As men are out of mind when dead:
　　I'm like a broken pot.
13 For slanders I of many heard,
　　fear compast me, while they
Against me did consult and plot,
　　to take my life away.
14 But as for me, O Lord, my trust
　　upon thee I did lay:
And I to thee, thou art my God,
　　did confidently say.
15 My times are wholly in thine hand:
　　do thou deliver me
From their hands, that mine enemies
　　and persecutors be.
16 Thy countenance to shine do thou
　　upon thy servant make:
Unto me give salvation,
　　for thy great mercies' sake.
17 Let me not be asham'd, O Lord,
　　for on thee call'd I have:
Let wicked men be sham'd, let them
　　be silent in the grave.
18 To silence put the lying lips,
　　that grievous things do say,
And hard reports in pride and scorn,
　　on righteous men do lay.

19 How great's the goodness thou for them
    that fear thee keep'ſt in ſtore,
And wrought'ſt for them that truſt in thee,
    the ſons of men before!
20 In ſecret of thy preſence, thou
    ſhalt hide them from man's pride:
From ſtrife of tongues thou cloſely ſhalt
    as in a tent, them hide.
21 All praiſe and thanks be to the Lord:
    for he hath magnify'd
His wond'rous love to me, within
    a city fortify'd.
22 For from thine eyes cut off I am,
    (I in my haſte had ſaid;)
My voice yet heard'ſt thou, when to thee
    with cries my moan I made.
23 O love the Lord, all ye his Saints:
    becauſe the Lord doth guard
The faithful, and he plenteouſly
    proud doers doth reward.
24 Be of good courage, and he ſtrength
    unto your hearts ſhall ſend,
All ye whoſe hope and confidence
    doth on the Lord depend.

PSALM XXXII.

A Pſalm of David, Maſchil.

David in this Pſalm deſcribeth the bleſſedneſs of the man juſtified by faith, by way of general doctrine, ſet down, ver. 1, 2. Which he cleareth by his own experience, ver. 3, 4, 5. Then he ſheweth the uſes both of the general doctrine, and of his own experience; Firſt, for inducing the godly, to go to God by prayer in trouble, ver. 6. Secondly, for confirming of his own faith, ver. 7. Thirdly, For teaching all men ſubmiſſion to God, and not to ſtrive with him when he doth correct or exerciſe them, ver. 8, 9 Fourthly, For believing in God in all conditions, ver. 10.

And fifthly, For making the Lord the joy and delight of the juſtified man.

1 O Bleſſed is the man to whom
   is freely pardoned
  All the tranſgreſſions he hath done,
   whoſe ſin is covered.
2 Bleſt is the man to whom the Lord
   imputeth not his ſin,
  And in whoſe ſp'rit there is no guile,
   nor fraud is found therein.
3 When as I did refrain my ſpeech,
   and ſilent was my tongue:
  My bones then waxed old, becauſe
   I roared all day long.
4 For upon me both day and night
   thine hand did heavy ly:
  So that my moiſture turned is
   in ſummer's drought thereby.
5 I thereupon have unto thee
   my ſin acknowledged,
  And likewiſe mine iniquity
   I have not covered:
  I will confeſs unto the Lord
   my treſpaſſes, ſaid I;
  And of my ſin thou freely didſt
   forgive th' iniquity.
6 For this ſhall ev'ry godly one
   his prayer make to thee,
  In ſuch a time he ſhall thee ſeek
   as found thou may'ſt be:
  Surely, when floods of waters great
   do ſwell up to the brim,.
  They ſhall not overwhelm his ſoul,
   nor once come near to him.

7 Thou art my hiding place, thou shalt
   from trouble keep me free:
Thou with songs of deliverance
   about shall compass me.
8 I will instruct thee, and thee teach
   the way that thou shalt go:
And, with mine eye upon thee set,
   I will direction show.
9 Then be not like the horse or mule,
   which do not understand:
Whose mouth, least they come near to thee,
   a bridle must command.
10 Unto the man that wicked is
    his sorrow shall abound:
But him that trusteth in the Lord,
    mercy shall compass round.
11 Ye righteous, in the Lord be glad,
    in him do ye rejoice:
All ye that upright are in heart,
    for joy lift up your voice.

PSALM XXXIII.

This Psalm, in God's providence, hath no inscription, as also many others have none, that we may look upon Holy Scriptures as altogether inspired of God, and not put price upon it for the writers thereof, whether their name be expressed or not. In it there is, first an exhortation to praise God, ver. 1, 2, 3. for his powerful, wise, and righteous government of all things in general, ver. 4, 5. and more especially for his powerful guiding the works of Creation, ver. 6, 7. Secondly, An exhortation, as to praise God, so also to fear him, for his omnipotency, and his powerful over-ruling and disappointing all the devices of men against his Church, and his powerful executing all his own will, ver. 8, 9, 10, 11. Thirdly, A proclaiming the blessedness of the Lord's Church and people, and of God's praises in reaching his providence over all the world, in favour of his people, ver. 12, 13, 14, 15. In special, for disappointing and evacuating all vain confidences of men great and small, who do not trust in him, ver. 16, 17. and taking care of such as fear him, and trust in him, to deliver them from all evil, ver. 18, 19. Fourthly, The use is set down which the godly do make of this doctrine and song of Praise.

1 YE righteous in the Lord rejoice:
    it comely is, and right,
That upright men with thankful voice
    should praise the Lord of might.
2 Praise God with harp; and unto him
    sing with the psaltery,
Upon a ten string'd instrument
    make ye sweet melody.
3 A new song to him sing, and play
    with loud noise skilfully.
4 For right is God's word: all his works
    are done in verity.
5 To judgment and to righteousness
    a love he beareth still:
The loving-kindness of the Lord
    the earth throughout doth fill.
6 The Heavens by the word of God
    did their beginning take:
And by the breathing of his mouth
    he all their hosts did make.
7 The waters of the seas he brings
    together as an heap:
And in store-houses, as it were
    he layeth up the deep.
8 Let earth and all that live therein,
    with rev'rence fear the Lord:
Let all the world's inhabitants
    dread him with one accord.
9 For he did speak the word, and done
    it was without delay:

Eſtabliſhed it firmly ſtood
whatever he did ſay.
10 God doth the counſel bring to nought
which heathen folk do take;
And what the people do deviſe,
of none effect doth make.
11 O! but the counſel of the Lord
doth ſtand for ever ſure,
And of his heart the purpoſes
from age to age endure.
12 That nation bleſſed is, whoſe God
JEHOVAH is: and thoſe
A bleſſed people are, whom for
his heritage he choſe.
13 ·The Lord from Heav'n ſees and beholds
all ſons of men full well.
14 He views all from his dwelling-place
that in the earth do dwell.
15 He forms their hearts alike: and all
their doings he obſerves.
16 Great hoſts ſave not a king: much ſtrength
no mighty man preſerves.
17 An horſe for preſervation
is a deceitful thing:
And by the greatneſs of his ſtrength
can no deliv'rance bring.
18 Behold, on thoſe that do him fear,
the Lord doth ſet his eye:
Ev'n thoſe who on his mercy do
with confidence rely
19 From death to free their ſoul, in dearth
·life unto them to yield.

20 Our soul doth wait upon the Lord:
 he is our help and shield.
21 Sith in his holy name we trust,
 our heart shall joyful be.
22 Lord, let thy mercy be on us,
 as we do hope in thee.

PSALM XXXIV.

A Psalm of David, when he changed his behaviour before Abimelech, who drove him away, and he departed.

In this Psalm, David praiseth God for his delivery from the King of Gath, and exhorteth others to praise God with him, for his expxrience of God's mercy, ver. 1, 2, 3, 4, 5, 6. Then for making farther use of this mercy, he gives out general doctrines concerning God's protection and care of his children, with the use thereof, ver. 7, 8, 9, 10. Thirdly, He gives counsel how to lead a blessed life, ver. 11, 12, 13, 14. Fourthly, He enforceth his counsel by promises to the godly, who obey God's counsel; and threatnings to the wicked man, who obeyeth not, ver. 15, 16, 17, 18, 19, 20, 21, 22.

1 GOD will I bless all times; his praise
 my mouth shall still express.
2 My soul shall boast in God: the meek
 shall hear with joyfulness.
3 Extol the Lord with me, let us
 exalt his name together.
4 I sought the Lord, he heard, and did
 me from all fears deliver.
5 They look'd to him, and light'ned were:
 not shamed were their faces.
6 This poor man cry'd, God heard, and sav'd
 him from all his distresses.
7 The Angel of the Lord encamps,
 and round encompasseth
 All those about that do him fear,
 and them delivereth.

8 O taste and see that God is good:
   who trusts in him is blest.
9 Fear God, his Saints: none that him fear,
   shall be with want opprest.
10 The lions young may hungry be,
    and they may lack their food:
  But they that truly seek the Lord
    shall not lack any good.
11 O children, hither do ye come,
    and unto me give ear:
  I shall you teach to understand
    how ye the Lord should fear.
12 What man is he that life desires,
    to see good would live long?
13 Thy lips refrain from speaking guile,
    and from ill words thy tongue.
14 Depart from ill, do good, seek peace,
    pursue it earnestly.
15 God's eyes are on the just: his ears
    are open to their cry.
16 The face of God is set against
    those that do wickedly,
  That he may quite out from the earth
    cut off their memory.
17 The righteous cry unto the Lord,
    he unto them gives ear,
  And they out of their troubles all
    by him deliv'red are.
17 The Lord is ever nigh to them
    that be of broken sp'rit;
  To them he safety doth afford,
    that are in heart contrite.

19 The troubles that afflict the just,
　　in number many be:
　But yet at length out of them all
　　the Lord doth set him free.
20 He carefully his bones doth keep,
　　whatever can befall:
　That not so much as one of them
　　can broken be at all.
21 Ill shall the wicked slay: laid waste
　　shall be, who hate the just.
22 The Lord redeems his servants' souls:
　　none perish that him trust.

PSALM XXXV.
A Psalm of David.

This Psalm is a representation of Christ's hottest contest with his adversaries, wherein they are about to do their worst against him, and his kingdom; and he denounceth the hottest wrath of God against them, for their everlasting overthrow, set forth under the shadow of David's contest with his irreconcilable enemies. Wherein he prayeth God to arise for him, ver. 1, 2, 3. and take order with his deceitful enemies, ver. 4, 5, 6, 7, 8. which as it may comfort the supplicant, so shall it serve also for God's glory, ver. 9, 10. A main reason of which petition, is the unjust and ingrate dealing of his enemies with him, ver. 11, 12, 13, 14, 15, 16. Whereupon he reneweth his petition the second time, ver. 17, 18, 19. pressing his so mer reason from the enemies unjust and insolent disposition, ver. 20, 21. And then reneweth his petition the third time for himself against his enemies, ver. 22, 23, 24, 25, 26. and for all the favourers of his cause, ver. 27, 28.

1 PLEAD, Lord, with those that plead, and
　　with those that fight with me. [fight
2 Of shield and buckler take thou hold,
　　stand up mine help to be.
3 Draw also out the spear, and do
　　against them stop the way
　That me pursue: unto my soul,
　　I'm thy salvation, say.

4 Let them confounded be, and ſham'd,
　　that for my ſoul have ſought:
　Who plot my hurt, turn'd back be they,
　　and to confuſion brought.
5 Let them be like unto the chaff
　　that flies before the wind:
　And let the Angel of the Lord
　　purſue them hard behind.
6 With darkneſs cover thou their way,
　　and let it ſlipp'ry prove,
　And let the Angel of the Lord
　　purſue them from above.
7 For without cauſe have they for me
　　their net hid in a pit,
　They alſo have without a cauſe
　　for my ſoul digged it.
8 Let ruin ſeize him unawares,
　　his net he hid withal
　Himſelf let catch; and in the ſame
　　deſtruction let him fall.
9 My ſoul in God ſhall joy; and glad
　　in his ſalvation be.
10 And all my bones ſhall ſay, O Lord,
　　who is like unto thee.
　Which doſt the poor ſet free from him
　　that is for him too ſtrong;
　The poor and needy from the man
　　that ſpoils and does him wrong?
11 Falſe witneſſes roſe; to my charge
　　things I not knew they laid.
12 They, to the ſpoiling of my ſoul,
　　me ill for good repaid.

13 But as for me, when they were sick,
   in sackcloth sad I mourn'd:
 My humbled soul did fast, my pray'r
   into my bosom turn'd.
14 Myself I did behave, as he
   had been my friend or brother:
 I heavily bow'd down, as one
   that mourneth for his mother.
15 But in my trouble they rejoic'd,
   gath'ring themselves together:
 Yea, abjects vile together did
   themselves against me gather;
 I knew it not, they did me tear,
   and quiet would not be.
16 With mocking hypocrites, at feasts,
   they gnash'd their teeth at me.
17 How long, Lord, look'st thou on? from
   destructions they intend,   [those
 Rescue my soul, from lions young
   my darling do defend.
18 I will give thanks to thee, O Lord,
   within th' assembly great:
 And, where much people gath'red are,
   thy praises forth will set.
19 Let not my wrongful enemies
   proudly rejoice o'er me:
 Nor, who me hate without a cause,
   let them wink with the eye.
20 For peace they do not speak at all:
   but crafty plots prepare
 Against all those within the land
   that meek and quiet are.

21 With mouths set wide, they 'gainst me
 Ha, ha, our eye doth see. [said,
22 Lord, thou hast seen, hold not thy peace:
 Lord. be not far from me.
23 Stir up thyself; wake, that thou may'st
 judgment to me afford.
 Ev'n to my cause, O thou that art
 my only God and Lord.
24 O Lord my God, do thou me judge
 after thy righteousness,
 And let them not their joy 'gainst me
 triumphantly express.
25 Nor let them say within their hearts,
 Ah, we would have it thus:
 Nor suffer them to say, that he
 is swallowed up by us.
26 Sham'd and confounded be they all
 that at my hurt are glad
 Let those, against me that do boast,
 with shame and scorn be clad.
27 Let them that love my righteous cause
 be glad, shout, and not cease
 To say, the Lord be magnify'd
 who loves his servant's peace.
28 Thy righteousness shall also be
 declared by my tongue,
 The praises that belong to thee
 speak shall it all day long.

PSALM XXXVI.

*To the chief Musician, a Psalm of David,
the Servant of the Lord.*

This Psalm hath three parts. In the first, David sets down
the perverseness of the wicked in their sinful course and de-

vices against the godly and himself, ver. 1, 2, 3, 4. In the second, He comforts himself, and doth settle his faith on the praises and properties of God, ver. 5, 6, 7, 8, 9. In the third, He prayeth in the behalf of God's children, and for himself, to be delivered from the wicked, ver. 10, 11, 12.

1 THE wicked man's transgression
    within my heart thus says,
Undoubtedly the fear of God
    is not before his eyes.
2 Because himself he flattereth
    in his own blinded eye,
Until the hatefulness be found
    of his iniquity.
3 Words from his mouth proceeding are,
    fraud and iniquity:
He to be wise and to do good,
    hath left off utterly.
4 He mischief, lying on his bed,
    most cunningly doth plot,
He sets himself in ways not good;
    ill he abhorreth not.
5 Thy mercy, Lord, is in the Heav'ns;
    thy truth doth reach the clouds.
6 Thy justice is like mountains great;
    thy judgments deep as floods:
Lord, thou preservest man and beast.
7   How precious is thy grace!
Therefore in shadow of thy wings
    mens' sons their trust shall place.
8 They with the fatness of thy house
    shall be well satisfy'd,
From rivers of thy pleasures thou
    wilt drink to them provide.

9 Because of life the fountain pure
   remains alone with thee:
And in that purest light of thine
   we clearly light shall see.
10 Thy loving-kindness unto them
   continue that thee know;
And still on men upright in heart
   thy righteousness bestow.
11 Let not the foot of cruel pride
   come and against me stand,
And let me not removed be,
   Lord, by the wicked's hand.
12 There fall'n are they, and ruined,
   that work iniquities:
Cast down they are, and never shall
   be able to arise.

PSALM XXXVII.
A Psalm of David.

This Psalm tendeth to guard the godly against the ordinary tentation unto envy, emulation, fretting, and discouragement in the way of godliness, arising from the temporal prosperity of the wicked, and that by eight directions or councils from the Lord, each of them confirmed by reasons; most of which are comparisons of the blessed estate of the godly at the worst, with the estate of the wicked at their best. Their first direction or council, ver. 1, 2. the second, ver. 3. the third, ver. 4. the fourth, ver. 5, 6. the fifth, ver. 7. the sixth, ver. 8, 9, 10, 11, 12, to ver. 26. the seventh, ver. 27, to ver. 33. the eighth direction, ver. 34, to the end.

1 FOR evil-doers fret thou not
   thyself unquietly,
Nor do thou envy bear to those
   that work iniquity.

2 For, even like unto the grafs,
    foon be cut down fhall they,
And, like the green and tender herb,
    they wither fhall away.
3 Set thou thy truft upon the Lord,
    and be thou doing good;
And fo thou in the land fhalt dwell,
    and verily have food.
4 Delight thyfelf in God: he'll give
    thine heart's defire to thee.
5 Thy way to God commit: him truft,
    it bring to pafs fhall he.
6 And like unto the light he fhall
    thy righteoufnefs difplay,
And he thy judgments fhall bring forth
    like noon-tide of the day.
7 Reft in the Lord, and patiently
    wait for him: do not fret
For him, who, profp'ring in his way,
    fuccefs in fin doth get.
8 Do thou from anger ceafe, and wrath
    fee thou forfake alfo:
Fret not thyfelf in any wife,
    that evil thou fhould'ft do.
9 For thofe that evil-doers are,
    fhall be cut off and fall:
But thofe that wait upon the Lord,
    the earth inherit fhall.
10 For yet a little while, and then
    the wicked fhall not be:
His place thou fhalt confider well,
    but it thou fhalt not fee.

11 But, by inheritance, the earth
    the meek ones shall possess:
  They also shall delight themselves
    in an abundant peace.
12 The wicked plots against the just,
    and at him whets his teeth.
13 The Lord shall laugh at him, because
    his day he coming seeth.
14 The wicked have drawn out the sword,
    and bent their bow, to slay
  The poor and needy, and to kill
    men of an upright way.
15 But their own sword which they have
    shall enter their own heart;   [drawn,
  Their bows which they have bent shall
    and into pieces part   [break,
16 A little that a just man hath
    is more, and better far,
  Than is the wealth of many such
    as lewd and wicked are.
17 For sinners' arms shall broken be;
    but God the just sustains.
18 God knows the just man's days, and still
    their heritage remains.
19 They shall not be asham'd, when they
    the evil time do see;
  And when the days of famine are,
    they satisfy'd shall be.
20 But wicked men, and foes of God,
    as fat of lambs decay;
  They shall consume: yea, into smoke
    they shall consume away.

21 The wicked borrows, but the same
    again he doth not pay;
Whereas the righteous mercy shows,
    and gives his own away.
22 For such as blessed be of him,
    the earth inherit shall;
And they that cursed are of him,
    shall be destroyed all.
23 A good man's footsteps by the Lord
    are ordered aright:
And in the way wherein he walks,
    he greatly doth delight.
24 Although he fall, yet shall he not
    be cast down utterly;
Because the Lord, with his own hand,
    upholds him mightily.
25 I have been young, and now am old;
    yet have I never seen
The just man left, nor that his seed
    for bread have beggars been.
26 He's ever merciful, and lends:
    his seed is blest therefore.
27 Depart from evil, and do good;
    and dwell for evermore.
28 For God loves judgment, and his Saints
    leaves not in any case;
They are kept ever: but cut off
    shall be the sinner's race.
29 The just inherit shall the land,
    and ever in it dwell.
30 The just man's mouth doth wisdom speak,
    his tongue doth judgment tell.

31 In's heart the law is of his God,
    his steps slide not away.
32 The wicked man doth watch the just,
    and seeketh him to slay.
33 Yet him the Lord will not forsake,
    nor leave him in his hands;
  The righteous will he not condemn
    when he in judgment stands.
34 Wait on the Lord, and keep his way,
    and thee exalt shall he,
  Th' earth to inherit: when cut off
    the wicked thou shalt see.
35 I saw the wicked great in pow'r,
    spread like a green-bay tree.
36 He past, yea, was not: him I sought,
    but found he could not be.
37 Mark thou the perfect, and behold
    the man of uprightness:
  Because that surely of this man
    the latter end is peace.
38 But those men that transgressors are,
    shall be destroy'd together;
  The latter end of wicked men,
    shall be cut off for ever.
39 But the salvation of the just
    is from the Lord above;
  He, in the time of their distress,
    their stay and strength doth prove.
40 The Lord shall help, and them deliver:
    he shall them free and save
  From wicked men, because in him
    their confidence they have.

PSALM XXXVIII.

A Psalm of David, to bring in remembrance.

In this Psalm, David in trouble both of soul and body, as an example of the hardest exercises that Christ's followers can fall into; First, Prayeth for the mitigation of his trouble and removal of wrath, ver. 1. And secondly, Layeth out this sense of the trouble which he felt immediately from God, ver. 2, 3, 4, 5, 6, 7, 8. Thirdly, Having put up his confused desires to God, for Prayers, in the sense of his inability to express himself ver. 9, 10. He lays out his sense of the grief and troubles which he felt from men, and endured with great patience, ver. 11, 12, 13, 14. Fourthly, He sets down the wrestling he had in prayer to God, because of his persecution by his adversaries, ver 15, 16, 17, 18, 19, 20. And closeth the Psalm, not having gotten comfort for the time, ver. 21, 22.

1 IN thy great indignation,
 O Lord, rebuke me not:
Nor on me lay thy chast'ning hand,
 in thy displeasure hot.
2 For in me fast thine arrows stick,
 thine hand doth press me sore.
3 And in my flesh there is no health,
 nor soundness any more:
This grief I have, because thy wrath
 is forth against me gone;
And in my bones there is no rest,
 for sin that I have done.
4 Because gone up above mine head
 my great transgressions be:
And, as a weighty burthen, they
 too heavy are for me.
5 My wounds do stink, and are corrupt:
 my folly makes it so.
6 I troubled am, and much bow'd down:
 all day I mourning go.

D 3

7 For a disease that loathsome is
 so fills my loins with pain,
That in my weak and weary flesh
 no soundness doth remain.
8 So feeble and infirm am I,
 and broken am so sore;
That, through disquiet of my heart,
 I have been made to roar.
9 O Lord, all that I do desire
 is still before thine eye:
And of my heart the secret groans
 not hidden are from thee.
10 My heart doth pant incessantly,
 my strength doth quite decay:
As for mine eyes, their wonted light
 is from me gone away.
11 My lovers and my friends do stand
 at distance from my sore:
And those do stand aloof that were
 kinsmen, and kind before.
12 Yea, they that seek my life, lay snares:
 who seek to do me wrong,
Speak things mischievous, and deceits
 imagine all day long.
13 But, as one deaf, that heareth not,
 I suffer'd all to pass:
I as a dumb man did become,
 whose mouth not open'd was.
14 As one that hears not, in whose mouth
 are no reproofs at all.
15 For, Lord, I hope in thee: my God,
 thou'lt hear me when I call.

16 For I said, hear me, lest they should
    rejoice o'er me with pride;
And o'er me magnify themselves,
    when as my foot doth slide.
17 For I am near to halt, my grief
    is still before mine eye.
18 For I'll declare my sin: and grieve
    for mine iniquity.
19 But yet mine en'mies lively are,
    and strong are they beside:
And they that hate me wrongfully,
    are greatly multiply'd.
20 And they for good that render ill,
    as en'mies me withstood:
Yea, ev'n for this, because that I
    do follow what is good.
21 Forsake me not, O Lord: my God,
    far from me never be.
22 O Lord, thou my salvation art,
    haste to give help to me.

PSALM XXXIX.

*To the chief Musician, even to Jeduthan,
a Psalm of David.*

Another such like hard exercise as in the former Psalm, wherein David acknowledgeth his infirmity in a passionate expression, when he was in trouble, ver. 1, 2, 3, 4. Secondly, He recovereth and comforted himself, ver. 5, 6, 7. Thirdly, What was his prayer in this exercise, ver. 8, 9, 10, 11, 12, 13.

1 I said, I will look to my ways
    lest with my tongue I sin:
In sight of wicked men, my mouth
    with bridle I'll keep in.

2 With silence I as dumb became,
   I did myself restrain
  From speaking good; but then the more
   increased was my pain.
3 My heart within me waxed hot,
   and while I musing was,
  The fire did burn; and from my tongue
   these words I did let pass:
4 Mine end, and measure of my days,
   O Lord, unto me show,
  What is the same; that I thereby
   my frailty well may know.
5 Lo, thou my days an hand-breadth mad'st,
   mine age is in thine eye
  As nothing: sure each man at best
   is wholly vanity.
6 Sure each man walks in a vain show;
   they vex themselves in vain:
  He heaps up wealth, and doth not know
   to whom it shall pertain.
7 And now, O Lord, what wait I for?
   my hope is fix'd on thee.
8 Free me from all my trespasses,
   the fool's scorn make not me.
9 Dumb was I, op'ning not my mouth,
   because this work was thine.
10 Thy stroke take from me: by the blow
   of thine hand I do pine.
11 When with rebukes thou dost correct
   man for iniquity,
  Thou wastes his beauty like a moth:
   sure each man's vanity.

12 Attend my cry, Lord, at my tears,
 and pray'rs not silent be:
I sojourn as my fathers all,
 and stranger am with thee.
13 O spare thou me, that I my strength
 recover may again,
Before from hence I do depart,
 and here no more remain.

PSALM XL.

To the chief Musician, a Psalm of David.

David as a Type of Christ in the whole Psalm, and as an example of the exercise of the godly, giveth thanks for the experience of God's delivering of him out of a notable trouble, ver. 1, 2, 3, 4. In the second place, He is led on in his thanksgiving to praise God for the great work of Redemption by Christ the son of God coming into the world, which is the fountain of all other mercies to the Saints, ver. 5, 6, 7, 8. In the third place, David in Type, and Christ in the accomplishment, giving account of his prophetical office, intercedeth and prayeth for the evidence of God's favour to himself personally and mystically considered, ver. 9, 10, 11, 12, 13. and for disappointment of his enemies, ver. 14, 15. and for the comfort of all the godly beholding his exercise and his delivery, which he confidently doth expect, ver. 16, 17.

1 I Waited for the Lord my God,
 and patiently did bear;
At length to me he did incline
 my voice and cry to hear.
2 He took me from a fearful pit,
 and from a miry clay,
And on a rock he set my feet,
 establishing my way.
3 He put a new song in my mouth,
 our God to magnify:
Many shall see it, and shall fear,
 and on the Lord rely.

4 O blessed is the man whose trust
    upon the Lord relies:
  Respecting not the proud, nor such
    as turn aside to lies.
5 O Lord my God, full many are
    the wonders thou hast done;
  Thy gracious thoughts to us-ward far
    above all thoughts are gone:
  In order none can reckon them
    to thee: if them declare,
  And speak of them I would, they more
    than can be numb'red are.
6 No sacrifice nor offering
    didst thou at all desire;
  Mine ears thou bor'd: sin-off'ring thou
    and burnt didst not require.
7 Then to the Lord these were my words,
    I come, behold and see:
  Within the volume of thy book
    it written is of me:
8 To do thy will I take delight,
    O thou my God that art:
  Yea, that most holy law of thine
    I have within my heart.
9 Within the congregation great,
    I righteousness did preach:
  Lo, thou dost know, O Lord, that I
    refrained not my speech.
10 I never did within my heart
    conceal thy righteousness;
  I thy salvation have declar'd,
    and shown thy faithfulness:

Thy kindneſs, which moſt loving is,
  concealed have not I;
Nor from the congregation great
  have hid thy verity.
11 Thy tender mercies, Lord, from me
  O do thou not reſtrain:
 Thy loving-kindneſs and thy truth,
  let them me ſtill maintain.
12 For ills paſt reck'ning compaſs me,
  and mine iniquities
Such hold upon me taken have,
  I cannot lift mine eyes:
They more than hairs are on mine head,
  thence is my heart diſmay'd.
13 Be pleaſed, Lord, to reſcue me:
  Lord, haſten to mine aid.
14 Sham'd and confounded be they all
  that ſeek my ſoul to kill:
Yea, let them backward driven be,
  and ſham'd that wiſh me ill.
15 For a reward of this their ſhame,
  confounded let them be,
That in this manner ſcoffing ſay,
  Aha! aha! to me.
16 In thee let all be glad and joy,
  who ſeeking thee abide:
Who thy ſalvation love, ſay ſtill,
  the Lord be magnify'd.
17 I'm poor and needy, yet the Lord
  of me a care doth take:
Thou art my help, and Saviour,
  my God, no tarrying make.

PSALM XLI.

To the chief Musician, a Psalm of David.

David as a Type of Christ, and one of his afflicted followers, after prayer comforteth himself against the uncharitable Judgment, which the wicked had of him in his affliction, ver. 1, 2, 3, 4. In the second place, he complaineth of his enemies cursed disposition against him, and prayeth to be delivered out of his trouble, ver. 5, 6, 7, 8, 9, 10. In the third place, he is answered comfortably, and praiseth God for it, ver. 11, 12, 13.

1 BLESSED is he that wisely doth
    the poor man's case consider;
For when the time of trouble is,
    the Lord will him deliver.
2 God will him keep; yea, save alive,
    on earth he blest shall live;
And to his enemies' desire
    thou wilt him not up give.
3 God will give strength, when he on bed
    of languishing doth mourn:
And in his sickness sore, O Lord,
    thou all his bed wilt turn.
4 I said, O Lord, do thou extend
    thy mercy unto me;
O do thou heal my soul; for why?
    I have offended thee.
5 Those that to me are enemies,
    of me do evil say;
When shall he die, that so his name
    may perish quite away?
6 To see me if he comes, he speaks
    vain words: but then his heart
Heaps mischief to it, which he tells
    when forth he doth depart.

7 My haters jointly whispering,
  'gainst me my hurt devise.
8 Mischief, say they, cleaves fast to him:
  he ly'th, and shall not rise.
9 Yea, ev'n mine own familiar friend,
  on whom I did rely,
 Who ate my bread, ev'n he his heel
  against me lifted high.
10 But, Lord, be merciful to me,
  and up again me raise,
 That I may justly them requite,
  according to their ways.
11 By this I know that certainly
  I favour'd am by thee,
 Because my hateful enemy
  triumphs not over me.
12 But as for me, thou me uphold'st
  in mine integrity,
 And me before thy countenance
  thou sett'st continually.
13 The Lord, the God of Israel,
  be blest for ever then;
 From age to age eternally,
  Amen, yea, and amen.

PSALM XLII.

To the chief Musician, Maschil, for the sons of Korah.

In this Psalm David sheweth what was his longing after the fellowship of the Saints in their public worship and service of God in the time of his banishment, by the persecution of Saul, ver. 1, 2, 3, 4. and how he wrestled with discouragements, by checking himself for it, and by praying to God, whereby he was erected unto hope and confidence to be answered, ver. 5, 6, 7, 8, 9, 10, 11.

1 LIKE as the hart for water-brooks
    in thirſt doth pant and bray,
  So pants my longing ſoul, O God,
    that come to thee I may.
2 My ſoul for God, the living God,
    doth thirſt: when ſhall I near
  Unto thy countenance approach,
    and in God's ſight appear?
3 My tears have unto me been meat,
    both in the night and day;
  While unto me continually,
    Where is thy God? they ſay.
4 My ſoul is poured out in me,
    when this I think upon;
  Becauſe that with the multitude
    I heretofore had gone;
  With them unto God's houſe I went,
    with voice of joy and praiſe,
  Yea, with the multitude that kept
    the ſolemn holy days.
5 O why art thou caſt down, my ſoul?
    why in me ſo diſmay'd?
  Truſt God, for I ſhall praiſe him yet,
    his count'nance is mine aid.
6 My God, my ſoul's caſt down in me:
    thee therefore mind I will
  From Jordan's land, the Hermonites,
    and ev'n from Mizar hill.
7 At the noiſe of thy water-ſpouts,
    deep unto deep doth call:
  Thy breaking waves paſs over me,
    yea, and thy billows all.

8 His loving-kindnefs yet the Lord
   command will in the day;
 His fong's with me by night: to God,
   by whom I live, I'll pray.
9 And I will fay to God my rock,
   why me forgett'ft thou fo?
 Why, for my foes oppreffion,
   thus mourning do I go?
10 'Tis as a fword within my bones,
   when my foes me upbraid:
 Ev'n when by them, Where is thy God?
   'tis daily to me faid.
11 O why art thou caft down my foul?
   why thus with grief oppreft,
 Art thou difquieted in me?
   in God ftill hope and reft:

 For yet I know I fhall him praife,
   who gracioufly to me
 The health is of my countenance,
   yea, mine own God is he.

PSALM XLIII.

This Pfalm tendeth to the fame purpofe with the former; for David in exile complaineth of his perfecutors, and prayeth for delivery, and regretteth his fad condition, ver. 1, 2. Prayeth for reftitution unto the liberty of the public ordinances, promifing to praife God at his returning chearfully, ver. 3, 4. and wreftleth with his difcouragements as he did in the former Pfalm, ver. 5.

1 JUDGE me, O God, and plead my caufe
   againft th' ungodly nation;
 From the unjuft and crafty man
   O be thou my falvation.

2 For thou the God art of my strength;
    why thrusts thou me thee fro'?
  For th' enemies' oppression,
    why do I mourning go?
3 O send thy light forth and thy truth;
    let them be guides to me,
  And bring me to thine holy hill,
    ev'n where thy dwellings be.
4 Then will I to God's altar go,
    to God my chiefest joy:
  Yea, God, my God, thy name to praise
    my harp I will employ.
5 Why art thou then cast down, my soul?
    what should discourage thee?
  And why with vexing thoughts art thou
    disquieted in me?
  Still trust in God, for him to praise
    good cause I yet shall have;
  He of my count'nance is the health,
    my God that doth me save.

PSALM XLIV.

To the chief Musician, Maschil, for the sons of Korah.

The Church under heavy persecution, First, Strengtheneth her faith in God before she enter upon her lamentation, ver. 1, 2, 3, 4, 5, 6, 7, 8. In the second place, She layeth forth her sad sufferings under the hands of cruel persecutors, ver. 9, 10, 11, 12, 13, 14, 15. 16. In the third, She professeth her constant adherence unto God, and doth avow his truth for time by-past, and her purpose to continue for time to come, ver. 17, 18, 19, 20, 21, 22. In the last place, They pray unto the Lord to arise, and relieve them from their cruel persecutors, for the glory of both his justice and mercy, ver. 23, 24, 25.

1 O God, we with our ears have heard,
   Our fathers have us told
 What works thou in their days had'ſt done
   ev'n in the days of old.
2 Thy hand did drive the heathen out,
   and plant them in their place;
 Thou didſt afflict the nations,
   but them thou didſt increaſe.
3 For neither got their ſword the land,
   nor did their arm them ſave:
 But thy right hand, arm, countenance,
   for thou them favour gave.
4 Thou art my King; for Jacob, Lord,
   deliv'rances command.
5 Thro' thee we ſhall puſh down our foes
   that do againſt us ſtand;
 We, thro' thy name, ſhall tread down thoſe
   that ris'n againſt us have.
6 For in my bow I ſhall not truſt,
   nor ſhall my ſword me ſave.
7 But from our foes thou haſt us ſav'd,
   our haters put to ſhame.
8 In God we all the day do boaſt;
   and ever praiſe thy name.
9 But now we are caſt off by thee,
   and us thou putt'ſt to ſhame;
 And, when our armies do go forth,
   thou go'ſt not with the ſame.
10 Thou mak'ſt us from the enemy,
   faint-hearted to turn back:
 And they who hate us, for themſelves
   our ſpoils away do take.

11 Like sheep for meat thou gaveft us:
    'mong heathen caft we be.
12 Thou didft for nought thy people fell,
    their price enrich d not thee.
13 Thou mak'ft us a reproach to be
    unto our neighbours near;
  Derifion, and a fcorn to them
    that round about us are.
14 A by-word alfo thou doft us
    among the heathen make:
  The people, in contempt and fpite,
    at us their heads do fhake.
15 Before me my confufion
    continually abides,
  And of my bafhful countenance
    the fhame me ever hides.
16 For voice of him that doth reproach,
    and fpeaketh blafphemy;
  By reafon of th' avenging foe,
    and cruel enemy.
17 All this is come on us, yet we
    have not forgotten thee,
  Nor falfely in thy covenant,
    behav'd ourfelves have we.
18 Back from thy way our heart not turn'd,
    our fteps no ftraying made:
19 Tho' us thou brak'ft in dragon's place,
    and cov'redft with death's fhade.
20 If we God's name forgot, or ftretcht
    to a ftrange God our hands;
21 Shall not God fearch this out? for he
    heart's fecrets underftands.

22 Yea, for thy sake we're kill'd all day;
    counted as slaughter-sheep.
23 Rise, Lord, cast us not ever off;
    awake, why dost thou sleep?
24 O wherefore hidest thou thy face,
    forgett'st our case distrest,
25 And our oppression? for our soul
    is to the dust down prest:

  Our belly also on the earth,
    fast cleaving hold doth take.
26 Rise for our help, and us redeem,
    ev'n for thy mercies' sake.

PSALM XLV.

To the chief Musician upon Shoshanim, for the sons of Korah, Maschil, a song of Loves.

Laying aside what useth to be spoken here of Solomon's marrying of Pharoah's daughter, and of some typical things therein, (tending to the extenuation of Solomon's fault) as conjectural, and serving nothing to the advantage of that marriage, presuppose the conjecture did hold, both concerning the occasion, and also what might seem typical in it, because similitudes taken from, and types made of what things soever God pleaseth, do serve to make clear what the Spirit will have taken up about Christ, or about any spiritual Antitype; but doth not serve to make clear the thing resembled by the Antitype from being sinful, as by the Type of Agar, and of the brazen serpent, and of Jonas his punishment, and sundry other similitudes and parables set down in Scripture doth appear: But we are sure this Psalm is a song, describing the mystical marriage of the Messiah Christ Jesus our Lord, and his Church, wherein Christ the bridegroom is praised, ver. 1, 2, 3, 4, 5, 6, 7, 8, 9. and the Church his spouse is instructed in her duty to him, ver. 10, 11, 12, 13, 14, 15. and the end of the song declared to be the everlasting praise of Christ, ver. 16, 17.

1 MY heart brings forth a goodly thing;
    my words that I indite
  Concern the King: my tongue's a pen
    of one that swift doth write.

2 Thou fairer art than sons of men:
  into thy lips is store
    Of grace infus'd: God therefore thee
      hath blest for evermore.
3 O thou that art the mighty One,
    thy sword gird on thy thigh:
  Ev'n with thy glory excellent,
    and with thy majesty.
4 For meekness, truth and righteousness
    in state ride prosp'rously;
  And thy right hand shall thee instruct
    in things that fearful be.
5 Thine arrows sharply pierce the hearts
    of th' enemies of the King;
  And under thy subjection
    the people down do bring.
6 For ever and for ever is,
    O God, thy throne of might:
  The sceptre of thy kingdom is
    a sceptre that is right.
7 Thou lovest right, and hatest ill:
    for God, thy God most high,
  Above thy fellows have with th' oil
    of joy anointed thee.
8 Of aloes, myrrh and cassia,
    a smell thy garments had;
  Out of th' iv'ry palaces,
    whereby they made thee glad.
9 Among thy women honourable
    king's daughters were at hand:
  Upon thy right hand did the Queen
    in gold of Ophir stand.

10 O daughter, hearken and regard,
   and do thine ear incline;
  Likewife forget thy father's houfe,
   and people that are thine.
11 Then of the King defir'd fhall be
   thy beauty veh'mently;
  Becaufe he is thy Lord, do thou
   him worfhip rev'rently.
12 The daughter there of Tyre fhall be
   with gifts and off'rings great;
  Thofe of the people that are rich,
   thy favour fhall intreat.
13 Behold, the daughter of the King
   all glorious is within;
  And with embroideries of gold
   her garments wrought have been.
14 She fhall be brought unto the King
   in robes with needle wrought:
  Her fellow-virgins following
   fhall unto thee be brought.
15 They fhall be brought with gladnefs
   and mirth on ev'ry fide,   [great,
  Into the palace of the King,
   and there they fhall abide.
16 Inftead of thofe thy fathers dear,
   thy children thou may'ft take,
  And, in all places of the earth,
   them noble princes make.
17 Thy name rememb'red I will make
   through ages all to be:
  The people therefore evermore
   fhall praifes give to thee.

Another of the fame.

1 MY heart inditing is
    good matter in a fong:
  I fpeak the things that I have made,
    which to the King belong:
  My tongue fhall be as quick,
    his honour to indite,
  As is the pen of any fcribe
    that ufeth faft to write.
2 Thou'rt faireft of all men,
    grace in thy lips doth flow:
  And therefore bleffings evermore
    on thee doth God beftow.
3 Thy fword gird on thy thigh,
    thou that art moft of might:
  Appear in dreadful majefty,
    and in thy glory bright.
4 For meeknefs, truth and right,
    ride profp'roufly in ftate:
  And thy right-hand fhall teach to thee
    things terrible and great.
5 Thy fhafts fhall pierce their hearts
    that foes are to the King;
  Whereby into fubjection
    the people thou fhalt bring.
6 Thy royal feat, O Lord,
    for ever fhall remain:
  The fceptre of thy kingdom doth
    all righteoufnefs maintain.
7 Thou lov'ft right, and hat'ft ill:
    for God, thy God moft High,
  Above thy fellows have with th' oil
    of joy anointed thee.

8 Of myrrh and spices sweet
 a smell thy garments had:
Out of the iv'ry palaces,
 whereby they made thee glad.
9 And in thy glorious train
 king's daughters waiting stand:
And thy fair Queen, in Ophir gold,
 doth stand at thy right hand.
10 O daughter take good heed,
 incline, and give good ear:
Thou must forget thy kindred all,
 and father's house most dear.
11 Thy beauty to the King
 shall then delightful be:
And do thou humbly worship him
 because thy Lord is he.
12 The daughter then of Tyre
 there with a gift shall be;
And all the wealthy of the land
 shall make their suit to thee.
13 The daughter of the King
 all glorious is within;
And with embroideries of gold,
 her garments wrought have been.
14 She cometh to the King
 in robes with needle wrought;
The virgins that do follow her
 shall unto thee be brought.
15 They shall be brought with joy,
 and mirth on ev'ry side,
Into the palace of the King,
 and there they shall abide.

16 And, in thy father's ftead,
    thy children thou may'ft take;
  And in all places of the earth
    them noble princes make.
17 I will fhew forth thy name
    to generations all:
  Therefore the people evermore
    to thee give praifes fhall.

PSALM XLVI.

*To the chief Mufician, for the fons of Korah,
  a fong upon Alamoth.*

After fome notable delivery of the Church from her ene*[...]*, the Lord's people do confirm themfelves in their refolution to truft in God, and not to be afraid of trouble, becaufe of his comfortable prefence among them, which is like unto a river of continual refrefhment, as late experience did give evidence, ver. 1, 2, 3, 4, 5, 6. and do exhort all men in the world to obferve this his late work, and make ufe of it for their humiliation, ver. 7, 8, 9, 10. as the Church doth make ufe of it for confirmation, ver. 11.

1 GOD is our refuge, and our ftrength,
    in ftraits a prefent aid.
2 Therefore, altho' the earth remove,
    we will not be afraid,
  Though hills amidft the feas be caft:
3   Though waters roaring make,
  And troubled be, yea, tho' the hills
    by fwelling feas do fhake.
4 A river is, whofe ftreams do glad
    the city of our God:
  The holy place wherein the Lord
    moft High hath his abode.

5 God in the midst of her doth dwell,
    nothing shall her remove:
  The Lord to her an helper will,
    and that right early, prove.
6 The heathen rag'd tumultuously,
    the kingdoms moved were:
  The Lord God uttered his voice,
    the earth did melt with fear.
7 The Lord of hosts upon our side
    doth constantly remain;
  The God of Jacob's our refuge,
    us safely to maintain.
8 Come and behold what wond'rous works
    have by the Lord been wrought:
  Come, see what desolations
    he on the earth hath brought.
9 Unto the ends of all the earth
    wars into peace he turns;
  The bow he breaks, the spear he cuts,
    in fire the chariot burns.
10 Be still, and know that I am God:
    among the heathen I
  Will be exalted, I on earth
    will be exalted high.
11 Our God, who is the Lord of hosts,
    is still upon our side;
  The God of Jacob our refuge,
    for ever will abide.

PSALM XLVII.

To the chief Musician, a Psalm for the sons of Korah.

E

This Psalm is a prophecy of the enlargement of Christ's Kingdom, and of the conjunction of Jews and Gentiles, in one body under Christ their head and Lord, delivered by way of exhortation to Jews and Gentiles, joyfully to praise the God and Saviour of the people, Jesus Christ, on whom the Psalmist looketh as now ascended into Heaven triumphantly, after the full payment made of the price of redemption, and as going about the gathering in of the redeemed Gentiles, till he bring in the fulness of them into one Church with the Jews: The exhortation is prefixed, ver. 1. and repeated, ver. 6, 7. The reasons of the exhortation to a joyful praising of him are seven: The first, ver. 2. The second, ver. 3. The third, ver. 4. The fourth, ver. 5. The fifth, ver. 7. The sixth, ver. 8. The seventh, ver. 9.

1 ALL people, clap your hands to God,
    with voice of triumph shout:
2 For dreadful is the Lord most High;
    great King the earth throughout.
3 The heathen people under us
    he surely shall subdue;
And he shall make the nations
    under our feet to bow.
4 The lot of our inheritance
    chuse out for us shall he,
Of Jacob whom he loved well,
    ev'n the excellency.
5 God is with shouts gone up, the Lord
    with trumpets sounding high.
6 Sing praise to God, sing praise: sing praise,
    praise to our God sing ye.
7 For God is King of all the earth,
    with knowledge praise express.
8 God rules the nations: God sits on
    his throne of holiness.
9 The princes of the people are
    assembled willingly;
Ev'n of the God of Abraham
    they who the people be:

For why? the shields that do defend
   the earth, are only his:
They to the Lord belong; yea, he
   exalted greatly is.

PSALM XLVIII.

A Song and Pſalm, for the ſons of Korah.

In this Pſalm the Lord is magnified for all his mercies beſtowed on his Church, (reſembled by Jeruſalem), ver. 1, 2, 3. And in ſpecial for a late mercy manifeſted in a paſſage of his care to preſerve Jeruſalem, a Type of the Church univerſal, againſt the aſſault of mighty Kings, ver. 4, 5, 6. The uſes of which mercies are ſet down in number ſeven: The firſt, ver. 7. The ſecond, ver. 8. The third, ver. 9. The fourth, ver. 10. The fifth, ver. 11. The ſixth, ver. 12, 13. The ſeventh, ver. 14.

GREAT is the Lord, and greatly he
   is to be praiſed ſtill,
Within the city of our God,
   upon his holy hill.
2 Mount Zion ſtands moſt beautiful,
   the joy of all the land;
The city of the mighty King
   on her north ſide doth ſtand.
3 The Lord within her palaces
   is for a refuge known:
4 For lo, the Kings that gather'd were
   together by have gone.
But, when they did behold the ſame,
   they wond'ring would not ſtay;
But, being troubled at the ſight,
   they thence did haſte away.
Great terror there took hold on them,
   they were poſſeſs'd with fear;
Their grief came like a woman's pain
   when ſhe a child doth bear.

7 Thou Tarshish ships with east-wind [break'st:
8   As we have heard it told,
So in the city of the Lord
   our eyes did it behold:
In our God's city, which his hand
   for ever 'stablish will.
9 We of thy loving-kindness thought,
   Lord, in thy temple still.
10 O Lord, according to thy name,
   thro' all the earth's thy praise;
And thy right hand, O Lord, is full
   of righteousness always.
11 Because thy judgments are made known
   let Zion mount rejoice,
Of Judah let the daughters all
   send forth a chearful voice.
12 Walk about Zion, and go round:
   the high tow'rs thereof tell.
13 Consider ye her palaces,
   and mark her bulwarks well;
That ye may tell posterity.
14   For this God doth abide
Our God for evermore; he will
   ev'n unto death us guide.

PSALM XLIX.

To the chief Musician, a Psalm for the sons of Korah.

This Psalm sets forth the gloriation of a Believer in the grace of God, and in his blessed condition, wherein he is lifted up above all the wealthy and honourable men in the world, who are not reconciled unto God; and this the Psalmist delivereth out of his own feeling and experience. And first, Because it is a main matter and worthy of all acceptation, he maketh a preface to his gloriation, ver. 1, 2,

3, 4. Then he cometh out with it, making his boast in God, That by faith in God he was so secured against sin and misery that they should not be able to mar his happiness, ver. 5. Thirdly, He doth prefer his blessedness above whatsoever wealth or riches could yield to a man, ver. 6, 7, 8, 9, 10. and above whatsoever dominion over air lands, or honour among men could yield to any man, either living or after his death, either to himself or to any of his posterity, ver. 11, 12, 13, 14. Fourthly, He giveth reason of his gloriation, because being justified by faith, and at peace with God, he was sure of delivery from every evil, and to be received out of his grave into glory and fellowship with God, ver 15. Fifthly, He guards every true Believer against every temptation which might disquiet him when he seeth himself and other godly reason in outward trouble, and the wicked in posterity, ver. 16, 17, 18, 19, 20.

1 HEAR this, all people, and give ear,
    'all in the world that dwell:
  Both low and high, both rich and poor.
    My mouth shall wisdom tell;
3 My heart shall knowledge meditate.
4   I will incline mine ear
  To parables; and on the harp
    my sayings dark declare.
5 Amidst those days that evil be,
    why should I, fearing, doubt?
  When of my heels th' iniquity
    shall compass me about.
6 Whoe'er they be that in their wealth
    their confidence do pitch,
  And boast themselves because they are
    become exceeding rich.
7 Yet none of these his brother can
    redeem by any way,
  Nor can he unto God for him
    sufficient ransom pay:
8 (Their soul's redemption precious is,
    and it can never be).

L 3

9 That still he should for ever live,
   and not corruption see.
10 For why? he seeth that wise men die,
   and brutish fools also
 Do perish, and their wealth, when dead,
   to others they let go.
11 Their inward thought is, that their house
   and dwelling-places shall
 Stand thro' all ages; they their lands
   by their own names do call.
12 But yet in honour shall not man
   abide continually:
 But, passing hence, may be compar'd
   unto the beasts that die.
13 Thus brutish folly plainly is
   their wisdom and their way;
 Yet their posterity approve
   what they do fondly say.
14 Like sheep they in the grave are laid,
   and death shall them devour;
 And, in the morning, upright men
   shall over them have pow'r:
 Their beauty, from their dwelling, shall
   consume within the grave.
15 But from hell's hand God will me free,
   for he shall me receive.
16 Be thou not then afraid, when one
   enriched thou dost see,
 Nor when the glory of his house
   advanced is on high.
17 For he shall carry nothing hence,
   when death his days doth end:

Nor shall his glory after him
  into the grave descend.
18 Although he his own soul did bless,
  whilst he on earth did live,
(And when thou to thyself dost well,
  men will thee praises give).
19 He to his father's race shall go,
  they never shall see light.
20 Man honour'd, wanting knowledge, is
  like beasts that perish quite.

PSALM L.
A Psalm of Asaph.

This Psalm is a citing of the visible Church before God, the Judge of all the earth, (who at last shall judge all flesh in the day of Judgment, and shall take vengeance on the wicked), to compear before the tribunal of God; now in time when mercy may be had, and now then timeously to consider the Lord's controversy against sinners in his Church, that they may repent and be saved. And first, The dreadfulness of the Judgment is set down, ver. 1, 2, 3. Secondly, The citation of the party, that is, the visible Church with the witnesses, ver. 4, 5. 6. Thirdly, There is a challenge of self-work Justiciaries, Legalists, and formal Ceremonialists, who did rest upon outward good behaviour, and upon the outward discharge of the ordinances, as if the sacrifices of the law or any performance of external duties, had been sufficient to expiate sin, and justify a man, ver. 7, 8, 9, 10, 11, 12, 13. Fourthly, There is a direction unto them how to come off their legal righteousness, and carnal way of worship, and to turn themselves to the right way of worshipping God in spirit and truth, ver. 14, 15. Fifthly, There is a challenge of those who were grosly wicked, ver. 16, 17, 18, 19, 20, 21. And lastly, There is a direction also to them to repent, and to give God glory in time, with an encouragement to the upright Believers to go on their way, ver. 22, 23.

1 THE mighty God, the Lord
    hath spoken, and did call
  The earth, from rising of the sun,
    to where he hath his fall.

2 From out of Zion hill,
　　which of excellency
　And beauty the perfection is,
　　God shined gloriously.
3 Our God shall surely come,
　　keep silence shall not he:
　Before him fire shall waste, great storms
　　shall round about him be.
4 Unto the heavens clear
　　he from above shall call,
　And to the earth likewise, that he
　　may judge his people all.
5 Together let my Saints
　　unto me gather'd be:
　Those that by sacrifice have made
　　a covenant with me.
6 And then the Heav'ns shall
　　his righteousness declare:
　Because the Lord himself is he
　　by whom men judged are.
7 My people Isra'l hear,
　　speak will I from on High;
　Against thee I will testify:
　　God, ev'n thy God, am I.
8 I, for thy sacrifice,
　　no blame will on thee lay,
　Nor for burnt-off'rings, which to me
　　thou off'red'st ev'ry day.
9 I'll take no calf, nor goats,
　　from house or fold of thine.
10 For beasts of forests, cattle all
　　on thousand hills are mine.

11 The fowls on mountains high
     are all to me well kown :
Wild beasts, which in the fields do lye,
     ev'n they are all mine own.
12 Then, if I hungry were,
     I would not tell it thee :
Becaufe the world, and fulnefs all
     thereof, belongs to me.
13 Will I eat flefh of bulls?
     or goats blood drink will I?
14 Thanks offer thou to God, and pay
     thy vows to the moft High.
15 And call upon me when
     in trouble thou fhalt be ;
I will deliver thee, and thou
     my Name fhalt glorify.
16 But to the wicked man
     God faith, My laws and truth
Shouldft thou declare? how dar'ft thou take
     my cov'nant in thy mouth?
17 Sith thou inftruction hat'ft,
     which fhould thy ways direct :
And fith my words behind thy back
     thou caft'ft, and doft reject.
18 When thou a thief didft fee,
     with him thou didft confent,
And with the vile adulterers
     partaker on thou went.
19 Thou giv'ft thy mouth to ill,
     thy tongue deceit doth frame.
20 Thou fitt'ft and 'gainft thy brother fpeak'ft
     thy mother's fon doft fhame.

21 Becaufe I filence kept,
   while thou thefe things haft wrought;
That I was altogether like
   thyfelf, hath been thy thought:
Yet I will thee reprove,
   and fet before thine eyes
In order ranked thy mifdeeds,
   and thine iniquities.
22 Now, ye that God forget,
   this carefully confider,
Left I in pieces tear you all,
   and none can you deliver.
23 Whofo doth offer praife,
   me glorifies: and I
Will fhew him God's falvation,
   that orders right his way.

Another of the fame.

1 THE mighty God, the Lord, hath fpoke,
   and call'd the earth upon,
Ev'n from the rifing of the fun,
   unto his going down.
2 From out of Zion his own hill,
   where the perfection high
Of beauty is, from thence the Lord
   hath fhined glorioufly.
3 Our God fhall come, and fhall no more
   be filent, but fpeak out:
Before him fire fhall wafte, great ftorms
   fhall compafs him about.
4 He to the Heavens from above,
   and to the earth below
Shall call, that he his judgments may
   before his people fhow.

5 Let all my Saints together be
    unto me gathered ;
  Those that by sacrifice with me
    a covenant have made.
6 And then the Heavens shall declare
    his righteousness abroad ;
  Because the Lord himself doth come,
    none else is judge but God.
7 Hear, O my people, and I'll speak ;
    O Israel by name,
  Against thee I will testify ;
  God, ev'n thy God I am.
8 I, for thy sacrifices few,
    reprove thee never will,
  Nor for burnt-off 'rings to have been
    before me off'red still.
9 I'll take no bullock, nor he goats,
    from house nor folds of thine.
10 For beasts of forests, cattle all
    on thousand hills are mine.
11 The fowls are all to me well known,
    that mountains high do yield :
  And I do challenge as mine own
    the wild beasts of the field.
12 If I were hungry, I would not
    to thee for need complain ;
  For earth, and all its fulness, doth
    to me of right pertain.
13 That I to eat the flesh of
    take pleasure, dost thou
  Or that I need to quench
    the blood of goats :

14 Nay, rather unto me, thy God,
    thanksgiving offer thou;
  To the most High perform thy word,
    and fully pay thy vow.
15 And in the day of trouble great,
    see that thou call on me:
  I will deliver thee, and thou
    my name shalt glorify.
16 But God unto the wicked saith,
    Why shouldst thou mention make
  Of my commands? how dar'st thou in
    thy mouth my cov'nant take?
17 Sith it is so, that thou dost hate
    all good instruction,
  And sith thou cast'st behind thy back,
    and slight'st my words each one.
18 When thou a thief didst see, then straight
    thou joind'st with him in sin,
  And with the vile adulterers
    thou hast partaker been.
19 Thy mouth to evil thou dost give,
    thy tongue deceit doth frame.
20 Thou sitt'st and 'gainst thy brother speak'st
    thy mother's son to shame.
21 These things thou wickedly hast done,
    and I have silent been:
  Thou thought'st that I was like thyself,
    and did approve thy sin:
  But I will sharply thee reprove,
    and I will order right
  Thy sins and thy transgressions,
    in presence of thy sight.

22 Confider this, and be afraid,
    ye that forget the Lord,
Left I in pieces tear you all,
    when none can help afford.
23 Who off'reth praife, me glorifies:
    I will fhew God's falvation
To him that ordereth aright
    his life and converfation.

PSALM LI.

To the chief Mufician, a Pfalm of David, when Nathan the Prophet came unto him, after he had gone in to Bathfheba.

The Pfalmift in the fad fenfe of his guiltinefs, prayeth for remiffion of fin, with an eye to the Lord's large mercy, ver. 1, 2. and followeth his petition with a deep and hearty confeffion of his finfulnefs, ver. 3, 4, 5, 6. He prayeth the fecond time for remiffion of fin, with an eye toward the blood of the Meffiah, ver. 7. and followeth it with another petition for comfort to his afflicted fpirit, ver. 8. He prayeth for remiffion of fins the third time, ver. 9. and followeth it with another petition for renewed comfort of the Holy Spirit, and for removal of felt wrath, with a promife of making ufe thereof, to the edification of God's people, ver. 10, 11, 12, 13. He prayeth for remiffion of fin the fourth time, and namely of that particular fin, wherewith for the prefent his confcience was moft troubled, ver. 14 and he followeth it with another petition, for enabling of him for a more fpiritual and fincere manner of ferving God hereafter, renouncing all confidence in the external ceremonies of the law, ver. 15, 16, 17. And laft of all, he prayeth for mercy to the Church, ver. 18, 19.

1 AFTER thy loving-kindnefs, Lord,
    have mercy upon me:
For thy compaffions great, blot out
    all mine iniquity.
2 Me cleanfe from fin, and th'roughly wafh
    from mine iniquity.
3 For my tranfgreffions I confefs:
    my fin I ever fee.

4 'Gainſt thee, thee only have I ſinn'd,
   in thy ſight done this ill:
  That when thou ſpeak'ſt thou may'ſt be
   and clear in judging ſtill.   [juſt,
5 Behold, I in iniquity
   was form'd the womb within:
  My mother alſo me conceiv'd
   in guiltineſs and ſin.
6 Behold, thou in the inward parts
   with truth delighted art:
  And wiſdom thou ſhalt make me know
   within the hidden part.
7 Do thou with hyſſop ſprinkle me
   I ſhall be cleanſed ſo:
  Yea, waſh thou me, and then I ſhall
   be whiter than the ſnow.
8 Of gladneſs and of joyfulneſs
   make me to hear the voice:
  That ſo theſe very bones, which thou
   haſt broken, may rejoice.
9 All mine iniquities blot out;
   thy face hide from my ſin.
10 Create a clean heart, Lord, renew,
   a right ſp'rit me within.
11 Caſt me not from thy ſight; nor take
   thy holy Sp'rit away.
12 Reſtore me thy Salvation's joy;
   with thy free Sp'rit me ſtay.
13 Then will I teach thy ways unto
   thoſe that tranſgreſſors be;
  And thoſe that ſinners are, ſhall then
   be turned unto thee.

14 O God, of my salvation God,
   me from blood-guiltiness
 Set free: then shall my tongue aloud
   sing of thy righteousness.
15 My closed lips, O Lord, by thee
   let them be opened;
 Then shall thy praises by my mouth
   abroad be published.
16 For thou desir'st not sacrifice,
   else would I give it thee:
 Nor wilt thou with burnt-offering
   at all delighted be.
17 A broken spirit is to God
   a pleasing sacrifice:
 A broken and a contrite heart,
   Lord, thou wilt not despise.
18 Shew kindness, and do good, O Lord,
   to Zion, thine own hill,
 The walls of thy Jerusalem
   build up, of thy good will.
19 Then righteous off'rings shall thee please,
   and off'rings burnt, which they,
 With whole burnt-off'rings, and with
   shall on thine altar lay.   [calves,

PSALM LII.

To the chief Musician, Maschil, a Psalm of David, when Doeg, the Edomite, came and told Saul, and said unto him, David is come to the house of Abimelech.

The scope of the Psalmist is to shew, that Doeg his enemy had no reason to glory in the favour of the court, purchased by his false and cruel calumnies against him, and the Lord's Priests, which he proveth by four reasons: First, Because God's kindness could not be taken away by Doeg's cruel calumnies, ver. 1. Secondly, Because God should root out

Doeg out of the world for his wicked calumnies, ver. 3, 4, 5. Thirdly, Becaufe Doeg would be made a laughing-ftock and matter of derifion to the Godly, ver. 6, 7. Fourthly, Becaufe maugre his malice, David fhould be bleffed as a Believer in God, and a true worfhipper of him, ver. 8. Whereupon he concludeth with praife to God, ver. 9.

1 WHY doft thou boaft, O mighty man,
   of mifchief and of ill?
 The goodnefs of Almighty God
   endureth ever ftill.
2 Thy tongue mifchievous calumnies
   devifeth fubtilly:
 Like to a razor, fharp to cut,
   working deceitfully.
3 Ill more than good, and more than truth
   thou loveft to fpeak wrong.
4 Thou loveft all devouring words,
   O thou deceitful tongue.
5 So God fhall thee deftroy for ay;
   remove thee, pluck thee out
 Quite from thy houfe, out of the land
   of life he fhall thee root.
6 The righteous fhall it fee, and fear,
   and laugh at him they fhall.
7 Lo, this the man is, that did not
   make God his ftrength at all:
 But he, in his abundant wealth,
   his confidence did place;
 And he took ftrength unto himfelf
   from his own wickednefs.
8 But I am in the houfe of God
   like to an olive green:
 My confidence for ever hath
   upon God's mercy been.

9 And I for ever will thee praise,
  because thou hast done this:
I on thy name will wait, for good
  before thy Saints it is.

PSALM LIII.

To the chief Musician, upon Mahalath, Maschil, a Psalm of David.

As in the fourteenth Psalm, so here, David comforteth himself, and the rest of the Godly in their sad sufferings which they felt from godless men, lying in the miserable condition of nature, ver. 1, 2, 3. The grounds of comfort are three: The first, Because God was engaged in the sufferings of his own, and would plead their controversy against the wicked, ver. 4. The next, Because God's judgments were to come on all the persecutor's of the Godly, ver. 5. And the third, Because there is hope of the full salvation of the Godly in Christ, ver. 6. Comparing this Psalm with Psalm 14. wherein the enmity of the wicked against the Godly, and the comfort of the godly in that case, in this place are the same which are set down there; We learn, that as the Godly may fall oftner than once, in one case, under one and the same tentation, some sort of hard exercise and grief; so may they, and should they make use of some comforts, and bring to memory the same doctrines for that end, as the Church is taught to do, Psalm 14. and here in this Psalm.

1 THAT there is not a God, the fool
    doth in his heart conclude:
They are corrupt, their works are vile;
    not one of them doth good.
2 The Lord upon the sons of men
    from Heav'n did cast his eyes
To see if any one there was,
    that sought God, and was wise.
3 They altogether filthy are,
    they all are backward gone;
And there is none that doeth good,
    no not so much as one.

4 These workers of iniquity,
 do they not know at all,
That they my people eat as bread,
 and on God do not call?
5 Ev'n there they were afraid, and stood
 with trembling all dismay'd;
Whereas there was no cause at all
 why they should be afraid:
For God his bones that thee besieg'd
 hath scattered all abroad;
Thou hast confounded them, for they
 despised are of God.
6 Let Isra'l's help from Zion come:
 when back the Lord shall bring
His captives, Jacob shall rejoice,
 and Israel shall sing.

PSALM LIV.

To the chief Musician, on Neginoth, Maschil, a Psalm of David when the Ziphims came and said to Saul, Doth not David hide himself with us?

David being betrayed by the Ziphims, First, Doth make his prayer to God, for delivery, ver. 1, 2. Secondly, He strengtheneth his faith by some reasons, ver. 3. Thirdly, He is confident of his own delivery, and of God's judgments on the Ziphims, whereunto he subscribes, ver. 4, 5. And last of all, he promiseth praise to God for his own assured deliverance, ver. 6, 7.

1 SAVE me, O God, by thy great name,
  and judge me by thy strength.
2 My prayer hear, O God; give ear
  unto my my words at length.
3 For they that strangers are to me,
  do up against me rise;
 Oppressors seek my soul, and God
  set not before their eyes.

4 The Lord my God my helper is,
   lo, therefore I am bold:
He taketh part with ev'ry one
   that doth my soul uphold.
5 Unto mine enemies he shall
   mischief and ill repay:
O for thy truth's sake cut them off,
   and sweep them clean away.
6 I will a sacrifice to thee
   give with free willingness;
Thy name, O Lord, because 'tis good,
   with praise I will confess.
7 For he hath me delivered
   from all adversities;
And his desire mine eye hath seen
   upon mine enemies.

PSALM LV.

To the chief Musician, on Neginoth, Maschil, a Psalm of David.

This Psalm containeth this doctrine, That albeit Christ and his followers may be in great straits by the treachery of their pretended friends, yet through God's favour they shall be delivered, as David felt in experience. The use of which doctrine is subjoined in the end of the Psalm, which well agreeth with the Psalmist's condition in the time of Absalom's and Achitophel's conspiracy.

The parts of the Psalm we may make these three. In the first is set down his sorrowful supplication, to ver. 16. In the next, his comforting of himself in the Lord his deliverer, to ver. 22. In the third, Use of his experience, in the two last verses.

In his supplication he prayeth in the first place for a gracious hearing, because of the calumnies and cruelties of his enemies, ver. 1, 2, 3. In the next place, He setteth down his pitiful condition of mind, ver. 4, 5. Making him to wish to be far from the company of these conspirators, which were combined against him, ver. 6, 7, 8. In the third place, he prayeth to God to confound their counsels, because the whole city was in an uproar against him, seeking how to execute their mischievous plot, ver. 9, 10, 11. In the fourth place, he condescends upon a more particular reason of his prayer for confounding their councils, because the plotter of the conspiracy had been most intimate in his familiarity, and deep upon his counsel, ver. 12, 13, 14. Whereupon in the last place by way of prayer, he prophesieth of the curse of God to come upon them, ver. 15.

In the second part of the Psalm he comforteth himself in God. First, By his resolution constantly to depend upon God, and hopefully to pray, ver. 16, 17. Secondly, By his former experiences of deliverances granted to him before, ver. 18. Thirdly, Because he was assured God should take order with his enemies for their treacherous breach of covenant, and plaistering of their malicious designs with fair pretences, and deep dissimulation, ver 19, 20, 21.

In the third part of the Psalm are the uses of this experience, ver. 22, 23.

1 LORD, hear my pray'r, hide not thyself
    from my intreating voice:
2 Attend and hear me, in my plaint
    I mourn, and make a noise.
3 Because of th' en'my's voice, and for
    lewd men's oppression great:
On me they cast iniquity,
    and they in wrath me hate.
4 Sore pain'd within me is my heart:
    death's terrors on me fall.
5 On me comes trembling, fear, and dread,
    o'erwhelmed me withal.
6 O that I like a dove had wings!
    said I, then would I flee
Far hence, that I might find a place
    where I in rest might be.
7 Lo, then far off I wander would,
    and in the desart stay.
8 From windy storm, and tempest I
    would haste to 'scape away.
9 O Lord, on them destruction bring,
    and do their tongues divide;

> For in the city violence
>   and strife I have espy'd.
> 10 They day and night upon the walls
>   do go about it round:
> There mischief is, and sorrow there
>   in midst of it is found.
> 11 Abundant wickedness there is
>   within her inward part:
> And from her streets, deceitfulness
>   and guile do not depart.
> 12 He was no foe that me reproach'd,
>   then that endure I could;
> Nor hater that did 'gainst me boast,
>   from him me hide I would.
> 13 But thou, man, who mine equal, guide,
>   and mine acquaintance wast.
> 14 We join'd sweet counsels to God's house,
>   in company we past.
> 15 Let death upon them seize,—and down
>   let them go quick to hell:
> For wickedness doth much abound
>   among them where they dwell.
> 16 I'll call on God; God will me save.
> 17   I'll pray, and make a noise
> At ev'ning, morning, and at noon;
>   and he shall hear my voice.
> 18 He hath my soul delivered,
>   that it in peace might be,
> From battle that against me was:
>   for many were with me.
> 19 The Lord shall hear and them afflict,
>   of old who hath abode:

Becaufe they never changes have,
  therefore they fear not God.
20 'Gainſt thoſe that were at peace with him
  he hath put forth his hand:
  The covenant that he had made,
  by breaking he profan'd.
21 More ſmooth than butter were his words
  while in his heart was war:
  His ſpeeches were more ſoft than oil,
  and yet drawn ſwords they are.
22 Caſt thou thy burthen on the Lord,
  and he ſhall thee ſuſtain:
  Yea, he ſhall cauſe the righteous man
  unmoved to remain.
23 But thou, O Lord my God, thoſe men
  in juſtice ſhalt o'erthrow,
  And in deſtruction's dungeon dark
  at laſt ſhall lay them low:
  The bloody and deceitful men
  ſhall not live half their days,
  But unto thee with confidence
  – I will depend always.

PSALM LVI.

To the chief Muſician, upon Jonath-elem-rechokim, Michtam of David, when the Philiſtines took him in Gath.

David flying from Saul to the country of the Philiſtines, (as we read, 1 Sam. xxi, 13) is apprehended, he prayeth to God, and is delivered. There are two parts of the Pſalm: In the former part there are three conflicts of David's faith with his trouble and tentation, and three victories. The firſt conflict is in prayer, laying forth his enemies carriage againſt him, ver. 1, 2. And his victory by faith, ver. 3, 4. The ſecond conflict in his complaint he maketh againſt his enemies, ver. 5, 6. And his ſecond victory by faith, ver. 7. His third conflict is by laying forth his mournful condition before God, with hope to be regarded, ver. 8. And his third and greatest victory by faith, ver. 9, 10, 11. In the latter part of the Psalm is David's obligation, thankfully to acknowledge his merciful delivery, with a petition for grace to persevere in the course of obedience under God's protection, ver. 12, 13.

1 SHEW mercy, Lord, to me, for man
  would swallow me outright. :
He me oppresseth, while he doth
  against me daily fight.
2 They daily would me swallow up,
  that hate me spitefully :
For they be many that do fight
  against me, O most High.
3 When I'm afraid, I'll trust in thee.
4 In God I'll praise his word :
I will not fear what flesh can do,
  my trust is in the Lord.
5 Each day they wrest my words their thoughts
  'gainst me are all for ill.
6 They meet, they lurk, they mark my steps,
  waiting my soul to kill.
7 But shall they by iniquity
  escape thy judgment so ?
O God, with indignation, down
  do thou the people throw.
8 My wand'rings all what they have been
  thou know'st, their number took :
Into thy bottle put my tears ;
  are they not in thy book ?
9 My foes shall, when I cry, turn back :
  I know't, God is for me.
10 In God his word I'll praise : his word
  in God shall praised be.

11 In God I trust: I will not fear
    what man can do to me.
12 Thy vows upon me are, O God:
    I'll render/praise to thee.
13 Wilt thou not, who from death me sav'd,
    my feet from falls keep free,
To walk before God in the light
    of those that living be?

PSALM LVII.

To the chief Musician, Al-taschith, Michtam of David, when he fled from Saul in the cave.

This Psalm of David, as many other his Psalms, doth represent the condition of his spirit, both in the time of his trouble, and after the delivery: What was his exercise in the cave, and what was his condition after he was delivered out of that danger, whereof we read, 1 Sam. xxiv. There are two parts of the Psalm: The first containeth his prayer for deliverance, which is pressed by six arguments, all serving to strengthen his faith: The first because he trusted in God, ver. 1. The second, because he resolved to insist in prayer till he were heard, ver. 2. The third, Because he hoped certainly to find notable delivery from his extraordinary danger, ver. 3. The fourth, Because his enemies were beastly cruel, ver. 4. The fifth, Because this mercy might contribute much to the glorifying of God, ver. 5. The sixth is from the low condition whereunto his spirit is brought, by their crafty and cruel pursuit of him, ver. 6. In the rest of the Psalm is his thanksgiving, consisting of five parts. The first is the acknowledgement of the mercy and delivery granted, ver. 6. The next is his fixt resolution to praise God for it, ver. 7. The third is the up-stirring of tongue and hand, and the whole man to praise God, ver. 8. The fourth is a promise to transmit the knowledge of God's mercy to other nations, ver. 9. The fifth is the acknowledgement of the glory of this mercy, with a wish that it might be more and more seen and acknowledged, by giving new experience of it, ver. 10, 11.

1 BE merciful to me, O God,
    thy mercy unto me
Do thou extend, because my soul
    doth put her trust in thee:

Yea, in the shadow of thy wings
     my refuge I will place,
Until these sad calamities
   do wholly over pass.
2 My cry I will cause to ascend
     unto the Lord most High;
To God, who doth all things for me
     perform most perfectly.
3 From Heav'n he shall send down, and me
     from his reproach defend,
That would devour me: God his truth
     and mercy forth shall send.
4 My soul among fierce lions is,
     I fire-brands live among;
Mens' sons, whose teeth are spears and darts,
     a sharp sword is their tongue
5 Be thou exalted very high
     above the Heav'ns, O God:
Let thou thy glory be advanc'd
     o'er all the earth abroad.
6 My soul's bow'd down, for they a net
     have laid, my steps to snare:
Into the pit, which they have digg'd
     for me, they fall'n are.
7 My heart is fix'd, my heart is fix'd,
     O God: I'll sing, and praise.
8 My glory wake, wake psalt'ry, harp:
     myself I'll early raise.
9 I'll praise thee 'mong the people, Lord,
     'mong nations sing will I.
10 For great to Heav'n thy mercy is,
     thy truth is to the sky.

F

11 O Lord, exalted be thy name
above the Heav'ns to ſtand:
Do thou thy glory far advance
above both ſea and land.

PSALM LVIII.

To the chief Muſician, Al-taſchith, Michtam, of David.

The Pſalmiſt being oppreſſed by the calumnies of the courtiers of King Saul, and by the Senators of the courts of juſtice, who ſhould have provided againſt the oppreſſion of the ſubjects, chargeth them in the firſt part of this Pſalm, as moſt guilty of injuſtice done to him, ver. 1, 2, 3, 4, 5. In the ſecond part, He prayeth againſt them, that God would execute judgment upon them, ver. 6, 7, 8. And in the third part, He pronounceth the ſentence of their deſerved deſtruction, ver. 9, 10, 11. From this experience of the Prophet, we may ſee what ſtrong parties, and hard oppoſition the Godly may meet with in the defence of a good cauſe, and how neceſſary it is in ſuch trials to exerciſe our faith, and to exalt God above all oppoſite powers, that we may be borne out, and get conſolation and victory in the Lord.

1 DO ye, O congregation,
indeed ſpeak righteouſneſs?
O ye that are the ſons of men,
judge ye with uprightneſs?
2 Yea, ev'n within your very hearts
ye wickedneſs have done,
And ye the vi'lence of your hands
do weigh the earth upon.
3 The wicked men eſtranged are,
ev'n from the very womb:
They, ſpeaking lies, do ſtray as ſoon
as to the world they come.
4 Unto a ſerpent's poiſon like
their poiſon doth appear;
Yea, they are like the adder deaf,
that cloſely ſtops her ear:

5 That so she may not hear the voice
    of one that charm her would,
  No, not tho' he most cunning were,
    and charm most wisely could.
6 Their teeth, O God, within their mouth
    break thou in pieces small:
  The great teeth break thou out, O Lord,
    of these young lions all.
7 Let them like waters melt away,
    which downward still do flow:
  In pieces cut his arrows all,
    when he shall bend his bow.
8 Like to a snail that melts away,
    let each of them be gone:
  Like woman's birth untimely, that
    they never see the sun.
9 He shall them take away before
    your pots the thorns can find,
  Both living, and in fury great,
    as with a stormy wind.
10 The righteous, when he vengeance sees,
    he shall be joyful then:
  The righteous one shall wash his feet
    in blood of wicked men.
11 So men shall say, The righteous man
    reward shall never miss:
  And, verily, upon the earth
    a God to judge there is.

PSALM LIX.

To the chief Musician, Al-taschith, Michtam of David, when Saul sent, and they watched the house to kill him.

David in prefent danger of his life by Saul, (who having David inclofed within the city and within his own houfe, thought furely to have killed him, as we read, 1 Sam. xix. 11.) prayeth to God for deliverance, ver. 1, 2. and for a reafon of his prayer, maketh a complaint againft his enemies, ver. 3, 4. In the next place, He prayeth the fecond time for delivery to himfelf, and judgment againft his enemies, ver. 5. and complaineth of them the fecond time, ver 6, 7. In the third place, He declareth his confidence to be delivered, ver. 8, 9, 10. In the fourth place, He maketh imprecation againft his enemies for their wickednefs, ver. 11, 12, 13, 14, 15. And in the laft place, He promifeth thanks to God for his delivery, whereof he was affured before it came, ver. 16, 17.

1 MY God, deliver me from thofe
    that are mine enemies:
And do thou me defend from thofe
    that up againft me rife.

2 Do thou deliver me from them
    that work iniquity;
And give me fafety from the men
    of bloody cruelty.

3 For lo, they for my foul laid wait;
    the mighty do combine
Againft me, Lord, not for my fault,
    nor any fin of mine.

4 They run, and without fault in me,
    themfelves do ready make:
Awake to meet me with thy help,
    and do thou notice take.

5 Awake therefore, Lord God of hofts,
    thou God of Ifrael,
To vifit heathen all: fpare none
    that wickedly rebel.

6 At ev'ning they go to and fro:
    they make great noife and found
Like to a dog, and often walk
    about the city round.

7 Behold, they belch out with their mouth,
 and in their lips are 'fwords;
 For they do fay thus, Who is he
 that now doth hear our words?
8 But thou, O Lord, fhalt laugh at them,
 and all the heathen mock.
9 While he's in pow'r, I'll wait on thee:
 for God is my high rock.
10 He of my mercy that is God,
 betimes fhall me prevent:
 Upon mine en'mies God fhall let
 me fee mine heart's content.
11 Them flay not, left my folk forget;
 but fcatter them abroad
 By thy ftrong pow'r; and bring them
 O thou our fhield, and God. |down
12 For their mouth's fin; and for the words
 that from their lips do fly,
 Let them be taken in their pride,
 becaufe they curfe and lye.
13 In wrath confume them, them confume,
 that fo they may not be:
 And, that in Jacob God doth rule,
 to th' earth's ends let them fee.
14 At ev'ning let thou them return,
 making great noife and found
 Like to a dog, and often walk
 about the city round.
15 And let them wander up and down,
 in feeking food to eat;
 And let them grudge, when they fhall not
 be fatisfy'd with meat.

16 But of thy pow'r I'll sing aloud,
    at morn thy mercy praise:
For thou to me my refuge wast,
    and tow'r in troublous days.
17 O God, thou art my strength, I will
    sing praises unto thee:
For God is my defence, a God
    of mercy unto me.

PSALM LX.

To the chief Musician, upon Shushan-eduth, Michtam of David, to teach, when he strove with Aram-naharaim, and with Aram-zobeth, when Joab returned and smote of Edom in the Valley of Salt, twelve thousand.

This Psalm is a prayer for the victory of Israel over their enemies, indited upon the Prophet when Israel was fighting with the Syrians and Edomites. It may be divided into three parts: In the first whereof, the Psalmist prayeth for help more largely, ver. 1, 2, 3, 4, 5. In the second part David is made confident of the victory, ver. 6, 7, 8, 9, 10. In the third part he repeateth his prayer more briefly, and his confidence of having the victory, ver. 11, 12.

1 O Lord, thou hast rejected us,
    and scatt'red us abroad;
Thou justly hast displeased been;
    return to us, O God.
2 The earth to tremble thou hast made;
    therein didst breaches make:
Do thou thereof the breaches heal,
    because the land doth shake.
3 Unto thy people thou hard things
    hast shew'd, and on them sent;
And thou hast caused us to drink
    wine of astonishment.

4 And yet a banner thou haſt giv'n
    to them who thee do fear;
  That it by them, becauſe of truth,
    diſplayed may appear.
5 That thy beloved people may
    deliver'd be from thrall:
  Save with the pow'r of thy right hand,
    and hear me when I call.
6 God in his holineſs hath ſpoke,
    herein I will take pleaſure;
  Shechem I will divide, and forth
    will Succoth's valley meaſure.
7 Gilead I claim as mine by right;
    Manaſſeh mine ſhall be;
  Ephra'm is of mine head the ſtrength;
    Judah gives laws for me.
8 Moab's my waſhing pot; my ſhoe
    I'll over Edom throw;
  And over Paleſtina's land
    I will in triumph go.
9 O who is he will bring me to
    the city fortify'd?
  O who is he that to the land
    of Edom will me guide?
10 O God, which hadeſt us caſt off,
    this thing wilt thou not do?
  Ev'n thou, O God, which dideſt not
    forth with our armies go.
11 Help us from trouble: for the help
    is vain which man ſupplies.
12 Thro' God we'll do great acts: he ſhall
    tread down our enemies.

To the chief Musician, upon Neginoth, a Psalm of David.

David now in his exile maketh his address to God in a sad condition, ver. 1, 2, 3. And is comforted in the Lord, and persuaded of his present and future happiness, ver. 4, 5. And of the perpetuity of the Kingdom of Christ, represented by him, to the comfort of all Christ's subjects in all ages, ver. 6, 7, 8.

1 O God, give ear unto my cry,
 unto my pray'r attend.
2 From th' utmost corner of the land
 my cry to thee I'll send.
 What time my heart is overwhelm'd,
 and in perplexity:
 Do thou me lead unto the rock
 that higher is than I.
3 For thou hast for my refuge been
 a shelter by thy pow'r;
 And for defence against my foes
 thou hast been a strong tow'r.
4 Within thy tabernacle I
 for ever will abide:
 And under covert of thy wings
 with confidence me hide.
5 For thou the vows that I did make,
 O Lord, my God, didst hear:
 Thou hast giv'n me the heritage
 of those thy name that fear.
6 A life prolong'd for many days,
 thou to the King shalt give:
 Like many generations be
 the years which he shall live.

7 He in God's presence his abode
  for evermore shall have:
 O do thou truth and mercy both
  prepare, that may him save.
8 And so will I perpetually
  sing praise unto thy name;
 That, having made my vows, I may
  each day perform the same.

PPALM LXII.

To the chief Musician, to Jeduthun, a Psalm of David.

This Psalm is the issue of a sore conflict, and inward combat, which David felt from the strong opposition of his irreconcileable adversaries, and from the lasting troubles which he sustained by their persecution, and by his friends forsaking of him, whereby he was put hard to it what to think or what to do: At length faith in God giveth him victory, and maketh him first to break forth in avowing of his faith and hope in God, ver. 1, 2. Next, To insult over his enemies as dead men, because of their sinful course, ver. 3, 4. Thirdly, To strengthen himself in his faith and hope, ver. 5, 6, 7. Fourthly, To exhort all men to trust in God, and to depend on him, for reasons set down, ver. 8, 9. and not to trust in oppression and robbery, for reasons set down, ver. 10, 11, 12.

1 MY soul with expectation
   depends on God indeed:
 My strength and my salvation doth
   from him alone proceed.
2 He only my salvation is,
   and my strong rock is he;
 He only is my sure defence:
   much mov'd I shall not be.
3 How long will ye against a man
   plot mischief? ye shall all
 Be slain: ye as a tott'ring fence
   shall be, and bowing wall.

4 They only plot to cast him down
    from his excellency:
They joy in lyes: with mouth they bless,
    but they curse inwardly.
5 My soul, wait thou with patience
    upon thy God alone:
On him dependeth all my hope
    and expectation.
6 He only my salvation is,
    and my strong rock is he:
He only is my sure defence;
    I shall not moved be.
7 In God my glory placed is,
    and my salvation sure:
In God the rock is of my strength,
    my refuge most secure.
8 Ye people, place your confidence
    in him continually;
Before him pour ye out your heart:
    God is our refuge high.
9 Surely mean men are vanity,
    and great men are a lye:
In balance laid, they wholly are
    more light than vanity.
10 Trust ye not in oppression,
    in robb'ry be not vain:
On wealth set not your hearts, when as
    increased is your gain.
11 God hath it spoken once to me;
    yea, this I heard again,
That power to Almighty God
    alone doth appertain.

12 Yea, mercy also unto thee
 belongs, O Lord, alone:
For thou according to his work
 rewardest ev'ry one.

PSALM LXIII.

A Psalm of David, when he was in the wilderness of Judah.

We have in this Psalm David's exercise in his banishment, when he was hiding himself from Saul in the wilderness of Judah, wherein is set down his longing, and prayer after the benefit of the public ordinances, ver. 1, 2. and the fruits of a gracious and comfortable answer given to his prayer, in number four. The first is a resolution to follow spiritual duties, and in special to praise God, ver. 3. and to be a constant supplicant depending on God, ver. 4. and to take his contentment in God and in his praises, ver. 5, 6. and joyfully to trust in God's mercy, ver. 7. The second fruit is the acknowledgement of God's power, sustaining him in his adherence unto God, practised by him for time past, and purposed for time to come, ver. 8. The third fruit is confidence of the destruction of his enemies, ver. 9, 10. The fourth is assurance that he shall receive the Kingdom promised unto him, to the confusion of all such as did slander him as a traitor.

1 LORD, thee my God I'll early seek:
 my soul doth thirst for thee;
My flesh longs in a dry parch'd land,
 wherein no waters be:
2 That I thy pow'r may behold,
 and brightness of thy face,
As I have seen thee heretofore
 within thy holy place.
3 Since better is thy love than life,
 my lips thee praise shall give.
4 I in thy name will lift my hands,
 and bless thee while I live.

5 Ev'n as with marrow, and with fat,
   my foul fhall filled be:
Then fhall my mouth with joyful lips
   fing praifes unto thee.
6 When I do thee upon my bed
   remember with delight,
And when on thee I meditate
   in watches of the night.
7 In fhadow of thy wings I'll joy,
   for thou mine help haft been.
8 My foul thee follows hard: and me
   thy right hand doth fuftain.
9 Who feek my foul to fpill, fhall fink
   down to earth's loweft room.
10 They by the fword fhall be cut off,
   and foxes prey become.
11 Yet fhall the King in God rejoice,
   and each one glory fhall
That fwear by him; but ftopp'd fhall be
   the mouth of liars all.

PSALM LXIV.

To the chief Mufician, a Pfalm of David.

This Pfalm hath two parts: In the former is David's heavy complaint unto God againft his deadly enemies, laid forth before God in fundry particular evidences of their malice, ver. 1, 2, 3, 4, 5, 6. And in the latter part is the Lord's comfortable anfwer unto him, by giving him affurance of God's judgment coming on them, to their own and others aftonifhment, and to the comfort of the Godly, ver. 7, 8, 9, 10.

1 WHEN I to thee my prayer make,
   Lord to my voice give ear;
My life fave from the enemy
   of whom I ftand in fear:

2 Me from their secret counsel hide
   who do live wickedly;
From insurrection of those men
   that work iniquity:
3 Who do their tongues with malice whet,
   and make them cut like swords;
In whose bent bows are arrows set,
   ev'n sharp and bitter words:
4 That they may at the perfect man
   in secret aim their shot;
Yea, suddenly they dare at him
   to shoot, and fear it not.
5 In ill encourage they themselves,
   and their snares close do lay:
Together conference they have,
   who shall them see? they say.
6 They have search'd out iniquities,
   a perfect search they keep:
Of each of them the inward thought,
   and every heart is deep.
7 God shall an arrow shoot at them,
   and wound them suddenly.
8 So their own tongue shall them confound:
   all who them see shall fly.
9 And on all men a fear shall fall;
   God's works they shall declare;
For they shall wisely notice take
   what these his doings are.
10 In God the righteous shall rejoice,
   and trust upon his might;
Yea, they shall greatly glory all,
   in heart that are upright.

PSALM LXV.

To the chief Musician, a Psalm and Song of David.

This Psalm is all of God's praises. The proposition that he is to be praised, is set down, ver. 1. The reasons of his praise unto the end, are nine. The first whereof, is, Because he heareth prayer, ver. 2. The second, Because he mercifully pardoneth sins, ver. 3. The third, Because of his gracious purpose, and powerful prosecution of the decree of election, of his own redeemed ones, ver. 4. The fourth, Because of his defending of his Church in all places, ver. 5. The fifth, Is from the strength manifested in the framing and settling of the mountains, ver. 6. The sixth, From the wise and powerful over-ruling of all unruly and raging creatures, ver. 7. The seventh, Is from his preventing of troubles, which are coming to his Church, by terrifying all nations at the beholding of the tokens of his displeasure against the enemies of his people, ver. 8. The eighth argument is taken from the joyful peace granted sometimes to his people, ver. 8. The ninth argument of God's praise, is from the rich plenty of all necessary food, from year to year, which God provideth for maintenance of man and beast, and especially of his people Israel in their land, ver. 9, 10, 11, 12, 13.

1 PRAISE waits for thee in Zion, Lord:
    to thee vows paid shall be.
2 O thou that hearer art of pray'r,
    all flesh shall come to thee.
3 Iniquities, I must confess,
    prevail against me do:
But as for our transgressions,
    them purge away shalt thou.

4 Blest is the man whom thou dost chuse,
    and mak'st approach to thee,
That he within thy courts, O Lord,
    may still a dweller be:
We surely shall be satisfy'd
    with thy abundant grace,
And with the goodness of thy house,
    ev'n of thy holy place.

5 O God of our salvation,
   thou in thy righteousness,
By fearful works unto our pray'rs
   thine answer dost express:
Therefore the ends of all the earth,
   and those afar that be
Upon the sea, their confidence,
   O Lord, will place in thee.
6 Who being girt with pow'r, sets fast,
   by his great strength, the hills:
7 Who noise of seas, noise of their waves,
   and people's tumult, stills.
8 Those in the utmost parts that dwell,
   are at thy signs afraid:
Th' out-goings of the morn and ev'n
   by thee are joyful made.
9 The earth thou visit'st, wat'ring it:
   thou mak'st it rich to grow
With God's full flood: thou corn prepar'st,
   when thou provid'st it so.
10 Her rigs thou wat'rest plenteously:
   her furrows setteleft:
With show'rs thou dost her mollify,
   her spring by thee is blest.
11 So thou the year most lib'rally
   doft with thy goodness crown;
And all thy paths abundantly
   on us drop fatness down.
12 They drop upon the pastures wide,
   that do in desarts ly:
The little hills on ev'ry side
   rejoice right pleasantly.

13 With flocks the pastures clothed be;
   the vales with corn are clad:
And now they shout and sing to thee,
   for thou hast made them glad.

PSALM LXVI.
To the chief Musician, a Song or Psalm.

This Psalm being all of praises, may be divided into three parts. In the first the Psalmist exhorteth all the earth to praise God, ver. 1, 2, 3, 4. and that because of the works which God did of old for his people, ver. 5, 6. and because he is able to do the like when he pleaseth, ver. 7. In the second part he exhorts the Church of Israel living with him in that age, to praise God for the late experience of God's goodness towards them, in the delivery granted to them out of their late trials, troubles, and sore vexations, ver. 8, 9, 10, 11, 12. In the third place, the Prophet expresseth his own purpose of thankfulness unto God for the large experience which he had in particular of God's mercies to himself, from ver. 13. to the end.

1 ALL lands, to God in joyful sounds,
    aloft your voices raise.
2 Sing forth the honour of his name
    and glorious make his praise.
3 Say unto God, How terrible
    in all thy works art thou?
Through thy great pow'r thy foes to thee
    shall be constrain'd to bow.
4 All on the earth shall worship thee,
    they shall thy praise proclaim
In songs; they shall sing cheerfully
    unto thy holy Name.
5 Come, and the works that God hath
    with admiration see: [wrought,
In's working to the sons of men,
    most terrible is he.

6 Into dry land the sea he turn'd,
  and they a passage had;
 Ev'n marching thro' the flood on foot,
  there we in him were glad.
7 He ruleth ever by his pow'r,
  his eyes the nations see:
 O let not the rebellious ones
  lift up themselves on high.
8 Ye people, bless our God, aloud
  the voice speak of his praise.
9 Our soul in life who safe preserves,
  our foot from sliding stays.
10 For thou didst prove and try us, Lord,
  as men do silver try:
11 Brought'st us into the net, and mad'st
  bands on our loins to lie.
12 Thou hast caus'd men ride o'er our heads;
  and tho' that we did pass
 Through fire and water, yet thou brought'st
  us to a wealthy place.
13 I'll bring burnt off'rings to thy house:
  to thee my vows I'll pay.
14 Which my lips utter'd, my mouth spake
  when trouble on me lay.
15 Burnt-sacrifices of fat rams
  with incense I will bring:
 Of bullocks and of goats I will
  present an offering.
16 All that fear God, come here, I'll tell
  what he did for my soul.
17 I with my mouth unto him cry'd,
  my tongue did him extol.

18 If in my heart I sin regard,
   the Lord me will not hear.
19 But surely God me heard, and to
   my prayer's voice gave ear.
20 O let the Lord, our gracious God,
   for ever blessed be,
Who turned not my pray'r from him,
   nor yet his grace from me.

PSALM LXVII.

To the chief Musician, on Neginoth, a Psalm or Song.

This Psalm is a prophetical prayer for a blessing upon the Church of the Jews, for the good of the Gentiles, and enlarging of the Kingdom of Christ among them. The Petition is propounded, ver. 1, 2. In the next place is an acclamation with the Gentiles, glorifying of God at their in-bringing, now foreseen that it should come most certainly, ver. 3, 4. In the third place, the Church of the Jews do applaud the second time the conversion of the Gentiles, and their praising of God, promising to themselves, that by that means the increase of God's blessing on them shall follow, and the enlarging of the Kingdom of God through all the world, ver. 5, 6, 7.

1 LORD, bless and pity us:
   shine on us with thy face.
2 That th' earth thy way, and nations all
   may know thy saving grace.
3 Let people praise thee, Lord,
   let people all thee praise.
4 O let the nations be glad,
   in songs their voices raise:

Thou'lt justly people judge,
   on earth rule nations all.
5 Let people praise thee, Lord; let them
   praise thee, both great and small.

[P.68.] OF DAVID. 139

6 The earth her fruit shall yield:
 our God shall blessing send.
7 God shall us bless, men shall him fear,
 unto earth's utmost end.

Another of the same.

1 LORD, unto us be merciful,
 do thou us also bless:
 And graciously cause shine on us
 the brightness of thy face:
2 That so thy way upon the earth
 to all men may be known,
 Also among the nations all
 thy saving health be shown.
3 O let the people praise thee, Lord;
 let people all thee praise.
4 O let the nations be glad,
 and sing for joy always;
 For rightly thou shalt people judge,
 and nations rule on earth.
5 Let people praise thee, Lord; let all
 the folk praise thee with mirth.
6 Then shall the earth yield her increase;
 God, our God bless us shall.
7 God shall us bless; and of the earth
 the ends shall fear him all.

PSALM LXVIII.

To the chief Musician, a Psalm or Song of David.

This Psalm is very suitable to that time, when David having gotten the victory over his enemies round about, did assemble all Israel, and carried the ark of God, now returned from the land of the Philistines, triumphantly out of the house of Obed-Edom, into the city of David, as a type of Christ.

ascension after the work of Redemption in the word. In which Psalm, after the manner that Moses prayed unto God, or to Christ who was to be incarnate, when the ark did march, David prayeth here first against the Lord's enemies, ver. 1, 2. And then for the Lord's people, ver. 3. In the next place, He exhorteth all the Lord's people to praise God, ver. 4. and giveth twelve or thirteen reasons for it: First, Because of his mercy to the desolate and afflicted, ver. 5, 6. Secondly, Because of his wonderfulness and terribleness in delivering of his people out of bondage, as appeared in his bringing of his people out of Egypt, and thro' the wilderness, ver. 7, 8. Thirdly, Because of his fatherly care to entertain his redeemed people, as did appear in his nourishing of his Church in Canaan, ver. 9, 10. Fourthly, Because of the victories which he giveth usually to his people, when their enemies do invade them, ver. 11, 12. Fifthly, Because of the delivery which he will give to his people out of their most sad calamities, as he hath oftentimes given proof, ver. 13, 14. Sixthly, Because his Church is the most glorious kingdom in the world, being compared therewith, ver. 15, 16. Seventhly, Because Christ the King of the Church, hath all the Angels at his command to serve him; and having ended the Work of Redemption, was to ascend gloriously, for sending down gifts to his Church, and ruling of it, ver. 17, 18. Eighthly, Because of God's bounty to his people, in daily renewed mercies, till he perfect the work of their Salvation, ver. 19, 20. Ninthly, Because of his avenging of himself upon all his enemies, ver. 21. Tenthly, because God hath undertaken to work over again in effect, as need shall require, what he hath done in bringing his people out of Egypt, and in giving them victory over the Canaanites, ver. 22, 23. whereof the experience of his power, already manifested for Israel, was a proof and pledge sufficient, ver. 24, 25, 26, 27. Eleventhly, Because it was decreed by God, to establish his Church, and to make her strong by making Kings to become converts, ver. 28, 29. and that partly by treading down some of her enemies, ver. 30 and partly by making others, even some of her greatest enemies, to seek reconciliation with God, even her God, ver. 31. Twelfthly, He exhorteth to praise God, because of his omnipotent power, in conversion of kingdoms ready to be let forth for the defence of his people, ver. 32, 33, 34. and ready to overthrow their enemies, and all for the strengthening of his Church: for all which he exhorteth all to bless the Lord, ver. 35.

1 LET God arise, and scattered
 let all his en'mies be:
And let all those that do him hate,
 before his presence flee.

2 As smoke is driv'n, so drive thou them:
  as fire melts wax away,
 Before God's face let wicked men
  so perish and decay.
3 But let the righteous be glad:
  let them before God's sight
 Be very joyful, yea, let them
  rejoice with all their might.
4 To God sing, to his name sing praise:
  extol him with your voice,
 That rides on Heav'n by his name JAH,
  before his face rejoice.
5 Because the Lord a father is
  unto the fatherless;
 God is the widow's judge within
  his place of holiness.
6 God doth the solitary set
  in fam'lies; and from bands
 The chain'd doth free; but rebels do
  inhabit parched lands.
7 O God, what time thou did'st go forth
  before thy people's face;
 And when thro' the great wilderness
  thy glorious marching was;
8 Then at God's presence shook the earth,
  then drops from Heaven fell:
 This Sinai shook before the Lord,
  the God of Israel.
9 O God, thou to thine heritage
  didst send a plenteous rain,
 Whereby thou, when it weary was,
  didst it refresh again.

10 Thy congregation then did make
   their habitation there:
  Of thine own goodnefs for the poor,
   O God, thou didft prepare.
11 The Lord himfelf did give the word,
   the word abroad did fpread;
  Great was the company of them
   the fame who publifhed.
12 Kings of great armies foiled were,
   and forc'd to flee away:
  And women who remain'd at home,
   did diftribute the prey.
13 Tho' ye have lain among the pots,
   like doves ye fhall appear,
  Whofe wings with filver and with gold
   whofe feathers cov'red are.
14 When there th' Almighty fcatt'red kings,
   like Salmon's fnow 'twas white.
15 God's hill is like to Bafhan hill,
   like Bafhan hill for height.
16 Why do ye leap, ye mountains high?
   this is the hill where God
  Defires to dwell, yea, God in it
   for ay will make abode.
17 God's chariots twenty thoufand are,
   thoufands of Angels ftrong;
  In's holy place God is, as in
   mount Sinai them among.
18 Thou haft O Lord, moft glorious
   afcended up on high;
  And, in triumph victorious, led
   captive captivity:

>   Thou hast received gifts for men,
>   for such as did rebel:
>   Yea, ev'n for them, that God the Lord
>   in midst of them might dwell.
>
> 19 Blest be the Lord, who is to us
>   of our salvation God;
>   Who daily with his benefits
>   us plenteously doth load.
> 20 He of salvation is the God,
>   who is our God most strong:
>   And, unto God the Lord, from death
>   the issues do belong.
> 21 But surely God shall wound the head
>   of those that are his foes;
>   The hairy scalp of him that still
>   on in his trespass goes.
> 22 God said, My people I will bring
>   again from Bashan hill;
>   Yea, from the sea's devouring depths,
>   them bring again I will.
> 23 That in the blood of enemies
>   thy foot imbru'd may be,
>   And of thy dogs dipt in the same
>   the tongues thou mayest see.
> 24 Thy goings they have seen, O God,
>   the steps of majesty
>   Of my God, and my mighty King,
>   within the sanctuary.
> 25 Before went singers, players next
>   on instruments took way;
>   And them among the damsels were
>   that did on timbrels play.

26 Within the congregations,
   bleſs God with one accord;
From Iſra'l's fountain do ye bleſs
   and praiſe the mighty Lord.
27 With their prince, little Benjamin,
   princes and counſel there
Of Judah were, there Zabulon's
   and Napht'li's princes were.   [ſtrong
28 Thy God commands thy ſtrength: make
   what thou wrought'ſt for us, Lord.
29 For thy houſe at Jeruſalem,
   kings ſhall thee gifts afford.
30 The ſpear-men's hoſt, the multitude
   of bulls which fiercely look,   [ſent,
Thoſe calves, which people have forth
   O Lord, our God, rebuke,
Till every one ſubmit himſelf,
   and ſilver pieces bring:
The people that delight in war,
   diſperſe, O God and King.
31 Thoſe that be princes great, ſhall then
   come out of Egypt lands,
And Ethiopia to God
   ſhall ſoon ſtretch out her hands.
32 O all ye kingdoms of the earth,
   ſing praiſes to this King,
For he is Lord that ruleth all,
   unto him praiſes ſing.
33 To him that rides on heav'ns of heav'ns,
   which he of old did found;
Lo, he ſends out his voice, a voice
   in might that doth abound.

34 Strength unto God do ye ascribe;
    for his excellency
  Is over Israel; his strength
    is in the clouds most high.

35 Thou'rt from thy temple dreadful, Lord,
    Isra'l's own God is he,
  Who gives his people strength and pow'r;
    O let God blessed be.

PSALM LXIX.

To the chief Musician upon Shoshannim, a Psalm of David.

David, as a Type of Christ, earnestly dealeth with God for a delivery from his perplexed condition, and from the malice of his adversaries; and doth find a comfortable event. There are three parts of the Psalm. In the first, is his Prayer, six times presented, and strengthened with new reasons, to ver. 22. In the second part of the Psalm, is his imprecation of ten plagues against his enemies, with some reasons added for the justice of the inflicting the plagues, mentioned to ver. 29. In the third part, are four evidences of his victory from ver. 29. to the end. In all which, whatsoever is proper to the Type, is to be referred to the Type only; and whatsoever is fit also to be applied unto Christ the Antitype, must be referred to him only, in that sense which is suitable to his Majesty.

His prayer at first, is pronounced in few words: "Save me." The reasons are four. The first, from the danger he was in, ver. 1, 2. The next, from his long and patient waiting for an answer to his prayer, ver. 3. The third, from the multitude, malice, and iniquity of his enemies, ver. 4. The fourth, is by way of attestation of God, that he was innocent of that whereof he was charged by his enemies, joined in with his humble acknowledging of whatsoever other sins justice could charge upon him in any other respect, ver. 5.

1 SAVE me, O God, because the floods
    do so environ me,
  That ev'n unto my very soul
    come in the waters be.

2 I downward in deep mire do sink,
   where standing there is none :
I am into deep waters come,
   where floods have o'er me gone.
3 I weary with my crying am,
   my throat is also dry'd.
Mine eyes do fail, while for my God
   I waiting do abide.
4 Those men that do without a cause
   bear hatred unto me,
Than are the hairs upon mine head
   in number more they be :
They that would me destroy, and are
   mine en'mies wrongfully,
Are mighty : so, what I took not,
   to render forc'd was I.
5 Lord, thou my folly know'st ; my sins
   not cover'd are from thee.
6 Let none that wait on thee be sham'd,
   Lord God of hosts, for me.
O Lord, the God of Israel,
   let none who search do make,
And seek thee, be at any time
   confounded for my sake.
7 For I have borne reproach for thee ;
   my face is hid with shame.
8 To brethern strange, to mother's sons
   an alien I became.
9 Because the zeal did eat me up,
   which to thine house I bare :
And the reproaches cast at thee,
   upon me fallen are.

10 My tears and fasts, t' afflict my soul,
   were turned to my shame.
11 When sackcloth I did wear, to them
   a proverb I became.
12 The men that in the gate do sit,
   against me evil spake:
 They also that vile drunkards were,
   of me their song did make.
13 But in an acceptable time
   my pray'r, Lord, is to thee:
 In truth of thy salvation, Lord,
   and mercy great, hear me.
14 Deliver me out of the mire;
   from sinking do me keep:
 Free me from those that do me hate,
   and from the waters deep.
15 Let not the flood on me prevail,
   whose water overflows;
 Nor deep me swallow, nor the pit
   her mouth upon me close.
16 Hear me, O Lord, because thy love
   and kindness is most good:
 Turn unto me according to
   thy mercies' multitude.
17 Nor from thy servant hide thy face;
   I'm troubled, soon attend.
18 Draw near my soul, and it redeem:
   me from my foes defend.
19 To thee is my reproach well known,
   my shame and my disgrace:
 Those that mine adversaries be
   are all before thy face.

20 Reproach hath broke my heart, I'm full
   of grief : I look'd for one
   To pity me, but none I found ;
   comforters found I none.
21 They alſo bitter gall did give
   unto me for my meat ;
   They gave me vinegar to drink,
   when as my thirſt was great.
22 Before them let their table prove
   a ſnare : and do thou make
   Their welfare and proſperity
   a trap themſelves to take.
23 Let thou their eyes ſo dark'ned be,
   that ſight may them forſake ;
   And let their loins be made by thee
   continually to ſhake.
24 Thy fury pour thou out on them,
   and indignation ;
   And let thy wrathful anger, Lord,
   faſt hold take them upon.
25 All waſte and deſolate let be
   their habitation,
   And in their tabernacles all
   inhabitants be none.
26 Becauſe him they do perſecute,
   whom thou didſt ſmite before ;
   They talk unto the grief of thoſe
   whom thou haſt wounded ſore.
27 Add thou iniquity unto
   their former wickedneſs ;
   And do not let them come at all
   into thy righteouſneſs.

28 Out of the book of life let them
    be raz'd and blotted quite:
  Among the juſt and righteous
    let not their names be writ.
29 But now become exceeding poor
    and ſorrowful am I;
  By thy ſalvation, O my God,
    let me be ſet on high.
30 The name of God I with a ſong
    moſt cheerfully will praiſe;
  And I, in giving thanks to him,
    his name ſhall highly raiſe.
31 This to the Lord a ſacrifice
    more gracious ſhall prove,
  Than bullock, ox, or any beaſt
    that hath both horn and hoof.
32 When this the humble men ſhall ſee,
    it joy to them ſhall give:
  O all ye that do ſeek the Lord,
    your hearts ſhall ever live.
33 For God the poor hears, and will not
    his priſoners contemn.
34 Let heav'n and earth, and ſeas him praiſe,
    and all that move in them.
35 For God will Judah's cities build,
    and he will Zion ſave:
  That they may dwell therein, and it
    in ſure poſſeſſion have.
36 And they that are his ſervants' ſeed
    inherit ſhall the ſame:
  So ſhall they have their dwelling there,
    that love his bleſſed name.

PSALM LXX.

To the chief Musician, a Psalm of David, to bring to remembrance.

This Psalm is almost one in words with the latter end of Psalm xl. wherein David being in present danger of his life by his enemies, prayeth first, For speedy delivery, ver. 1. Next, For shameful disappointment to his enemies, ver 2, 3. And thirdly, For a comfortable life to all the Godly, ver. 4. From which condition albeit he himself was very far for the present, yet he professeth he doth rely on God by faith, and prayeth for a timeous delivery, ver. 5.

1 LORD, haste me to deliver;
 with speed, Lord, succour me.
2 Let them that for my soul do seek
 sham'd and confounded be:
Turn'd back be they and sham'd,
 that in my hurt delight:
3 Turn'd back be they, Ha, ha, that say,
 their shaming to requite.
4 In thee let all be glad,
 and joy that seek for thee:
Let them who thy salvation love,
 say still, God praised be.
5 I poor and needy am;
 come, Lord, and make no stay:
My help thou and deliv'rer art,
 O Lord, make no delay.

Another of the same.

1 MAKE haste, O God, me to preserve;
 with speed, Lord, succour me.
2 Let them that for my soul do seek,
 sham'd and confounded be:
Let them be turned back, and sham'd
 that in my hurt delight.
3 Turn'd back be they, Ha, ha, that say,
 their shaming to requite.

4 O Lord, in thee let all be glad,
    and joy that seek for thee:
Let them who thy salvation love
    say still, God praised be.
5 But I both poor and needy am;
    come, Lord, and make no stay:
My help thou and deliv'rer art;
    O Lord, make no delay.

PSALM LXXI.

This Psalm is a Prayer of David's in his old age, requesting for delivery from the conspiracy of Absalom, wherein he wrestleth with the Lord by fervent supplication, in seven petitions, all tending to this purpose, that he may be delivered, to ver. 14. and from ver. 14. to the end, we have his confidence to be delivered, set forth in four evidences thereof. Absalom here is not named, nor is the particular case set down, otherwise than in general expressions, that so it may serve the better for the larger use of the Church of God, and of the particular members thereof in their afflictions.

1 O Lord, my hope and confidence
    is plac'd in thee alone:
Then let thy servant never be
    put to confusion.
2 And let me, in thy righteousness,
    from thee deliv'rance have:
Cause me escape; incline thine ear
    unto me, and me save.
3 Be thou my dwelling rock, to which
    I ever may resort:
Thou gav'st commandment me to save,
    for thou'rt my rock and fort.
4 Free me, my God, from wicked hands,
    hands cruel and unjust:
5 For thou, O Lord God, art my hope,
    and, from my youth, my trust.

6 Thou from the womb didſt hold me up;
    thou art the ſame, that me
  Out of my mother's bowels took:
    I ever will praiſe thee.
7 To many I a wonder am;
    but thou'rt my refuge ſtrong.
8 Fill'd let my mouth be with thy praiſe,
    and honour all day long.
9 O do not caſt me off, when as
    old age doth overtake me:
  And, when my ſtrength decayed is,
    then do not thou forſake me.
10 For thoſe that are mine enemies
    againſt me ſpeak with hate:
  And they together counſel take
    that for my ſoul lay wait.
11 They ſaid, God leaves him: him purſue
    and take; none will him ſave.
12 Be thou not far from me, my God:
    thy ſpeedy help I crave.
13 Confound, conſume them, that unto
    my ſoul are enemies:
  Cloth'd be they with reproach and ſhame
    that do my hurt deviſe.
14 But I with expectation
    will hope continually:
  And yet with praiſes more and more
    I will thee magnify.
15 Thy juſtice and ſalvation
    my mouth abroad ſhall ſhow
  Ev'n all the day; for I thereof
    the numbers do not know.

16 And I will constantly go on
    in strength of God the Lord;
  And thine own righteousness, ev'n thine
    alone, I will record.
17 For, ev'n from my youth, O God,
    by thee I have been taught:
  And hitherto I have declar'd
    the wonders thou hast wrought.
18 And now, Lord, leave me not, when I
    old and grey-headed grow:
  Till to this age, thy strength and pow'r
    to all to come I show.
19 And thy most perfect righteousness,
    O Lord, is very high,
  Who hast so great things done: O God,
    who is like unto thee?
20 Thou, Lord, who great adversities,
    and sore to me didst show,
  Shalt quicken, and bring me again
    from depths of earth below.
21 My greatness and my pow'r thou wilt
    increase and far extend;
  On every side, against all grief,
    thou wilt me comfort send.
22 Thee, ev'n thy truth I'll also praise,
    my God, with psaltery:
  Thou holy One of Israel,
    with harp I'll sing to thee.
23 My lips shall much rejoice in thee,
    when I thy praises found;
  My soul, which thou redeemed hast,
    in joy shall much abound.

24 My tongue thy juſtice ſhall proclaim,
    continuing all day long:
For they confounded are and ſham'd,
    that ſeek to do me wrong.

PSALM LXXII.
A Pſalm for Solomon.

In this Pſalm, under the ſhadow of King Solomon's reign, Chriſt's gracious government is praiſed; and firſt, The Church is taught to pray for a bleſſing on King David and his ſon's government, including Chriſt's, ver. 1. Next, The anſwer is given by the Spirit of the Lord in a prophecy of the bleſſedneſs of the reign, and Kingdom of Chriſt the ſon of David, from ver. 2, to ver. 18. Thirdly, The uſe hereof is ſet down in thankſgiving unto God, ver. 18, 19. and herein is the accompliſhment of all the deſires of David, obtained by this ſatisfactory anſwer, ver. 20.

1 O Lord, thy judgments give the King,
    his ſon thy righteouſneſs.
2 With right he ſhall thy people judge,
    thy poor with uprightneſs.
3 The lofty mountains ſhall bring forth
    unto the people peace;
Likewiſe the little hills the ſame
    ſhall do by righteouſneſs.
4 The people's poor ones he ſhall judge,
    the needy's children ſave;
And thoſe ſhall he in pieces break,
    who them oppreſſed have.
5 They ſhall thee fear, while ſun and moon
    do laſt, through ages all.
6 Like rain on mown graſs he ſhall drop,
    or ſhow'rs on earth that fall.
7 The juſt ſhall flouriſh in his days,
    and proſper in his reign:
He ſhall, while doth the moon endure,
    abundant peace maintain.

8 His large and great dominion shall
  from sea to sea extend :
  It from the river shall reach forth
  unto earth's utmost end.
9 They in the wilderness that dwell,
  bow down before him must :
  And they that are his enemies
  shall lick the very dust.
10 The Kings of Tarshish, and the isles,
  to him shall presents bring :
  And unto him shall offer gifts
  'Sheba's and Seba's King.
11 Yea, all the mighty Kings on earth
  before him down shall fall :
  And all the nations of the world
  do service to him shall.
12 For he the needy shall preserve,
  when he to him doth call ;
  The poor also, and him that hath
  no help of man at all.
13 The poor man, and the indigent,
  in mercy he shall spare :
  He shall preserve alive the souls
  of those that needy are.
14 Both from deceit and violence,
  their soul he shall set free :
  And in his sight right precious
  and dear their blood shall be.
15 Yea, he shall live, and giv'n to him
  shall be of Sheba's gold ;
  For him still shall they pray, and he
  shall daily be extoll'd.

16 Of corn an handful in the earth
   on tops of mountains high,
  With prosp'rous fruit shall shake, like
   on Lebanon that be.   [trees
  The city shall be flourishing,
   her citizens abound
  In number shall, like to the grass
   that grows upon the ground.
17 His name for ever shall endure,
   last like the sun it shall:
  Men shall be blest in him, and blest
   all nations shall him call.
18 Now blessed be the Lord our God,
   the God of Israel,
  For he alone doth wond'rous works
   in glory that excel.
19 And blessed be his glorious name
   to all eternity:
  The whole earth let his glory fill:
   Amen, so let it be.
  [*The Prayers of David the son of Jesse are ended.*]

PSALM LXXIII.
A Psalm of Asaph.

The Psalmist setteth down here the doctrine of God's goodness to the faithful, however he seem to deal with him, ver. 1. and cleareth it by his own experience: Wherein first, After he had stumbled to see the wicked prosper in the world, comparing his own calamities with their prosperity, ver. 2, 3, 4, 5, 6, 7, 8, 9, 10, 11, 12. he was like to be overcome with the tentation, and to forsake the course of godliness, ver. 13, 14. Next, With this tentation he wrestles, ver. 15, 16. And thirdly, He getteth the victory, by consulting the word of God, ver. 17, 18, 19, 20. In the last place, He maketh a fourfold use of this experience: the first whereof is, the acknowledging of his own weakness under the tentation, ver. 21, 22. The next is, Confessing of God's kindness to him in the time of tentation, ver. 23.

The third is, The confirming of his own faith for time to come, ver. 24, 25, 26 The fourth is, His resolution to draw more near to God hereafter, ver. 27, 28.

1 YET God is good to Israel,
    to each pure hearted one.
2 But as for me, my steps near slipt,
    my feet were almost gone.
3 For I envious was, and grudg'd
    the foolish folk to see,
  When I perceiv'd the wicked sort
    enjoy prosperity.
4 For still their strength continueth firm;
    their death of bands is free:
5 They are not toil'd as other men,
    nor plagu'd as others be.
6 Therefore their pride, like to a chain,
    them compasseth about:
  And, as a garment, violence
    doth cover them throughout.
7 Their eyes stand out with fat, they have
    more than their hearts could wish.
8 They are corrupt, their talk of wrong
    both loud and lofty is.
9 They set their mouth against the heav'ns
    in their blasphemous talk;
  And their reproaching tongue throughout
    the earth at large doth walk.
10 His people oftentimes for this
    look back, and turn about;
  Sith waters of so full a cup
    to these are poured out.
11 And thus they say, How can it be
    that God these things doth know?
  Or, can there in the Highest be
    knowledge of things below?

12 Behold, these are the wicked ones,
    yet prosper at their will
  In worldly things, they do increase
    in wealth and riches still.
13 I verily have done in vain,
    my heart to purify;
  To no effect in innocence
    washed my hands have I.
14 For daily, and all day throughout,
    great plagues I suffer'd have;
  Yea, every morning I of new
    did chastisement receive.
15 If in this manner foolishly
    to speak I would intend,
  Thy children's generation
    behold, I should offend.
16 When I this thought to know, it was
    too hard a thing for me.
17 Till to God's sanctuary I went;
    then I their end did see.
18 Assuredly thou didst them set
    a slipp'ry place upon:
  Them suddenly thou castedst down
    into destruction.
19 How, in a moment, suddenly
    to ruin brought are they!
  With fearful terrors utterly
    they are consum'd away.
20 Ev'n like unto a dream, when one
    from sleeping doth arise;
  So thou, O Lord, when thou awak'st,
    their image shalt despise.

21 Thus grieved was my heart in me,
    and me my reins oppreſt.
22 So rude was I, and ignorant,
    and in thy ſight a beaſt.
23 Nevertheleſs continually,
    O Lord, I am with thee :
  Thou doſt me hold by my right hand,
    and ſtill upholdeſt me.
24 Thou with thy counſel, while I live,
    wilt me conduct and guide ;
  And to thy glory afterward
    receive me to abide.
25 Whom have I in the Heav'ns high,
    but thee, O Lord, alone ?
  And in the earth, whom I deſire,
    beſides thee there is none.
26 My fleſh and heart doth faint and fail,
    but God doth fail me never :
  For of my heart God is the ſtrength,
    and portion for ever.
27 For lo, they that are far from thee
    for ever periſh ſhall :
  Them that a-whoring from thee go
    thou haſt deſtroyed all.
28 But ſurely it is good for me
    that I draw near to God :
  In God I truſt, that all thy works
    I may declare abroad.

PSALM LXXIV.
Maſchil of Aſaph,

Of this Pſalm there are three parts. In the firſt the pitiful lamentation of the Church preſented unto God, becauſe of the deſtruction of Jeruſalem, and burning of the temple by the Chaldeans, to ver. 11. In the next, is the ſtrengthening of the faith and hope of God's people, that God would ſend a delivery, to ver. 18. In the third, There are ſundry petitions for relief of his people, reſtitution of his own work, and ſuppreſſion of his enemies, to the end of the Pſalm.

1 O God, why haſt thou caſt us off?
    is it for evermore?
  Againſt thy paſture-ſheep, why doth
    thine anger ſmoke ſo ſore?
2 O call to thy rememberance
    thy congregation,
  Which thou haſt purchaſed of old,
    ſtill think the ſame upon:
  The rod of thine inheritance,
    which thou redeemed haſt,
  This Zion hill, wherein thou hadſt
    thy dwelling in times paſt.
3 To theſe long deſolations
    thy feet lift, do not tarry:
  For all the ills thy foes have done
    within thy ſanctuary.
4 Amidſt thy congregations
    thine enemies do roar:
  Their enſigns they ſet up, for ſigns
    of triumph, thee before.
5 A man was famous, and was had
    in eſtimation,
  According as he lifted up
    his ax thick trees upon.
6 But all at once with axes now
    and hammers they go to;
  And down the carved work thereof
    they break and quite undo.

7 They fired have thy sanctuary,
    and have defil'd the same,
By casting down unto the ground
    the place where dwelt thy name.
8 Thus said they in their hearts, Let us
    destroy them out of hand:
They burnt up all the synagogues
    of God within the land.
9 Our signs we do not now behold;
    there is not us among
A prophet more, nor any one
    that knows the time how long.
10 How long, Lord, shall the enemy
    thus in reproach exclaim?
And shall the adversary thus
    always blaspheme thy name?
11 Thy hand, ev'n thy right hand of might,
    why dost thou thus draw back?
O from thy bosom pluck it out,
    for our deliv'rance sake.
12 For certainly God is my King,
    ev'n from the times of old,
Working, in midst of all the earth,
    salvation manifold.
13 The sea by thy great pow'r to part
    asunder thou didst make;
And thou the dragons' heads, O Lord,
    within the waters brake.
14 The leviathan's head thou brak'st
    in pieces, and didst give
Him to be meat unto the folk
    in wilderness that live.

15 Thou clav'ft the fountain and the flood,
   which did with ftreams abound;
 Thou dry'ft the mighty waters up
   unto the very ground.
16 Thine only is the day, O Lord,
   thine alfo is the night;
 And thou alone prepared haft
   the fun and fhining light
17 By thee the borders of the earth
   were fettled ev'ry where:
 The fummer and the winter both
   by thee created were.
18 That th' enemy reproached hath,
   O keep it in record;
 And that the foolifh people have
   blafphem'd thy name, O Lord.
19 Unto the multitude do not
   thy turtle's foul deliver;
 The congregation of thy poor
   do not forget for ever.
20 Unto thy cov'nant have refpect:
   for earth's dark places be
 Full of the habitations
   of horrid cruelty.
21 O let not thofe that be opprefs'd
   return again with fhame;
 Let thofe that poor and needy are
   give praife unto thy name.
22 Do thou, O God, arife and plead
   the caufe that is thine own:
 Remember how thou art reproach'd
   ftill by the foolifh one.

‘ 23 Do not forget the voice of those
 that are thine enemies:
Of those the tumult ever grows
 that do against thee rise.

PSALM LXXV.

To the chief Musician, Al-taschith, a Psalm or Song of Asaph.

This Psalm doth well agree with the time of David's entry into the kingdom after Saul's death, before he was established King over all the tribes: whe ein he with the Church, Fi.st, Doth thank God for bringing him wonderfully to a begun possession of a part of the kingdom, ver 1. Secondly, He promiseth that when the L id sh.ll give him the rest of the kingdom, to employ h s power for righteous governing and settling of it, after it shall be put once in a right fraire, ver. 2, 3. Thirdly, He begins to triumph over the wicked that followed Saul, bringing to their mind the advertisement he had given them not to be proud in their places, ver. 4, 5. Pa tly, Because God had the disposing of p eferments in his own hand, ve. 6, 7. And partly, Because albeit God gave to all his own children a taste of troubles, as he saw fit, yet the d.egs of wrath were reserved for the wicked, ver. 8. Fourthly, He promiseth to praise God continually, for casting down the wicked, and exalting of the Godly, ver. 9, 10.

1 TO thee, O God, do we give thanks,
 we do give thanks to thee:
Because thy wond'rous works declare
 thy great name near to be.
2 I purpose when I shall receive
 the congregation,
That I shall judgment uprightly
 render to ev'ry one.
3 Dissolved is the land, with all
 that in the same do dwell:
But I the pillars thereof do
 bear up, and stablish well.

4 I to the foolish people said,
    do not deal foolishly;
  And unto those that wicked are,
    lift not your horn on high.

5 Lift not your horn on high: nor speak
6   with stubborn neck. But know,
  That nor from east, nor west, nor south,
    promotion doth flow.
7 But God is judge: he puts down one
    and sets another up.
8 For in the hand of God most High
    of red wine is a cup:

  'Tis full of mixture, he pours forth,
    and makes the wicked all
  Wring out the bitter dregs thereof,
    yea, and they drink them shall.
9 But I for ever will declare;
    I Jacob's God will praise.
10 All horns of lewd men I'll cut off;
    but just men's horns will raise.

PSALM LXXVI.

To the chief Musician on Neginoth, a Psalm
or Song of Asaph.

This Psalm of praise, given forth upon occasion of some great deliverance of the Church, such as was that when Senacherib's host was destroyed, or some other like overthrow given to the enemy.
The sum of the Psalm is this, The Lord is glorious in his Church, and greatly to be praised by his people, set down, ver. 1, 2. The reasons given for this are six: The first, ver. 3. The second, ver. 4. The third, ver. 5, 6. The fourth, ver. 7. The fifth, ver. 8, 9. The sixth, ver. 10. The use whereof, with a reason for it, is set down, ver. 11, 12.

1 IN Judah's land God is well known:
    his name's in Ifra'l great.
2 In Salem is his tabernacle,
    in Zion is his feat.
3 There arrows of the bow he brake,
    the fhield, the fword, the war.
4 More glorious thou than hills of prey,
    more excellent art far.
5 Thofe that were ftout of heart are fpoil'd,
    they flept their fleep outright:
And none of thofe their hands did find
    that were the men of might.
6 When thy rebuke, O Jacob's God,
    had forth againft them paft,
Their horfes and their chariots both
    were in a dead fleep caft.
7 Thou, Lord, ev'n thou art he that fhould
    be fear'd, and who is he
That may ftand up before thy fight,
    if once thou angry be?   [heard;
8 From Heav'n thou judgment caus'd be
    the earth was ftill with fear.
9 When God to judgment rofe, to fave,
    all meek on earth that were.
10 Surely the very wrath of man
    unto thy praife redounds;
Thou to the remnant of his wrath
    wilt fet reftraining bounds.
11 Vow to the Lord your God, and pay;
    all ye that near him be,
Bring gifts and prefents unto him,
    for to be fear'd is he.

12 By him the sp'rits shall be cut off
    of those that princes are;
Unto the kings that are on earth
    he fearful doth appear.

PSALM LXXVII.

To the chief Musician, to Jeduthun, a Psalm of Asaph.

This Psalm doth express the deep exercise of the Psalmist, troubled with the sense of God's displeasure, and how he wrestled under this condition, and had deliverance from it, which is summarily propounded, ver. 1. and made plain more particularly in the rest of the Psalm; for first, he setteth down his trouble of mind, ver. 2, 3, 4. Secondly, His wrestling with the sense of felt wrath, ver. 5, 6, 7, 8, 9. Thirdly, His begun victory by faith, ver. 10, 11, 12. Fourthly, The settling of his mind by consideration of God's manner of dealing with his Church of old, to the end of the Psalm.

1 UNTO the Lord I with my voice,
    I unto God did cry
Ev'n with my voice, and unto me
    his ear he did apply.
2 I in my trouble sought the Lord:
    my sore by night did run,
And ceased not: my grieved soul
    did consolation shun.
3 I to rememb'rance God did call,
    yet trouble did remain;
And overwhelm'd my spirit was,
    whilst I did sore complain.
4 Mine eyes debarr'd from rest and sleep
    thou makest still to wake:
My trouble is so great, that I
    unable am to speak.

5 The days of old to mind I call'd,
    and oft did think upon
  The times and ages that are paſt
    full many years agone.
6 By night my ſong I call to mind,
    and commune with my heart;
  My ſp'rit did carefully enquire
    how I might eaſe my ſmart.
7 For ever will the Lord caſt off,
    and gracious be no more?
8 For ever is his mercy gone?
    fails his word evermore?
9 Is't true, that to be gracious
    the Lord forgotten hath?
  And that his tender mercies he
    hath ſhut up in his wrath?
10 Then did I ſay, That ſurely this
    is mine infirmity:
  I'll mind the years of the right hand
    of him that is moſt High.
11 Yea, I remember will the works
    performed by the Lord:
  The wonders done of old by thee,
    I ſurely will record.
12 I alſo will of all thy works
    my meditation make,
  And of thy doings to diſcourſe
    great pleaſure I will take.
13 O God, thy way moſt holy is
    within thy ſanctuary:
  And what God is ſo great in pow'r
    as is our God moſt High?

14 Thou art the God that wonders doſt
    by thy right hand moſt ſtrong;
 Thy mighty pow'r thou haſt declar'd
    the nations among.
15 To thine own people with thine arm
    thou didſt redemption bring,
 To Jacob's ſons, and to the tribes
    of Joſeph that do ſpring.
16 The waters, Lord, perceived thee,
    the waters ſaw thee well;
 And they for fear aſide did flee:
    the depths on trembling fell.
17 The clouds in water forth were pour'd,
    ſound loudly did the ſky:
 And ſwiftly through the world abroad
    thine arrows fierce did fly.
18 Thy thunder's voice alongſt the heav'n
    a mighty noiſe did make:
 By light'nings light'ned was the world,
    th' earth tremble did and ſhake.
19 Thy way is in the ſea, and in
    the waters great thy path;
 Yet are thy footſteps hid, O Lord,
    none knowledge thereof hath.
20 Thy people thou didſt ſafely lead
    like to a flock of ſheep,
 By Moſes' hand and Aaron's thou
    didſt them conduct and keep.

PSALM LXXVIII.
Maſchil of Aſaph.

In this Pſalm the Lord's Spirit doth ſtir up his people to make a right uſe of the Lord's work of juſtice and mercy ſet down in the holy Scripture; and to this end he giveth account of

God's dealing very mercifully with his people, and never in justice but when mercy was abused; and he sheweth also by the people's dealing with God unthankfully and deceitfully, whether he dealt mercifully or in justice with them.

The Psalm may be divided thus: After a preface to prepare the hearer for attention and observation of what he was to deliver, ver. 1, 2, 3, 4. he bringeth forth, first, The evidence of God's gracious care he had of his people, in giving them his blessed word, to teach unto them faith and obedience, ver. 5, 6, 7, 8. Secondly, The evidence of God's judgment against his people, who were put to flight before their foes, when they did not believe the Lord, and did not make use of his works among them, ver. 9, 10, 11. Thirdly, He setteth down how great things God did for them in Egypt, and in the wilderness, ver. 12, 13, 14, 15, 16. Fourthly, How they made no better use of these mercies, than to tempt God, and provoke him to wrath, ver. 17, 18, 19, 20. Fifthly, How for their tempting of God, he was angry at them for their unbelief, and not considering of the miraculous feeding of them with Manna, ver. 21, 22, 23, 24, 25. and how in wrath he satisfied their lust by sending quails for them, to eat flesh their fill, ver. 26, 27, 28, 29. Sixthly, How because they repented not of their provocation, the Lord did plague them, and they went on in their misbelief and disobedience; and God went on in the course of multiplying judgments on them, and cutting off multitudes of them, ver 30, 31, 32, 33. Seventhly, How they at last made a fashion of repenting and seeking of God, but proved in effect nothing but flattering and dissembling hypocrites, unconstant in the covenant, ver. 34, 35, 36, 37. Eighthly, How the Lord in mercy pitied and spared them many a time, notwithstanding all their provocations of his justice against them, ver. 38, 39, 40, 41. Ninthly, He setteth down the prime cause of all this their sin and misery, because they marked not, or made no use of the difference that God put between the Egyptians and them; nor how for their cause he had plagued the Egyptians with plague after plague, ver. 42, 43, 44, 45, 46, 47, 48, 49, 50, 51. and brought their fathers safely out of Egypt, when their enemies were drowned before their eyes, ver. 52, 53. Tenthly, He setteth down how the Lord perfected their journey to Canaan, and brought them to the possession of it, thrusting out the Canaanites, that they might have place, ver. 54, 55. Eleventhly, How they for all this, provoked God to anger with their idolatry and superstition, ver. 56, 57, 58. Twelfthly, How the Lord for this their oft repeated provocation, did miserably vex them in the days of Eli and Samuel, giving over his ark into the Philistines hand, and plaguing their country with variety of plagues, ver. 59, 60, 61, 62, 63, 64. Thirteenthly, How God of his free mercy put his enemies to shame, and restored Religion and Liberty to the Church and Kingdom, ver. 65, 66. And last of all, How he brought them to a settled condition under David, who was a Type of Christ, ver. 67, 68, 69, 70, 71, 72.

1 ATTEND, my people, to my law,
    thereto give thou an ear;
The words that from my mouth proceed
    attentively do hear.
2 My mouth shall speak a parable,
    and sayings dark of old:
3 The same which we have heard and known,
    and us our fathers told.

4 We also will them not conceal
    from their posterity;
Them to the generation
    to come declare will we:
The praises of the Lord our God,
    and his almighty strength,
The wond'rous works that he hath done
    we will shew forth at length.

5 His testimony and his law
    in Isra'l he did place,
And charg'd our fathers it to shew
    to their succeeding race.
6 That so the race which was to come
    might well them learn and know:
And sons unborn, who should arise,
    might to their sons them show.
7 That they might set their hope in God,
    and suffer not to fall
His mighty works out of their mind;
    but keep his precepts all:

8 And might not, like their fathers, be
    a ſtiff rebellious race;
  A race not right in heart, with God
    whoſe ſp'rit not ſtedfaſt was.
9 The ſons of Ephra'm, who nor bows,
    nor other arms did lack,
  When as the day of battle was,
    they faintly turned back.
10 They brake God's cov'nant, and refus'd
    in his commands to go:
11 His works and wonders they forgot,
    which he to them did ſhow.
12 Things marvellous he brought to paſs,
    their fathers them beheld,
  Within the land of Egypt done,
    yea, ev'n in Zoan's field.
13 By him divided was the ſea,
    he caus'd them through to paſs,
  And made the waters ſo to ſtand
    as like an heap it was.
14 With cloud by day, with light of fire
    all night he did them guide.
15 In deſert, rocks he clave, and drink
    as from great depths ſupply'd.
16 He from the rock brought ſtreams, like
    made waters to run down.   [floods
17 Yet ſinning more, in deſert they
    provok'd the higheſt One.
18 For in their heart they tempted God,
    and, ſpeaking with miſtruſt,
  They greedily did meat require
    to ſatisfy their luſt.

19 Againſt the Lord himſelf they ſpake;
 and, murmuring, ſaid thus,
A table in the wildernefs
 can God prepare for us?
20 Behold, he ſmote the rock, and thence
 came ſtreams and waters great;
But can he give his people bread,
 and ſend them fleſh to eat?
21 The Lord did hear, and waxed wroth
 ſo kindled was a flame
'Gainſt Jacob, and 'gainſt Iſrael
 up indignation came.
22 For they believ'd not God, nor truſt
 in his ſalvation had:
23 Tho' clouds above he did command,
 and Heav'n's doors open made;
24 And Manna rain'd on them, and gave
 them corn of Heav'n to eat.
25 Man Angels' food did eat: to them
 he to the full ſent meat.
26 And in the Heaven he did cauſe
 an eaſtern wind to blow;
And by his power he let out
 the ſouthern wind to go.
27 Then fleſh, as thick as duſt, he made
 to rain down them among,
And feather'd fowls, like as the ſand
 which ly'th the ſhore along.
28 At his command, amidſt their camp
 theſe ſhow'rs of fleſh down fell,
All round about the tabernacles
 and tentswhere they did dwell.

29 So did they eat abundantly,
   and had of meat their fill;
 For he did give to them what was
   their own defire and will.
30 They from their luft had not eftrang'd
   their heart and their defire:
 But while the meat was in their mouths,
   which they did fo require.
31 God's wrath upon them came, and flew
   the fatteft of them all;
 So that the choice of Ifrael,
   o'erthrown by death, did fall.
32 Yet, notwithftanding of all this,
   they finned ftill the more:
 And, tho' he had great wonders wrought,
   believ'd him not therefore.
33 Wherefore, their days in vanity
   he did confume and wafte:
 And by his wrath their wretched years
   away in trouble paft.
34 But when he flew them, then they did
   to feek him fhew defire:
 Yea, they returned, and after God
   right early did enquire.
35 And that the Lord had been their rock
   they did remember then;
 Ev'n that the high Almighty God
   had their Redeemer been.
36 Yet with their mouth they flatter'd him,
   and fpake but feignedly;
 And they unto the God of truth
   with their falfe tongues did lye.

37 For tho' their words were good, their
    with him was not sincere; [heart
  Unstedfast and perfidious
    they in his cov'nant were.
38 But, full of pity, he forgave
    their sin, them did not slay;
  Nor stirr'd up all his wrath, but oft
    his anger turn'd away.
39 For that they were but fading flesh
    to mind he did recall;
  A wind that passeth soon away,
    and not returns at all.
40 How often did they him provoke
    within the wilderness?
  And in the desert did him grieve
    with their rebelliousness?
41 Yea, turning back, they tempted God,
    and limits set upon
  Him, who in midst of Isra'l, is
    the only holy One.
42 They did not call to mind his pow'r,
    nor yet the day when he
  Deliver'd them out of the hand
    of their fierce enemy.
43 Nor how great signs in Egypt land
    he openly had wrought,
  What miracles in Zoan's field
    his hand to pass had brought.
44 How lakes and rivers ev'ry where,
    he turned into blood;
  So that no man nor beast could drink
    of standing lake or flood.

45 He brought among them swarms of flies,
    which did them sore annoy:
  And divers kinds of filthy frogs
    he sent them to destroy.
46 He to the caterpillar gave
    the fruits of all their soil;
  Their labours he deliver'd up
    unto the locusts' spoil.
47 Their vines with hail, their sycamores
    he with the frost did blast.
48 Their beasts to hail he gave, their flocks
    hot thunder-bolts did waste.
49 Fierce burning wrath he on them cast,
    and indignation strong,
  And troubles sore, by sending forth
    ill angels them among.
50 He to his wrath made way, their soul
    from death he did not save;
  But over to the pestilence
    the lives of them he gave.
51 In Egypt land the first-born all
    he smote down ev'ry where:
  Among the tents of Ham, ev'n these
    chief of their strength that were.
52 But his own people, like to sheep,
    thence to go forth he made;
  And he, amidst the wilderness
    them, as a flock, did lead.
53 And he them safely on did lead,
    so that they did not fear:
  Whereas their en'mies by the sea
    quite overwhelmed were.

54 To borders of his sanctuary
    the Lord his people led,
  Ev'n to the mount which his right hand,
    for them had purchased.
55 The nations of Canaan,
    by his almighty hand,
  Before their face he did expel
    out of their native land;
  Which for inheritance to them
    by line he did divide,
  And made the tribes of Israel
    within their tents abide.
56 Yet God most high they did provoke,
    and tempted ever still;
  And to observe his testimonies
    did not incline their will.
57 But, like their fathers, turned back,
    and dealt unfaithfully:
  Aside they turn'd, like a bow
    that shoots deceitfully.
58 For they to anger did provoke
    him with their places high,
  And with their graven images
    mov'd him to jealousy.
59 When God heard this, he waxed wroth,
    and much loath'd Isra'l then:
60 So Shiloth's tent he left, the tent
    which he had plac'd with men:
61 And he his strength delivered,
    into captivity;
  He left his glory in the hand
    of his proud enemy.

62 His people alſo he gave o'er
    unto the ſword's fierce rage,
So ſore his wrath inflamed was
    againſt his heritage.
63 The fire conſum'd their choice young
    their maids no marriage had.   [men:
64 And when their prieſts fell by the ſword,
    their wives no mourning made.
65 But then the Lord aroſe, as one
    that doth from ſleep awake;
And, like a giant, that, by wine
    refreſh'd, a ſhout doth make.
66 Upon his en'mies' hinder parts
    he made his ſtroke to fall:
And ſo upon them he did put
    a ſhame perpetual.
67 Moreover, he the tabernacle
    of Joſeph did refuſe:
The mighty tribe of Ephraim
    he would in no wiſe chuſe.
68 But he did chuſe Jehudah's tribe
    to be the reſt above;
And of mount Zion he made choice,
    which he ſo much did love.
69 And he his ſanctuary built
    like to a palace high,
Like to the earth, which he did found
    to perpetuity.
70 Of David, that his ſervant was,
    he alſo choice did make;
And even from the folds of ſheep
    was pleaſed him to take:

71 From waiting on the ewes with young,
    he brought him forth to feed
  Iſrael, his inheritance,
    his people, Jacob's feed.

72 So after the integrity
    he, of his heart, them fed:
  And by the good ſkill of his hands,
    them wiſely governed.

PSALM LXXIX.
A Pſalm of Aſaph.

The ſcattered and captive people of God, after the deſtruction of Jeruſalem and of the Temple, do put up a pitiful complaint unto God, to ver. 6. and do pray for a merciful relief to his Church, and for avenging their blood upon their enemies. As for the complaint, in it they lament four things, Firſt, the profanation and deſolation of the Lord's inheritance and temple by the heathen their enemies, ver. 1. Secondly, The barbarous cruelty and inhumanity uſed againſt them, ver. 2, 3. Thirdly, The contempt and mocking of their wicked neighbours in their miſery, ver. 4. Fourthly, As they acknowledge this to proceed from God's diſpleaſure, ſo they lament that it is like to be everlaſting, ver. 5.
In their Prayer, in the latter part of the Pſalm, they crave, Firſt, Juſtice upon their enemies, ver. 6, 7. Secondly, Pardon of their own ſins, and deliverance out of their miſery, for ſundry reaſons, ver. 8, 9, 10, 11. Thirdly, That God would reward their inhuman neighbours who mocked at their miſery, ver. 12. And do cloſe their petition with a promiſe of praiſe and thanks unto God by the Church in all ſucceeding ages.

1 O God, the heathen enter'd have
    thine heritage; by them
  Defiled is thy houſe: on heaps
    they laid Jeruſalem
2 The bodies of thy ſervants they
    have caſt forth, to be meat
  To rav'nous fowls, thy dear Saints' fleſh
    they gave to beaſts to eat.

3 Their blood about Jerusalem,
  like water, they have shed:
And there was none to bury them,
  when they were slain and dead.
4 Unto our neighbours a reproach
  most base become are we:
A scorn and laughing-stock to them
  that round about us be.
5 How long, Lord, shall thine anger last?
  wilt thou still keep the same?
And shall thy fervent jealousy
  burn like unto a flame?
6 On heathens pour thy fury forth,
  that have thee never known,
And on those kingdoms which thy Name
  have never call'd upon.
7 For these are they who Jacob have
  devoured cruelly.
And they his habitation
  have caused waste to lie.
8 Against us mind not former sins:
  thy tender mercies show:
Let them prevent us speedily;
  for we're brought very low.
9 For thy Name's glory, help us, Lord,
  who hast our Saviour been:
Deliver us, for thy Name's sake,
  O purge away our sin.
10 Why say the heathen, Where's their
  let him to them be known,   [God?
When those who shed thy servants' blood
  are in our sight o'erthrown.

11 O let the pris'ners' sighs ascend
     before thy sight on High;
  Preserve those in thy mighty pow'r,
     that are design'd to die.
12 And to our neighbour's bosom cause
     it sev'n-fold rendered be,
  Ev'n the reproach wherewith they have,
     O Lord, reproach'd thee.
13 So we thy folk, and pasture sheep,
     shall give thee thanks always:
  And unto generations all
     we will shew forth thy praise.

PSALM LXXX.

*To the chief Musician, upon Shoshannim,
a Psalm of Asaph.*

This Psalm given the Church to be made use of, is of the like sad subject with the former, and may be applied to the time of carrying away the ten tribes out of the holy Land, while Judah was yet in possession of it, and the temple was yet standing, and the Lord was dwelling between the Cherubims and the Sanctuary, where the ark and mercy-seat were yet remaining; or to the time of the begun desolation of the land by Nebuchadnezzar, or to any other desolation which did threaten their final rooting out. The sum of the Psalm is a lamenting of the miserable condition of the Israelites, and an earnest entreating of the Lord to give them repentance and delivery. In the first place, The Church maketh her address to God, and propoundeth the main petition, ver. 1, 2, 3. In the second place, They lament their misery, and repeat the same petition, ver. 4, 5, 6, 7. In the third place, They call to mind the Lord's care to plant his people in the land as a vine tree, and do lament the doleful change of their happy condition into that of their present misery, ver. 8, 9, 10, 11, 12, 13. In the fourth place, They pray for God's mercy and pity towards his desolate people, ver. 14, 15, 16. In the last place, They pray for the standing of the tribe of Judah, and that for Christ's cause, who was to take his human nature of this tribe; and do close the Psalm with repeating the third time their special petition for repentance and delivery to be granted unto them, ver. 17, 18, 19.

1 HEAR Ifra'l's fhepherd, like a flock
    thou that doft Jofeph guide;
  Shine forth, O thou that doft between
    the cherubims abide.
2 In Ephraim's, and Benjamin's,
    and in Manaffeh's fight,
  O come for our falvation,
    ftir up thy ftrength and might.
3 Turn us again, O Lord, our God:
    and upon us vouchfafe
  To make thy countenance to fhine,
    and fo we fhall be fafe.
4 O Lord of hofts, almighty God,
    how long fhall kindled be
  Thy wrath againft the prayer made
    by thine own folk to thee?
5 Thou tears of forrow giv'ft to them
    inftead of bread to eat:
  Yea, tears inftead of drink thou giv'ft
    to them in meafure great.
6 Thou makeft us a ftrife unto
    our neighbours round about:
  Our enemies among themfelves
    at us do laugh and flout.
7 Turn us again, O God of hofts,
    and upon us vouchfafe
  To make thy countenance to fhine,
    and fo we fhall be fafe.
8 A vine from Egypt brought thou haft,
    by thine out-ftretched hand:
  And thou the heathen out didft caft,
    to plant it in their land.

9 Before it thou a room didſt make,
 where it might grow and ſtand;
Thou cauſedſt it deep root to take,
 and it did fill the land.
10 The mountains veil'd were with its ſhade,
 as with a covering;
Like goodly cedars where the boughs
 which out from it did ſpring.
11 Upon the one hand, to the ſea
 her boughs ſhe did out ſend;
On th' other ſide, unto the flood
 her branches did extend.
12 Why haſt thou then thus broken down
 and ta'en her hedge away,
So that all paſſengers do pluck
 and make of her a prey?
13 The boar who from the foreſt comes,
 doth waſte it at his pleaſure;
The wild beaſt of the field alſo
 devours it out of meaſure.
14 O God of hoſts, we thee beſeech,
 return now unto thine:
Look down from Heav'n in love, behold
 and viſit this thy vine.
15 This vineyard, which thine own righthand
 hath planted us among,
And that ſame branch, which for thyſelf
 thou haſt made to be ſtrong.
16 Burnt up it is with flaming fire,
 it alſo is cut down:
They utterly are periſhed
 when as thy face doth frown.

17 O let thy hand be still upon
　　the man of thy right hand,
　The son of man, whom for thyself
　　thou madest strong to stand.
18 So henceforth we will not go back,
　　nor turn from thee at all:
　O do thou quicken us, and we
　　upon thy name will call.
19 Turn us again, Lord God of hosts,
　　and upon us vouchsafe
　To make thy countenance to shine,
　　and so we shall be safe.

PSALM LXXXI.

To the chief Musician, upon Gittith, a Psalm of Asaph.

This Psalm was appointed to be sung in their solemn feasts, new moons, and feast of tabernacles; in special, for a testimony of God's gracious and bountiful dealing with his people on the one hand, and of their provocation of God on the other hand, moving him to change his dispensation toward them, and to withhold many benefits from them, which otherwise they might have had, if they had not rejected God's counsel, and had chosen their own ways, that by this Psalm his people might learn to be wiser.

The parts of the Psalm are three. The first, is a preface, wherein there is a mutual stirring up of the Church-members to keep the solemn feasts, and blowing of trumpets, ver. 1, 2, 3 and a reason of this mutual exhortation, taken from God's institution of this ordinance when he brought his people out of Egypt from the service of strangers, ver. 4, 5.

In the second part is set down, how God delivered them from bondage in Egypt, and from troubles in their journey, ver. 6, 7. and how reasonable commands the Lord did give unto them, which commands are all summed up in this one, That God should be their God alone, ver. 8, 9, 10.

In the third part is set down, First, How they rejected God and his counsel, ver. 11. Next, How therefore they were plagued, by being given over to their own lusts, ver. 12. Thirdly, How they deprived themselves of God's benefits, which by following God's counsel, they might have enjoyed, ver. 13, 14, 15.

1 SING loud to God, our ſtrength: with joy
    to Jacob's God do ſing.
2 Take up a pſalm, the pleaſant harp,
    timbrel and pſalt'ry bring.
3 Blow trumpets at new-moon, what day
    our feaſt appointed is.
4 For charge to Iſra'l, and a law
    of Jacob's God was this.
5 To Joſeph this a teſtimony
    he made, when Egypt land
  He travell'd thro': where ſpeech I heard
    I did not underſtand.
6 His ſhoulder I from burdens took:
    his hands from pots did free.
7 Thou didſt in trouble on me call,
    and I deliver'd thee:

  In ſecret place of thundering,
    I did thee anſwer make;
  And at the ſtreams of Meribah,
    of thee a proof did take.
8 O thou my people, give an ear,
    I'll teſtify to thee:
  To thee, O Iſrael, if thou wilt
    but hearken unto me.
9 In midſt of thee there ſhall not be
    any ſtrange God at all:
  Nor unto any God unknown
    thou bowing down ſhalt fall.
10 I am the Lord thy God, which did
    from Egypt land thee guide:
  I'll fill thy mouth abundantly,
    do thou it open wide.

11 But yet my people to my voice
    would not attentive be :
And ev'n my chosen Israel
    he would have none of me.
12 So to the lust of their own hearts
    I them delivered :
And then in counsels of their own
    they vainly wandered.
13 O that my people had me heard,
    Isra'l my ways had chose !
14 I had their en'mies soon subdu'd,
    my hand turn'd on their foes.
15 The haters of the Lord to him
    submission should have feign'd ;
But as for them, their time should have
    for evermore remain'd.
16 He should have also fed them with
    the finest of the wheat :
Of honey from the rock, thy fill
    I should have made thee eat.

PSALM LXXXII.

A Psalm of Asaph.

This Psalm agreeth with the time of David's persecution by Saul and his counsellors, the Peers of the land ; wherein the Psalmist comforteth himself in God's supremacy, and his judging of all judges on the earth ; for executing whereof God cometh into their meeting, ver. 1. Then challengeth them for their injustice and oppression, ver. 2. Thirdly, Readeth the law and rule of their duty unto them, ver. 3, 4. Fourthly, Condemneth them as guilty, ver. 5. Fifthly, Pronounceth sentence of doom upon them, ver. 6, 7. And then the Psalmist closeth the Psalm with prayer, ver. 8.

1 IN Gods' assembly, God doth stand :
    he judgeth Gods among.
2 How long, accepting persons vile,
    will ye give judgment wrong ?

3 Defend the poor and fatherless:
 to poor oppress'd do right.
4 The poor and needy ones set free:
 rid them from ill men's might.
5 They know not, nor will understand;
 in darkness they walk on:
All the foundations of the earth
 out of their course are gone.
6 I said, that ye are Gods, and are
 sons of the Highest all.
7 But ye shall die like men, and as
 one of the princes fall.
8 O God, do thou raise up thyself,
 the earth to judgment call:
For thou, as thine inheritance,
 shalt take the nations all.

PSALM LXXXIII.
A Song or Psalm of Asaph.

This Psalm agreeth with such a condition of the Church, as we read of in the days of Jehosaphat, 2 Chron. xx. and serveth to comfort the Church in the greatest conspiracies of her enemies against her. The Psalm hath two parts. In the former, The Church doth cry to God to shew himself for his people, ver. 1. and complaineth of their conspiracy and preparation to come against her, ver 2, 3. and of their purpose to root out the Lord's people, ver. 4, 5. specifying a number of nations, who were upon the plot, ver. 6, 7, 8. In the latter part, They pray that judgment may so befall them, as befell other such their enemies before, who enterprised the same enterprise, ver. 9, 10, 11, 12. In particular, That the whole host may be overturned and consumed, ver. 13, 14. and the remnant may be chased and scattered, ver. 15. and ashamed and confounded for ever, ver. 16, 17. that so God may have the more glory among them, ver. 18.

1 KEEP not, O God, we thee entreat,
 O keep not silence now:
Do thou not hold thy peace, O God,
 and still no more be thou.

2 For lo, thine enemies a noise
   tumultuously have made:
And they that haters are of thee
   have lifted up the head.
3 Against thy chosen people they
   do crafty counsel take:
And they against thy hidden ones
   do consultations make.
4 Come, let us cut them off, said they,
   from being a nation,
That of the name of Isra'l may
   no more be mention.
5 For with joint heart they plot: in league
   against thee they combine.
6 The tents of Edom, Ishma'lites;
   Moab's and Hagar's line.
7 Gebal, and Ammon, Amalek,
   Philistines, those of Tyre:
8 And Assur join'd with them; to help
   Lot's children they conspire.
9 Do to them as to Midian,
   Jabin at Kison strand:
10 And Sis'ra; which at Endor fell,
   as dung to fat the land.
11 Like Oreb, and like Zeeb, make
   their noble men to fall:
Like Zeba, and Zalmunna-like,
   make thou their princes all:
12 Who said, for our possession
   let us God's houses take.
13 My God, them like a wheel, as chaff
   before the wind, them make.

14 As fire consumes the wood, as flame
   doth mountains set on fire :
15 Chase and affright them with the storm
   and tempest of thine ire.
16 Their faces fill with shame, O Lord,
   that they may seek thy name.
17 Let them confounded be, and vex'd,
   and perish in their shame:
18 That men may know, that thou to whom
   alone doth appertain
   The Name JEHOVAH, dost most high
   o'er all the earth remain.

PSALM LXXXIV.

To the chief Musician upon Gittith, a Psalm for the Sons of Korah.

This Psalm is of the same subject with Psalm xlii. and Psalm lxiii. Wherein the Psalmist lamenteth his banishment from the temple and the public ordinances of religion, to ver. 8. and then prayeth for his restoring to that privilege in the rest of the Psalm. This Psalm agreeth well with the time of David's parting with the ark, when he fled from Absalom.
In his lamentation, First, He commendeth the place of public Worship, ver. 1. Then sheweth his longing after it, ver. 2. Thirdly, He wisheth to be as a sparrow, in the meanest condition partaker of that privilege, ver. 3. Fourthly, He proclaimeth the blessedness of all the Lord's Ministers, who may always be there, ver. 4. Fifthly, He calleth them blessed who have liberty to come on foot from any part of the country to keep at least the solemn feasts, ver. 5, 6, 7. In his prayer, he requests in general terms, to be restored to the Lord's worship, ver. 8, 9. for two reasons, one is, Because he preferreth the meanest officer's condition in God's House to the most quiet dwelling among the wicked, ver. 10. Another reason, Because felicity is to be found in God, by the means of his ordinances, ver. 11. And mean time while his prayer should be granted, he resteth by faith on God, in whom Believers are made blessed, wherever they be.

1 HOW lovely is thy dwelling-place,
   O Lord of hosts, to me!
   The tabernacles of thy grace,
   how pleasant, Lord, they be!

2 My thirsty soul longs veh'mently,
    yea, faints thy courts to see:
My very heart and flesh cry out,
    O living God, for thee!
3 Behold, the sparrow findeth out
    an house wherein to rest;
The swallow also for herself,
    hath purchased a nest,
Ev'n thine own altars; where she safe
    her young ones forth may bring,
O thou Almighty, Lord of hosts,
    who art my God and King.
4 Blest are they in thy house that dwell,
    they ever give thee praise.
5 Blest is the man whose strength thou art:
    in whose heart are thy ways.
6 Who passing thorough Baca's vale,
    therein do dig up wells:
Also the rain that falleth down
    the pools with water fills.
7 So they from strength unwearied go
    still forward unto strength,
Until in Zion they appear,
    before the Lord at length.
8 Lord God of hosts, my prayer hear:
    O Jacob's God, give ear.
9 See, God, our shield, look on the face
    of thine anointed dear.
10 For in thy courts one day excels
    a thousand: rather in
My God's house will I keep a door,
    than dwell in tents of sin.

11 For God the Lord's a sun and shield:
    he'll grace and glory give:
And will withhold no good from them
    that uprightly do live.
12 O thou that art the Lord of hosts,
    that man is truly blest,
Who by assured confidence
    on thee alone doth rest.

PSALM LXXXV.

To the chief Musician, a Psalm for the Sons of Korah.

This Psalm agreeth well with the condition of the Church of the Jews, now fallen into new troubles, after their return from the captivity of Babylon. In the former part whereof they pray for a new proof and experience of God's mercy, to ver. 8. In the latter part is set down a comfortable answer to their prayer, and for the help of their faith in their prayer. First, They make mention of their gracious delivery from the captivity, ver. 1, 2, 3. Next, They pray for repentance, and removing of the tokens of God's wrath, ver. 4, 5. Thirdly, They pray for restoration of their miserable and dead condition wherein they were lying, by some merciful deliverance, ver. 6, 7.

As for the answer in the latter part, he prepareth himself to receive it from the Lord, and by inspiration receiveth indeed a comfortable prophecy of five notable fruits of mercy. The first is, Of peace to God's people, ver. 8. The next is, Of deliverance and salvation to his servants, ver. 9. The third is, of the grace of Christ unto justification, and the fruits of it, ver. 10, 11. The fourth is, Of temporal blessings, upon the place where the Lord's people do dwell, and that for his peoples' comfort, ver. 12. The fifth is, Of the grace of Christ unto sanctification, ver. 13.

1 O Lord, thou hast been favourable
    to thy beloved land;
Jacob's captivity thou hast
    recall'd with mighty hand.
2 Thou pardoned thy people hast
    all their iniquities,
Thou all their trespasses and sins
    hast cov'red from thine eyes.

3 Thou took'ft off all thine ire, and turn'dft
   from thy wrath's furioufnefs.
4 Turn us, God of our health, and caufe
   thy wrath 'gainft us to ceafe.
5 Shall thy difpleafure thus endure
   againft us without end?
   Wilt thou to generations all
   thine anger forth extend?
6 That in thee may thy people joy,
   wilt thou not us revive?
7 Shew us thy mercy; Lord, to us
   do thy falvation give.
8 I'll hear what God the Lord will fpeak:
   to his folk he'll fpeak peace,
   And to his faints: but let them not
   return to foolifhnefs.
9 To them that fear them, furely near
   is his falvation;
   That glory in our land may have
   her habitation.
10 Truth met with mercy, righteoufnefs
   and peace kifs'd mutually.
11 Truth fprings from earth, and righteoufnefs
   looks down from Heav'n high.
12 Yea, what is good the Lord fhall give:
   our land fhall yield increafe.
13 Juftice, to let us in his fteps,
   fhall go before his face.

PSALM LXXXVI.
A Prayer of David.

This Pfalm agreeth well with the time when David was in trouble, being perfecuted by Saul. The fum of it was a Prayer for relief, confifting of feven petitions, fome of them more generally, and fome of them more particularly expreffing his trouble, and his defire of relief: All which petitions have reafons joined unto them, ferving to ftrengthen the faith of the fuplpicant.

1 O Lord, do thou bow down thine ear,
    and hear me gracioufly;
Becaufe I fore afflicted am,
    and am in poverty.
2 Becaufe I'm holy, let my foul
    by thee preferved be:
O thou my God, thy fervant fave
    that puts his truft in thee.
3 Sith unto thee I daily cry,
    be merciful to me.
4 Rejoice thy fervant's foul: for, Lord,
    I lift my foul to thee.
5 For thou art gracious, O Lord,
    and ready to forgive;
And rich in mercy, all that call
    upon thee to relieve.
6 Hear, Lord, my pray'r: unto the voice
    of my requeft attend.
7 In troub'lous times I'll call on thee:
    for thou wilt anfwer fend.
8 Lord, there is none among the Gods
    that may with thee compare:
And like the works, which thou haft done,
    not any work is there.

9 All nations whom thou mad'st, shall come
 and worship rev'rently
Before thy face: and they, O Lord,
 thy Name shall glorify.
10 Because thou art exceeding great,
 and works by thee are done,
Which are to be admir'd: and thou
 art God thyself alone.
11 Teach me thy way, and in thy truth,
 O Lord, then walk will I:
Unite my heart, that I thy name
 may fear continually.
12 O Lord my God, with all my heart
 to thee I will give praise:
And I the glory will ascribe
 unto thy name always.
13 Because thy mercy toward me
 in greatness doth excel:
And thou deliver'd hast my soul
 out from the lowest hell.
14 O God, the proud against me rise,
 and vi'lent men have met,
That for my soul have sought, and thee
 before them have not set.
15 But thou art full of pity, Lord,
 a God most gracious;
Long-suffering, and in thy truth
 and mercy plenteous;
16 O turn to me thy countenance,
 and mercy on me have:
Thy servant strengthen, and the son
 of thine own hand-maid save.

I

17 Shew me a sign for good, that they
    which do me hate, may see,
And be asham'd: because thou, Lord,
    didst help and comfort me.

PSALM LXXXVII.

A Psalm or Song for the Sons of Korah.

When God loosed the captivity of the Jews by Cyrus, few of them did return from Babylon; the work of the reparation of church and state, temple and city, had few to assist it; their enemies were many, they were straitned with poverty and famine, and the hearts and hands of the Godly were weakened; they were like to faint and despair, that neither church or state should flourish any more amongst them. For comfort in such a time was this Psalm fitted, leading the Lord's people to live by faith, and to work on in the building of the Lord's house, and reparation of the city, looking to God the builder of his church, and maintainer of his people, to which purpose the Psalmist giveth them seven consolations, opposite to so many tentations unto discouragement. The first is, That they should look to God who had founded his own temple solidly, and so not faint for the weakness and fewness of the builders, ver. 1. The second, That they should look to God's love and good-will, and not be troubled for want of external power and riches, ver. 2. The third is, That they should look to the prophecies concerning the Church, and not be troubled for what present outward appearance and carnal reason did represent, ver. 3. The fourth is, That they should not be troubled for the multitude of their foes for the present time, but look to the multitude of friends and converts which they should have hereafter, ver. 4. The fifth is, That they should not be troubled with the fear of the ruin of the Church, but look to Almighty God, who would establish her so, that no power should overturn her, ver. 5. The sixth is, That they should not be troubled with the present contempt under which they did lie, but look to the glory and estimation which God should put in his own time upon the Church and her children, ver. 6. The seventh is, That they should not be troubled with the present grief they were in, but should look to the spiritual joy and causes thereof, which the Lord was to furnish to his people, ver. 7.

1 UPON the hills of holiness
    he his foundation sets.
2 God, more than Jacob's dwellings all,
    delights in Zion's gates.

3 Things glorious are said of thee,
 thou city of the Lord.
4 Rahab and Babel, I, to those
 that know me, will record:
Behold ev'n Tyrus, and with it
 the land of Palestine,
And likewise Ethiopia:
 this man was born therein.
5 And it of Zion shall be said,
 This man, and that man there
Was born: and He that is most high
 himself, shall 'stablish her.
6 When God the people writes, he'll count
 that this man born was there.
7 There be that sing and play: and all
 my well-springs in thee are.

PSALM LXXXVIII.

A Song or Psalm for the Sons of Korah, to the chief Musician upon Mahalath Leanoth, Maschil of Heman the Ezrahite.

This Heman the Ezrahite, was one of those four wisest men in all Israel, next after Solomon, who is preferred above them all, 1 Kings iv. 31. The exercise of this wise and holy man is set down here under the heaviest condition of a wounded spirit, of any that we read of; wherein, first, He prayeth for comfort to his soul, now afflicted under the sense of sad wrath and long desertion, ver. 1, 2. In the second place, He poureth out his soul to God, and layeth before him a most pitiful lamentation of his distressed condition, ver. 3, 4, 5, 6, 7, 8. In the third place, He wrestleth by faith in his prayer to God for comfort, ver. 9, 10, 11, 12, 13, 14. And lastly, Finding no comfort, he reneweth his lamentation, leaveth his prayer before the Lord, and writeth it for the edification of the Church in all time coming, as the matter of a joyful song.

1 LORD God, my Saviour, day and night
    before thee cry'd have I.
2 Before thee let my prayer come;
   give ear unto my cry.

3 For troubles great do fill my soul:
   my life draws nigh the grave.
4 I'm counted with those that go down
   to pit, and no strength have.
5 Ev'n free among the dead, like them
   that slain in grave do lie;
  Cut off from thy hand, whom no more
   thou hast in memory.
6 Thou hast me laid in lowest pit,
   in deep and darksome caves.
7 Thy wrath lies hard on me, thou hast
   me press'd with all thy waves.
8 Thou hast put far from me my friends:
   thou mad'st them to abhor me:
  And I am so shut up, that I
   find no evasion for me.
9 By reason of affliction,
   mine eye mourns dolefully:
  To thee, Lord, do I call, and stretch
   my hands continually.
10 Wilt thou shew wonders to the dead?
    shall they rise, and thee bless?
11 Shall in the grave thy love be told?
    in death thy faithfulness?
12 Shall thy great wonders in the dark,
    or shall thy righteousness
   Be known to any in the land
    of deep forgetfulness?
13 But, Lord, to thee I cry'd, my pray'r
    at morn prevent shall thee.
14 Why, Lord, dost thou cast off my soul
    and hid'st thy face from me?

15 Diſtreſt am I, and from my youth
  I ready am to die:
 Thy terrors I have borne, and am
  diſtracted fearfully.
16 The dreadful fierceneſs of thy wrath
  quite over me doth go:
 Thy terrors great have cut me off,
  they did purſue me ſo.
17 For round about me ev'ry day,
  like water, they did roll;
 And, gathering together, they
  have compaſſed my ſoul.
18 My friends thou haſt put far from me,
  and him that did me love;
 And thoſe that mine acquaintance were
  to darkneſs didſt remove.

PSALM LXXXIX.

Maſchil of Ethan the Ezrahite.

This Pſalm is intitled Maſchil, or a pſalm written for inſtruction of Ethan the Ezrahite, who, after Solomon, was another of the four wiſeſt men in Iſrael: This man ſurviving the glory of Solomon's kingdom, and beholding the diminiſhing of the glory of David's houſe, lamenteth the deſolation thereof unto God.

The Pſalm hath three parts. In the firſt part, he ſetteth his faith upon God, and laboureth to ſtrengthen it againſt the tentation which was boiling in his breaſt, ver. 19. In the ſecond part, he expoundeth the ſum of the covenant of grace, made between God and Chriſt, typified by David; wherein indeed, albeit David hath his own intereſt, yet the ſubſtance was to be found only in Chriſt, who came of David according to the fleſh, from ver. 19 to 38. In the third part, is a lamentation of the apparent diſſolving of this covenant with David's poſterity, and a prayer for repairing the ruins of that kingdom for the glory of God; which prayer he aſſureth himſelf ſhall be granted.

1 GOD's mercies I will ever sing,
    and with my mouth I shall
  Thy faithfulness make to be known
    to generations all.
2 For mercy shall be built, said I,
    for ever to endure;
  Thy faithfulness, ev'n in the Heav'ns,
    thou wilt establish sure.

3 I with my chosen one have made
    a cov'nant graciously;
  And to my servant, whom I lov'd,
    to David sworn have I:
4 That I thy seed establish shall
    for ever to remain,
  And will to generations all
    thy throne build and maintain.

5 The praises of thy wonders, Lord,
    the Heavens shall express;
  And in the congregation
    of Saints, thy faithfulness.
6 For who in Heaven with the Lord
    may once himself compare?
  Who is like God among the sons
    of those that mighty are?

7 Great fear in meeting of the Saints
    is due unto the Lord:
  And he, of all about him, should
    with rev'rence be ador'd.
8 O thou that art the Lord of hosts,
    what Lord in mightiness
  Is like to thee, who compass'd round
    art with thy faithfulness?

9 Ev'n in the raging of the sea
    thou over it doſt reign;
And when the waves thereof do ſwell,
    thou ſtilleſt them again.
10 Rahab in pieces thou didſt break,
    like one that ſlaughter'd is;
And with thy mighty arm thou haſt
    diſpers'd thine enemies.
11 TheHeav'ns are thine, thou for thine own
    the earth doſt alſo take;
The world, and fulneſs of the ſame,
    thy pow'r did found and make.
12 The north and ſouth from thee alone
    their firſt beginning had:
Both Tabor mount and Hermon hill
    ſhall in thy name be glad.
13 Thou haſt an arm that's full of pow'r:
    thy hand is great in might:
And thy right hand exceedingly
    exalted is in height.
14 Juſtice and judgment of thy throne
    are made the dwelling place:
Mercy, accompany'd with truth,
    ſhall go before thy face.
15 O greatly bleſt the people are,
    the joyful ſound that know:
In brightneſs of thy face, O Lord,
    they ever on ſhall go.
16 They in thy name ſhall all the day
    rejoice exceedingly;
And in thy righteouſneſs ſhall they
    exalted be on high.

17 Becaufe the glory of their ftrength
    doth only ftand in thee:
  And in thy favour fhall our horn
    and pow'r exalted be.
18 For God is our defence, and he
    to us doth fafety bring:
  The holy One of Ifrael
    is our almighty King.
19 In vifion to thy holy One
    thou faidft, I help upon
  A ftrong one laid: out of the folk
    I rais'd a chofen one:
20 Ev'n David, I have found him out
    a fervant unto me;
  And, with my holy oil, my King
    anointed him to be.
21 With whom my hand fhall ftablifh'd be,
    mine arm fhall make him ftrong.
22 On him the foe fhall not exact,
    nor fon of mifchief wrong.
23 I will beat down before his face
    all his malicious foes;
  I will them greatly plague, who do
    with hatred him oppofe.
24 My mercy and my faithfulnefs,
    with him yet ftill fhall be:
  And in my name his horn and pow'r
    men fhall exalted fee.
25 His hand and pow'r fhall reach afar,
    I'll fet it in the fea;
  And his right hand eftablifhed
    fhall in the rivers be.

26 Thou art my father, he shall cry,
    thou art my God alone;
  And he shall say, Thou art the rock
    of my salvation.
27 I'll make him my first-born, more high
    than Kings of any land.
28 My love I'll ever keep for him,
    my cov'nant fast shall stand.
29 His seed I by my pow'r will make
    for ever to endure;
  And, as the days of Heav'n, his throne
    shall stable be and sure.
30 But if his children shall forsake
    my laws, and go astray,
  And in my judgment shall not walk,
    but wander from my way:
31 If they my laws break, and do not
    keep my commandments:
32 I'll visit then their faults with rods,
    their sins with chastisements.
33 Yet I'll not take my love from him,
    nor false my promise make.
34 My cov'nant I'll not break, nor change
    what with my mouth I spake.
35 Once by my holiness I sware,
    to David I'll not lie.
36 His seed and throne shall as the sun
    before me last for ay.
37 It, like the moon, shall ever be
    establish'd stedfastly:
  And, like to that which in the heav'n,
    doth witness faithfully.

38 But thou, displeased, hast cast off,
　　thou didst abhor and loath;
　With him that thine anointed is
　　thou hast been very wroth.
39 Thou hast thy servant's covenant
　　made void, and quite cast by:
　Thou hast profan'd his crown, while it
　　cast on the ground doth lie.
40 Thou all his hedges hast broke down,
　　his strong holds down hast torn:
41 He to all passers by a spoil,
　　to neighbours is a scorn.
42 Thou hast set up his foes' right hand,
　　mad'st all his en'mies glad;
43 Turn'd his sword's edge, and him to stand
　　in battle hast not made.
44 His glory thou hast made to cease,
　　his throne to ground down cast:
45 Short'ned his days of youth, and him
　　with shame thou cover'd hast.
46 How long, Lord, wilt thou hide thyself,
　　for ever in thine ire?
　And shall thine indignation
　　burn like unto a fire?
47 Remember, Lord, how short a time
　　I shall on earth remain:
　O wherefore is it so, that thou
　　hast made all men in vain?
48 What man is he that liveth here,
　　and death shall never see?
　Or from the power of the grave,
　　what man his soul shall free?

49 Thy former loving-kindnesses,
   O Lord, where be they now?
 Those which in truth and faithfulness
   to David sworn hast thou.
50 Mind, Lord, thy servant's sad reproach,
   how I in bosom bear
 The scornings of the people all,
   who strong and mighty are.
51 Wherewith thy raging enemies
   reproach'd, O Lord, think on;
 Wherewith they have reproach'd the steps
   of thine anointed One.
52 All blessing to the Lord our God
   let be ascribed then:
 For evermore, so let it be.
   Amen, yea, and amen.

PSALM XC.
A Prayer of Moses, the Man of God.

This Psalm agreeth well with the latter end of Moses's life, when he being now to remove, did present this prayer to God, and delivered it unto the Church, for their comfort and direction, how to carry themselves towards God in their short and sorrowful life.

The Psalm may be divided into three parts. In the first, Is the Church's four-fold comfort against the temporal troubles and miseries in this world. The first, Is taken from the Lord's kindness to his people in all ages, ver. 1. The second, Is taken from the decree of their election, ver. 2. The third, from the hope of their resurrection, ver. 3. The fourth, From the shortness of time unto it, ver. 4. In the second part, The shortness and misery of life procured by sin, are lamentably set forth before the Lord, who is full of pity, ver. 5, 6, 7, 8, 9, 10, 11. In the last part are six petitions, some whereof are for the right use of the shortness and sorrows of this life, and some of them for a gracious deliverance from them, ver. 12, 13, 14, 15, 16, 17.

1 LORD, thou hast been our dwelling-
      in generations all: [place
2 Before thou ever hadst brought forth
     the mountains great or small.

E'er ever thou hadſt form'd the earth
 and all the world abroad;
Ev'n thou from everlaſting art
 to everlaſting, God.
3 Thou doſt unto deſtruction
 man that is mortal turn:
And unto them thou ſay'ſt, Again,
 ye ſons of men, return.
4 Becauſe a thouſand years appear
 no more before thy ſight,
Than yeſterday, when it is paſt,
 or than a watch by night.
5 As with an overflowing flood,
 thou carry'ſt them away:
They like a ſleep are, like the graſs
 that grows at morn, are they.
6 At morn it flouriſhes and grows,
 cut down at ev'n doth fade.
7 For by thine anger we're conſum'd,
 thy wrath makes us afraid.
8 Our ſins thou and iniquities
 doſt in thy preſence place,
And ſett'ſt our ſecret faults before
 the brightneſs of thy face.
9 For in thine anger all our days
 do paſs on to an end;
And as a tale that hath been told,
 ſo we our years do ſpend.
10 Threeſcore and ten years do ſum up
 our days and years, we ſee;
Or if, by reaſon of more ſtrength,
 in ſome fourſcore they be:

>   Yet doth the strength of such old men
>   but grief and labour prove;
>   For it is soon cut off, and we
>   fly hence, and soon remove.
> 11 Who knows the power of thy wrath?
>   according to thy fear,
> 12 So is thy wrath. Lord, teach thou us
>   our end in mind to bear:
>   And so to count our days, that we
>   our hearts may still apply
>   To learn thy wisdom and thy truth,
>   that we may live thereby.
> 13 Turn yet again to us, O Lord;
>   how long thus shall it be?
>   Let it repent thee now for those
>   that servants are to thee.
> 14 O with thy tender mercies, Lord,
>   us early satisfy;
>   So we rejoice shall all our days,
>   and still be glad in thee.
> 15 According as the days have been
>   wherein we grief have had,
>   And years wherein we ill have seen,
>   so do thou make us glad.
> 16 O let thy work and pow'r appear
>   thy servants' face before,
>   And shew unto their children dear
>   thy glory evermore.
> 17 And let the beauty of the Lord
>   our God be us upon:
>   Our handy-works establish thou,
>   establish them each one.

PSALM XCI.

Albeit this Psalm hath no inscription, nor the name of the penman who did write, yet Satan could not deny it to be the Lord's word, for out of this Psalm he brought one of his darts against our Saviour, Matth. iv. and the promises which are made here to the believer, are so much more strongly ours, as Christ, head of all his people, hath interest therein as a man, and hath taken them to him in our name.

1 HE that doth in the secret place
    of the most High reside,
Under the shade of him that is
    th' Almighty, shall abide.
2 I of the Lord, my God, will say,
    He is my refuge still,
He is my fortress, and my God,
    and in him trust I will.
3 Assuredly he shall thee save,
    and give deliverance
From subtile fowler's snare, and from
    the noisome pestilence.
4 His feathers shall thee hide; thy trust
    under his wings shall be:
His faithfulness shall be a shield
    and buckler unto thee.
5 Thou shalt not need to be afraid
    for terrors of the night,
Nor for the arrow that doth fly
    by day, while it is light:
6 Nor for the pestilence that walks
    in darkness secretly:
Nor for destruction that doth waste
    at noon-day openly.

7 A thousand at thy side shall fall,
   on thy right hand shall lie
 Ten thousand dead; yet unto thee
   it shall not once come nigh.
8 Only thou with thine eyes shalt look,
   and a beholder be;
 And thou therein the just reward
   of wicked men shalt see.
9 Because the Lord, who constantly
   my refuge is alone,
 Ev'n the most High, is made by thee
   thy habitation:
10 No plague shall near thy dwelling come,
   no ill shall thee befall:
11 For, thee to keep in all thy ways,
   his Angels charge he shall.
12 They in their hands shall bear thee up,
   still waiting thee upon,
 Lest thou at any time shouldst dash
   thy foot against a stone.
13 Upon the adder thou shalt tread,
   and on the lions strong;
 Thy feet on dragons trample shall,
   and on the lions young.
14 Because on me he set his love,
   I'll save and set him free:
 Because my great Name he hath known,
   I will him set on high.
15 He'll call on me, I'll answer him:
   I will be with him still
 In trouble, to deliver him,
   and honour him I will.

16 With length of days unto his mind
    I will him satisfy;
  I also my salvation
    will cause his eyes to see.

PSALM XCII.
A Psalm or Song for the Sabbath-day.

This Psalm is entitled, A Psalm for the Sabbath-day; wherein the Church is stirred up to praise God by sundry reasons, ver. 1, 2, 3. but especially for these three causes, first, For the great work of creation, sustenance and wise governing of the creatures, ver. 4, 5. The second cause is, For his wisdom and justice in punishing the wicked, ver. 6, 7, 8, 9. The third is, For his grace and goodness towards believers, ver. 10, 11, 12, 13, 14, 15.

1 TO render thanks unto the Lord
    it is a comely thing,
  And to thy Name, O thou most High,
    due praise aloud to sing:
2 Thy loving-kindness to shew forth,
    when shines the morning light,
  And to declare thy faithfulness,
    with pleasure ev'ry night.
3 On a ten stringed instrument,
    upon the psaltery:
  And on the harp with solemn sound,
    and grave sweet melody.
4 For thou, Lord, by thy mighty works,
    hast made my heart right glad;
  And I will triumph in the works
    which by thine hands were made.
5 How great, Lord, are thy works! each
    of thine, a deep it is: [thought
6 A brutish man it knoweth not:
    fools understand not this.

7 When those that lewd and wicked are,
    spring quickly up like grass,
  And workers of iniquity,
    do flourish all apace:
  It is that they for ever may
    destroyed be and slain:
8 But thou, O Lord, art the most High,
    for ever to remain.
9 For lo, thine enemies, O Lord,
    thine en'mies perish shall:
  The workers of iniquity
    shall be dispersed all.
10 But thou shalt, like unto the horn
    of th' unicorn, exalt
  My horn on high: thou with fresh oil
    anoint me also shalt.
11 Mine eyes shall also my desire
    see on mine enemies:
  Mine ears shall of the wicked hear
    that do against me rise.
12 But like the palm-tree flourishing
    shall be the righteous one:
  He shall like to the cedar grow
    that is in Lebanon.
13 Those that within the house of God
    are planted by his grace,
  They shall grow up, and flourish all
    in our God's holy place.
14 And in old age, when others fade,
    they fruit still forth shall bring:
  They shall be fat, and full of sap,
    and ay be flourishing:

15 To shew that upright is the Lord:
   he is a rock to me:
And he from all unrighteousness
   is altogether free.

PSALM XCIII.

In this Psalm, for the comfort of God's people, against the multitude and power of their enemies, and the greatness of Kings and Potentates in the world, who ofttimes are like to overflow, devour, and drown the Church, the glory of the Lord is described, in whom is the Church's defence, comfort, and victory. For this end first, The praises of God for the Church's comfort are set down absolutely, ver. 1, 2. Then the opposition of the enemies of the Church is compared to the growing flood and raging sea, ver. 3. And thirdly, The praises of God are set down in opposition to their power, ver. 4, 5. with the use of this doctrine.

1 THE Lord doth reign, and cloth'd is he
      with Majesty most bright:
His works do shew him cloth'd to be
      and girt about with might:
The world is also stablished,
      that it cannot depart.
2 Thy throne is fix'd of old, and thou
      from everlasting art.
3 The floods, O Lord, have lifted up,
      they lifted up their voice:
The floods have lifted up their waves,
      and made a mighty noise.
4 But yet the Lord, that is on high,
      is more of might by far
Than noise of many waters is,
      or great sea-billows are.
5 Thy testimonies ev'ry one
      in faithfulness excel:
And holiness for ever, Lord,
      thine house becometh well.

PSALM XCIV.

This Psalm is a prayer and complaint of the Church unto God in the time of her oppression by intestine enemies, in special by unjust and cruel rulers, whereunto sundry grounds of comfort to the Godly in this hard condition are subjoined. The prayer and complaint reach unto ver. 8. The grounds of comfort are four. The first is, the consideration of God's wisdom in the permission of this sore trouble of his people, with a check upon the oppressors for their atheism, ver. 8, 9, 10, 11. The second is, The consideration of the profit which God's people shall have by this exercise, ver. 12, 13. The third is, From a promise that God shall change the face of affairs to the joy of the Godly, ver. 14, 15. The fourth is, From the experience which the Psalmist had of God's helping of him in this case, set down at large to the end of the psalm.

1 O Lord God, unto whom alone
    all vengeance doth belong:
  O mighty God, who vengeance own'st,
    shine forth, avenging wrong.
2 Lift up thyself, thou of the earth
    the sov'reign Judge that art:
  And unto those that are so proud,
    a due reward impart.
3 How long, O mighty God, shall they
    who lewd and wicked be,
  How long shall they who wicked are
    thus triumph haughtily?
4 How long shall things most hard by them
    be uttered and told?
  And all that work iniquity
    to boast themselves be bold?
5 Thy folk they break in pieces, Lord,
    thine heritage oppress.
6 The widow they, and stranger slay,
    and kill the fatherless.

7 Yet fay they, God it fhall not fee:
  nor God of Jacob know.
8 Ye bruitfh people! underftand:
  fools! when wife will ye grow?
9 The Lord did plant the ear of man,
  and hear them fhall not he?
  He only form'd the eye, and then
  fhall he not clearly fee?
10 He that the nations doth correct,
  fhall he not chaftife you?
  He knowledge unto man doth teach,
  and fhall himfelf not know?
11 Man's thoughts to be but vanity,
  the Lord doth well difcern.
12 Bleft is the man thou chaft'neft, Lord,
  and mak'ft thy law to learn.
13 That thou may'ft give him reft from days
  of fad adverfity,
  Until the pit be digg'd for thofe
  that work iniquity.
14 For fure the Lord will not caft off
  thofe that his people be,
  Neither his own inheritance
  quit and forfake will he.
15 But judgment unto righteoufnefs
  fhall yet return again:
  And all fhall follow after it
  that are right-hearted men.
16 Who will rife up for me againft
  thofe that do wickedly?
  Who will ftand up for me 'gainft thofe
  that work iniquity?

17 Unless the Lord had been my help,
    when I was sore oppress'd,
  Almost my soul had in the house
    of silence been at rest.
18 When I had uttered this word,
    (my foot doth slip away)
  Thy mercy held me up, O Lord,
    thy goodness did me stay.
19 Amidst the multitude of thoughts
    which in my heart do fight,
  My soul, lest it be overcharg'd,
    thy comforts do delight.
20 Shall of iniquity the throne
    have fellowship with thee,
  Which mischief, cunningly contriv'd,
    doth by a law decree?
21 Against the righteous souls thy join,
    they guiltless blood condemn.
22 But of my refuge God's the rock,
    and my defence from them.
23 On them their own iniquity
    the Lord shall bring and lay,
  And cut them off in their own sin:
    our Lord God shall them slay.

PSALM XCV.

This Psalm is applied to Christ by the Apostle, Heb. iii. 7, 8, 9, 10, 11. Whereof there are two parts. In the first, is an exhortation to worship God in Christ, or Christ with God the Father and holy Spirit, dwelling among them in the temple, and representing unto them his future incarnation, and the execution of his offices in types and figures. The arguments of praising and worshipping of him are five. The first, Because he is the rock of our salvation, ver. 1, 2. The second, Because of his greatness, ver. 3. The third, For his power, ver. 4. The fourth, Because he created all things, and us his people, ver. 5, 6. The latter part of the Psalm is another exhortation unto the visible Church, to evidence their obedience of faith, and not to harden their hearts in the time of God's dealing with them by his word, as their fathers did, who perished in the wilderness for their provocation, ver. 8, 9, 10, 11.

1 O Come, let us sing to the Lord:
  come, let us ev'ry one
 A joyful noise make to the rock
  of our salvation.
2 Let us before his presence come,
  with praise and thankful voice:
 Let us sing psalms to him with grace,
  and make a joyful noise.
3 For God, a great God, and great King,
  above all Gods he is.
4 Depths of the earth are in his hand:
  the strength of hills is his.
5 To him the spacious sea belongs,
  for he the same did make:
 The dry land also from his hands
  its form at first did take.
6 O come, and let us worship him,
  let us bow down withal;
 And on our knees, before the Lord
  our Maker, let us fall.
7 For he's our God, the people we
  of his own pasture are,
 And of his hand the sheep: to-day,
  if ye his voice will hear.
8 Then harden not your hearts, as in
  the provocation,
 As in the desert, on the day
  of the tentation:

9 When me your fathers tempt'd and prov'd,
   and did my working fee:
10 Ev'n for the space of forty years
   this race hath grieved me:
   I said, this people errs in heart,
   my ways they do not know:
11 To whom I sware in wrath, that to
   my rest they should not go.

PSALM XCVI.

We find, 1 Chron. xvi. 23. a part of this Psalm, sung at the bringing up of the ark to Sion, to be in substance and almost in words also one and the same with this which is here; for as there, so here the Prophet foreseeth in the spirit the spreading of the kingdom of Christ among the nations; and therefore, first He exhorteth all people heartily to receive Christ and propagate his glory, ver. 1, 2, 3. and giveth reasons for it, ver. 4, 5, 6. Then he repeateth and enlargeth the exhortation to glorify God, and to rejoice in him, because Christ was indeed to come among the Gentiles, to reign among them righteously, ver. 7, 8, 9, 10, 11, 12, 13.

1 O Sing a new song to the Lord,
   sing all the earth to God.
2 To God sing, bless his Name: shew still
   his saving health abroad.
3 Among the heathen nations
   his glory do declare;
   And unto all the people show
   his works that wond'rous are.
4 For great's the Lord and greatly he
   is to be magnify'd:
   Yea, worthy to be fear'd is he,
   above all Gods beside:
5 For all the Gods are idols dumb
   which blinded nations fear:
   But our God is the Lord, by whom
   the Heav'ns created were.

6 Great honour is before his face,
    and majefty divine:
Strength is within his holy place,
    and there doth beauty fhine.
7 Do ye afcribe unto the Lord,
    of people ev'ry tribe,
Glory do ye unto the Lord,
    and mighty pow'r afcribe.
8 Give ye the glory to the Lord
    that to his Name is due:
Come ye into his courts, and bring
    an offering with you.
9 In beauty of his holinefs,
    O do the Lord adore:
Likewife let all the earth throughout
    tremble his face before.
10 Among the heathen fay, God reigns:
    the world fhall ftedfaftly
Be fixt from moving, he fhall judge
    the people righteoufly.
11 Let Heav'ns be glad before the Lord,
    and let the earth rejoice:
Let feas, and all that is therein,
    cry out, and make a noife.
12 Let fields rejoice, and ev'ry thing
    that fpringeth of the earth:
Then woods, and ev'ry tree, fhall fing
    with gladnefs and with mirth
13 Before the Lord: becaufe he comes,
    to judge the earth comes he:
He'll judge the world with righteoufnefs,
    the people faithfully.

PSALM XCVII.

This Psalm containeth a prophecy of the spiritual glory of Christ's Kingdom, to ver. 8. and the use of the doctrine. to the end of the Psalm. The comfort of Christ's Kingdom in relation to his Church is set down, ver. 1, 2. and the terribleness thereof in relation to his enemies, ver. 3, 4, 5, 6. with a curse upon image-worshippers, ver. 7. The uses of the doctrine they are four: The first is, That all excellency, and whatsoever is honourable in the world, should do homage to him, set down in the end of ver. 7. The second is, That the true Church should be glad at the hearing and the seeing of the execution of God's judgments upon idolators, with a reason for it, ver. 8, 9. The third use is, A direction to the Saints to beware of sin, with some reasons for it, ver. 10, 11. The fourth use is, That the righteous should rejoice, and thank God upon all occasions, ver. 12.

1 GOD reigneth: let the earth be glad,
    and isles rejoice each one.
2 Dark clouds him compass; and in right
    with judgment dwells his throne.
3 Fire goes before him, and his foes
    it burns up round about.
4 His light'nings lighten did the world:
    earth saw, and shook throughout.
5 Hills, at the presence of the Lord,
    like wax did melt away:
    Ev'n at the presence of the Lord,
    of all the earth, I say.
6 The Heav'ns declare his righteousness:
    all men his glory see.
7 All who serve graven images
    confounded let them be.
    Who do of idols boast themselves,
    let shame upon them fall:
    Ye that are called Gods, see that
    ye do him worship

8 Zion did hear, and joyful was,
    glad Judah's daughters were:
They much rejoic'd, O Lord, because
    thy judgments did appear.
9 For thou, O Lord, art high above
    all things on earth that are:
Above all other Gods thou art
    exalted very far.
10 Hate ill, all ye that love the Lord:
    his Saints' souls keepeth he;
And from the hands of wicked men
    he sets them safe and free.
11 For all those that be righteous,
    sown is a joyful light;
And gladness sown is for all those
    that are in heart upright.
12 Ye righteous in the Lord rejoice:
    express your thankfulness,
When ye into your memory
    do call his holiness.

PSALM XCVIII.

A Psalm.

This Psalm is an exhortation to Jew and Gentile, to rejoice and bless the Lord for Christ's coming, to set up his kingdom in the world, The exhortation is thrice pressed: First, In proper terms, requiring the Church to sing for joy, with reasons adjoined, ver. 1, 2, 3. Then it is repeated, and musical instruments called for, to shew that by the human voice the matter of the joy which is in Jesus Christ, is inexpressible, ver. 4, 5, 6. Thirdly, To shew that neither voice of man, nor musical instruments, are sufficient to express the joy which cometh by Christ's Kingdom; the whole creatures are called unto this work of rejoicing, and setting forth his glory, ver. 7, 8. and the reason is given, because Christ cometh to set up, and exercise his kingdom in righteousness, ver. 9. Faith.

1 O Sing a new song to the Lord,
    for wonders he hath done;
  His right hand, and his holy arm,
    him victory hath won.
2 The Lord God his salvation
    hath caused to be known:
  His justice in the heathen's sight
    he openly hath shown.
3 He mindful of his grace and truth
    to Isra'l's house hath been:
  And the salvation of our God
    all ends of th' earth have seen.
4 Let all the earth unto the Lord
    send forth a joyful noise:
  Lift up your voice aloud to him,
    sing praises, and rejoice.
5 With harp, with harp, and voice of psalms,
    unto JEHOVAH sing.
6 With trumpets, cornets, gladly sound
    before the Lord, the King.
7 Let seas, and all their fulness roar;
    the world, and dwellers there.
8 Let floods clap hands, and let the hills
    together joy declare
9 Before the Lord; because he comes,
    to judge the earth comes he;
  He'll judge the world with righteousness,
    his folk with equity.

PSALM XCIX.

For the comfort of the Church against a multitude of enemies round about her, there is in this Psalm a declaration of the Kingdom of Christ reigning as God, one with the Father and holy Spirit in the Church of Israel, before his incarnation, with a four-fold exhortation to all who shall hear tell of him. The first exhortation is, To stand in awe of him, because of his great majesty manifested in Sion, ver. 1, 2. Another exhortation is, To praise him for his greatness, terribleness, holiness and righteousness, ver. 3, 4. A third exhortation is, To glorify and worship him for sundry reasons, ver. 5, 6, 7, 8. for which he repeateth the exhortation the fourth time, ver. 9.

1 TH' eternal Lord doth reign as King,
    let all the people quake:
He sits between the cherubims,
    let th' earth be mov'd and shake.
2 The Lord in Zion great and high
    above all people is.
3 Thy great and dreadful Name (for it
    is holy) let them bless.
4 The King's strength also judgment loves,
    thou settlest equity;
Just judgment thou dost execute
    in Jacob righteously.
5 The Lord our God exalt on high,
    and rev'rently do ye
Before his footstool worship him:
    the holy One is he.
6 Moses and Aaron 'mongst his priests,
    Samuel with them that call
Upon his name: these call'd on God,
    and he them answer'd all.
7 Within the pillar of the cloud
    he unto them did speak:
The testimonies he them taught,
    and laws, they did not break.
8 Thou answer'dst them, O Lord our God,
    thou wast a God that gave
Pardon to them, tho' on their deeds
    thou wouldest vengeance have.

9 Do ye exalt the Lord our God,
    and at his holy hill
Do ye him worship: for the Lord
    our God is holy still.

PSALM C.

A Psalm of Praise.

The title of this Psalm sheweth the sum and scope thereof to be for stirring up of the whole Church to praise God cheerfully; unto which duty all are exhorted once, ver. 1, 2. for three reasons, first, Because he is God. Secondly, Because we are his creatures. Thirdly, Because we are his covenanted people, or members of the visible Church, whereof he taketh care, as a pastor doth of his own flock, ver. 3. And again, All are exhorted to thank, praise, and bless him, ver. 4. And that for his goodness, mercy, and truth, ver. 5.

1 ALL people that on earth do dwell,
    Sing to the Lord with chearful voice.
2 Him serve with mirth, his praise forth tell:
    Come ye before him and rejoice.
3 Know, that the Lord is God indeed,
    Without our aid he did us make;
We are his flock, he doth us feed,
    And for his sheep he doth us take.

4 O enter then his gates with praise,
    Approach with joy his courts unto:
Praise, laud, and bless his name always;
    For it is seemly so to do.
5 For why? the Lord our God is good;
    His mercy is for ever sure:
His truth at all times firmly stood,
    And shall from age to age endure.

Another of the same.

1 O All ye lands, unto the Lord
 make ye a joyful noise.
2 Serve God with gladness: him before
 come with a singing voice.
3 Know ye the Lord, that he is God;
 not we, but he us made:
 We are his people, and the sheep
 within his pasture fed.
4 Enter his gates and courts with praise,
 to thank him go ye thither:
 To him express your thankfulness,
 and bless his name together.
5 Because the Lord our God is good;
 his mercy faileth never:
 And to all generations
 his truth endureth ever.

PSALM CI.
A Psalm of David.

David, not being as yet entered in possession of his kingdom, doth by direction of the holy Spirit, fall upon a consideration of the duties of a righteous Prince, which he setteth down as a rule, to be followed by himself and all magistrates, obliging himself to endeavour to comfort his government thereto, wherein he is but a type and shadow of Christ, in whom alone the perfect performance of the duties here promised are to be found. The principal duties which David undertaketh to discharge may be for order's sake, reduced to the number of eight, according to the number of verses.

1 I Mercy will and judgment sing:
 Lord, I will sing to thee.
2 With wisdom in a perfect way
 shall my behaviour be:
 O when, in kindness unto me,
 wilt thou be pleas'd to come?
 With a perfect heart will walk
 within my house at home.

3 I will endure no wicked thing
    before mine eyes to be:
  I hate their work that turn aside,
    it shall not cleave to me.
4 A stubborn and a froward heart
    depart quite from me shall:
  A person given to wickedness
    I will not know at all.
5 I'll cut him off that slandereth
    his neighbour privily:
  The haughty heart I will not bear,
    nor him that looketh high.
6 Upon the faithful of the land
    mine eyes shall be, that they
  May dwell with me: he shall me serve
    that walks in perfect way.
7 Who of deceit a worker is,
    in my house shall not dwell:
  And in my presence shall he not
    remain that lyes doth tell.
8 Yea, all the wicked of the land
    early destroy will I:
  All from God's city to cut off
    that work iniquity.

PSALM CII.

A Prayer of the Afflicted when he is overwhelmed, and poureth out his complaint before the Lord

This Psalm agreeth well with the time of the Babylonish captivity of the Jews, about the end whereof the seventy years being now nigh expired, and weight of the misery of God's people, and the mockery of the Heathen, and the people's longing for delivery, did so afflict the Prophet, that in compassion towards the scattered Church, he poureth out this Prayer, and communicateth it at the Lord's direction, to all other feeling members of the body to be made use of.

for the waking up of their affections, and strengthening of their hope of delivery. The parts of it are three. In the first, He craveth audience to his Prayer because of his sad condition, wherein he sympathiseth with the Church in affliction, to ver. 12. In the second, He encourageth himself in the hope of being heard in behalf of the Church, to ver. 23. In the third, He layeth forth the occasion of all this grief, which was the fear he had of the cutting off of the Church of the Jews, before the coming of the Messiah, and sheweth how he strengtheneth his faith in Prayer against this temptation.

1 O Lord, unto my pray'r give ear,
   my cry let come to thee:
2 And in the day of my distress,
   hide not thy face from me.
Give ear to me: what time I call,
   to answer me make haste.
3 For as an hearth my bones are burnt:
   my days like smoke do waste.
4 My heart within me smitten is,
   and it is withered
Like very grass: so that I do
   forget to eat my bread.
5 By reason of my groaning voice,
   my bones cleave to my skin;
6 Like pelican in wilderness,
   forsaken I have been:

I like an owl in desart am,
   that nightly there doth moan.
7 I watch, and like a sparrow am,
   on the house-top alone.
8 My bitter en'mies all the day
   reproaches cast on me:
And being mad at me, with rage
   against me sworn they be.

9 For why? I ashes eaten have
    like bread, in sorrows deep;
  My drink I also mingled have
    with tears that I did weep:
10 Thy wrath and indignation
    did cause this grief and pain:
  For thou hast lift me up on high,
    and cast me down again.
11 My days are like unto a shade
    which doth declining pass:
  And I am dry'd and withered
    ev'n like unto the grass.
12 But thou, Lord, everlasting art,
    and thy remembrance shall
  Continually endure, and be
    to generations all.
13 Thou shalt arise, and mercy have
    upon thy Sion yet:
  The time to favour her is come,
    the time that thou hast set.
14 For in her rubbish, and her stones
    thy servants pleasure take,
  Yea, they the very dust thereof
    do favour for her sake.
15 So shall the heathen people fear,
    the Lords most holy Name:
  And all the Kings on earth shall dread
    thy glory and thy fame
16 When Sion by the mighty Lord
    built up again shall be,
  In glory then, and majesty,
    to men appear shall he.

17 The prayer of the destitute
    he surely will regard:
  Their prayer will he not despise;
    by him it shall be heard.
18 For generations yet to come
    this shall be on record:
  So shall the people that shall be
    created, praise the Lord.
19 He from his sanctuary's height
    hath downward cast his eye:
  And from his glorious throne in Heav'n
    the Lord the earth did spy:
20 That of the mournful prisoner
    the groanings he might hear,
  To set them free that unto death
    by men appointed are:
21 That they in Sion may declare
    the Lord's most holy Name,
  And publish in Jerusalem
    the praises of the same:
22 When as the people gather shall
    in troops with one accord,
  When kingdoms shall assembled be
    to serve the highest Lord.
23 My wonted strength and force he hath
    abated in the way:
  And he my days hath shortened;
24   Thus therefore did I say,
  My God, in mid-time of my days,
    take thou me not away:
  From age to age eternally
    thy years endure and stay.

25 The firm foundation of the earth
   of old time thou haſt laid :
The Heavens alſo are the work
   which thine own hands have made.
26 Thou ſhalt for evermore endure,
   but they ſhall periſh all :
Yea, ev'ry one of them wax old,
   like to a garment, ſhall.

Thou, as a veſture, ſhalt them change,
   and they ſhall changed be.
27 But thou the ſame art, and thy years
   are to eternity.
28 The children of thy ſervants ſhall
   continually endure ;
And in thy ſight, O Lord, their ſeed
   ſhall be eſtabliſh'd ſure.

Another of the ſame.

1 LORD, hear my pray'r, and let my cry
   Have ſpeedy acceſs unto thee.
2 In day of my calamity,
   O hide not thou thy face from me :
Hear when I call to thee, that day
   An anſwer ſpeedily return.
3 My days like ſmoke conſume away,
   And, as an hearth, my bones do burn.
4 My heart is wounded very ſore,
   And withered, like graſs, doth fade :
I am forgetful grown therefore
   To take and eat my daily bread.
5 By reaſon of my ſmart within,
   And voice of my moſt grievous groans,
My fleſh conſumed is, my ſkin
   All parch'd, doth cleave unto my bones.

6 The pelican of wilderneſs,
    The owl in deſart I do' match.
7 And, ſparrow-like, companionleſs,
    Upon the houſe's top, I watch.
8 I all day long am made a ſcorn,
    Reproach'd by my malicious foes;
    The madmen are againſt me ſworn,
    The men againſt me that aroſe.
9 For I have aſhes eaten up,
    To me as if they had been bread;
    And, with my drink, I in my cup
    Of bitter tears a mixture made:
10 Becauſe thy wrath was not appeas'd,
    And dreadful indignation;
    Therefore it was that thou me rais'd,
    And thou again didſt caſt me down.
11 My days are like a ſhade alway,
    Which doth declining ſwiftly paſs:
    And I am withered away,
    Much like unto the fading graſs.
12 But thou, O Lord, ſhalt ſtill endure,
    From change and all mutation free,
    And, to all generations ſure,
    Shall thy rememb'rance ever be.
13 Thou ſhalt ariſe, and mercy yet
    Thou to mount Sion ſhalt extend:
    Her time for favour which was ſet,
    Behold, is now come to an end.
14 Thy Saints take pleaſure in her ſtones,
    Her very duſt to them is dear.
15 All heathen lands, and kingly thrones
    On earth, thy glorious name ſhall fear.

16 God in his glory shall appear,
   When Sion he builds and repairs.
17 He shall regard and lend his ear
   Unto the needy's humble pray'rs.
   Th' afflicted's pray'r he will not scorn;
18 All times this shall be on record:
   And generations yet unborn
   Shall praise and magnify the Lord.
19 He from his holy place look'd down,
   The earth he view'd from Heav'n on high.
20 To hear the pris'ners' mourning groan,
   And free them that are doom'd to die:
21 That Sion, and Jerus'lem too,
   His name and praise may well record:
22 When people and the kingdoms do
   Assemble all to praise the Lord.
23 My strength he weak'ned in the way,
   My days of life he shortened.
24 My God, O take me not away
   In mid-time of my days, I said:
   Thy years throughout all ages last.
25 Of old thou hast established
   The earth's foundation firm and fast:
   Thy mighty hands the heav'ns have made.
26 They perish shall, as garments do,
   But thou shalt evermore endure:
   As vestures, thou shalt change them so:
   And they shall all be changed sure..
27 But from all changes thou art free,
   Thy endless years do last for ay:
28 Thy servants, and their seed who be,
   Establish'd shall before thee stay.

PSALM CIII.

A Psalm of David.

This is a Psalm of praise and thanksgiving to God, for his grace to his people, wherein the believer stirreth up himself, and by his own example others also to praise God, ver. 1, 2. And that for seventeen reasons or arguments of praise; some of them taken from mercies shewn to himself, some from mercie to all believers, and some taken from his sovereign dominion over all, unto ver. 20. And in the last three verses, there is an exhortation to all the creatures, to join in God's praises with the Prophet.

1 O Thou, my soul, bless God the Lord:
    and all that in me is,
Be stirred up, his holy name
    to magnify and bless.
2 Bless, O my soul, the Lord thy God,
    and not forgetful be
Of all his gracious benefits
    he hath bestow'd on thee.

3 All thine iniquities who doth
    most graciously forgive:
Who thy diseases all and pains
    doth heal, and thee relieve.
4 Who doth redeem thy life, that thou
    to death may'st not go down:
Who thee with loving-kindness doth
    and tender mercies crown.

5 Who with abundance of good things
    doth satisfy thy mouth:
So that, ev'n as the eagle's age,
    renewed is thy youth.
6 God righteous judgment executes
    for all oppressed ones.
7 His ways to Moses, he his acts
    made known to Isra'l's sons.

8 The Lord our God is merciful,
    and he is gracious,
  Long-suffering, and slow to wrath,
    in mercy plenteous.
9 He will not chide continually,
    nor keep his anger still.
10 With us he dealt not as we sinn'd,
    nor did requite our ill.
11 For as the heav'n in its height
    the earth surmounteth far:
  So great to those that do him fear
    his tender mercies are.
12 As far as east is distant from
    the west, so far hath he
  From us removed, in his love,
    all our iniquity.
13 Such pity as a father hath
    unto his children dear;
  Like pity shews the Lord to such
    as worship him in fear.
14 For he remembers we are dust,
    and he our frame well knows.
15 Frail man, his days are like the grafs,
    as flow'r in field he grows.
16 For over it the wind doth pass,
    and it away is gone,
  And of the place where once it was,
    it shall no more be known.
17 But unto them that do him fear,
    God's mercy never ends;
  And to their children's children still
    his righteousness extends:

18 To such as keep his covenant,
  and mindful are alway
Of his most just commandements,
  that they may them obey.
19 The Lord prepared hath his throne
  in heavens firm to stand:
And every thing that being hath,
  his kingdom doth command.
20 O ye his Angels that excel
  in strength, bless ye the Lord;
Ye who obey what he commands,
  and hearken to his word:
21 O bless and magnify the Lord,
  ye glorious hosts of his;
Ye ministers, that do fulfil
  whate'er his pleasure is.
22 O bless the Lord, all ye his works,
  wherewith the world is stor'd,
In his dominions ev'ry where:
  my soul, bless thou the Lord.

PSALM CIV.

As in the former Psalm, the Prophet stirred up himself, and all others to glorify God, specially for the works of grace; so here he stirreth up himself and others to glorify God, specially for the works of Creation and Providence: And in the first place, He sheweth the scope of all the Psalm, ver. 1. In the second place, He bringeth arguments for pressing the duty of praising God, from the first day's work of Creation, to wit, The light. And from the second day's work in spreading forth the Heavens, ver 2, 3, 4. And from the third day's work of bringing forth the earth, the sea, the flowers and plants, for the use of man and beast, which were the works of the sixth day, ver. 5, 6, 7, 8, 9, 10, 11, 12, 13, 14, 15, 16, 17, 18. And from the works of the fourth day, sun and moon, ver. 19, 20, 21, 22, 23, 24. And from the works of the fifth day, fishes greater and smaller, ver. 25, 26. In the third place, He bringeth arguments of God's praise, from the preservation, specially of living creatures, ver. 27, 28, 29, 30. In the fourth place is the conclusion of the Psalm, with some further reasons for praising of God, ver. 31, 32, 33, 34, 35.

1 Bless God, my soul, O Lord my God,
    thou art exceeding great,
  With honour and with majesty
    thou clothed art in state.
2 With light, as with a robe, thyself
    thou coverest about:
  And, like unto a curtain, thou
    the heavens stretchest out.
3 Who of his chambers doth the beams
    within the waters lay,
  Who doth the clouds his chariot make,
    on wings of wind make way.
4 Who flaming fire his ministers,
    his angels sp'rits doth make.
5 Who earth's foundations did lay,
    that it should never shake.
6 Thou didst it cover with the deep,
    as with a garment spread:
  The waters stood above the hills,
    when thou the word but said.
7 But at the voice of thy rebuke,
    they fled, and would not stay:
  They, at thy thunder's dreadful voice,
    did haste them fast away.
8 They by the mountains do ascend,
    and by the valley ground
  Descend, unto that very place
    which thou for them didst found.
9 Thou hast a bound unto them set
    that they may not pass over,
  That they do not return again
    the face of earth to cover.

10 He to the valleys sends the springs
   which run among the hills.
11 They to all beasts of field give drink:
   wild asses drink their fills.
12 By them the fowls of heav'n shall have
   their habitation,
 Which do among the branches sing
   with delectation.
13 He from his chambers watereth
   the hills, when they are dry'd:
 With fruit and increase of thy works
   the earth is satisfy'd.
14 For cattle he makes grass to grow,
   he makes the herb to spring
 For th' use of man, that food to him
   he from the earth may bring:
15 And wine, that to the heart of man
   doth chearfulness impart,
 Oil that his face makes shine, and bread
   that strengtheneth his heart.
16 The trees of God are full of sap:
   the cedars that do stand
 In Lebanon, which planted were
   by his almighty hand.
17 Birds of the air upon their boughs
   do chuse their nests to make;
 As for the stork, the fir-tree she
   doth for her dwelling take.
18 The lofty mountains for wild goats
   a place of refuge be,
 The conies also to the rocks
   do for their safety flee.

19 He sets the moon in heav'n, thereby
   the seasons to discern:
  From him the sun his certain time
   of going down doth learn.
20 Thou darkness mak'st, 'tis night: then
   of forests creep abroad.   [beasts
21 The lions young roar for their prey,
   and seek their meat from God.
22 The sun doth rise, and home they flock,
   down in their dens they lie.
23 Man goes to work, his labour he
   doth to the ev'ning ply.
24 How manifold, Lord, are thy works!
   in wisdom wonderful
  Thou ev'ry one of them hast made!
   earth's of thy riches full!
25 So is this great and spacious sea,
   wherein things creeping are,
  Which numbred cannot be, and beasts
   both great and small are there.
26 There ships go, there thou mak'st to play
   that leviathan great.
27 These all wait on thee, that thou may'st
   in due time give them meat.
28 That which thou givest unto them,
   they gather for their food:
  Thine hand thou op'nest lib'rally,
   they filled are with good.
29 Thou hid'st thy face, they troub'led are,
   their breath thou tak'st away,
  Then do they die, and to their dust
   return again do they.

30 Thy quick'ning fp'rit thou fendeſt forth,
    then they created be:
And then the earth's decayed face
    renewed is by thee.
31 The glory of the mighty Lord
    continue ſhall for ever:
The Lord JEHOVAH ſhall rejoice
    in all his works together.
32 Earth, as affrighted, trembleth all,
    if he on it but look;
And if the mountains he but touch,
    they preſently do ſmoke.
33 I will ſing to the Lord moſt high
    ſo long as I ſhall live:
And while I being have, I ſhall
    to my God praiſes give.
34 Of him my meditation ſhall
    ſweet thoughts to me afford:
And as for me I will rejoice
    in God, my only Lord.
35 From earth let let ſinners be confum'd,
    let ill men nó more be:
O thou my ſoul, bleſs thou the Lord:
    praiſe to the Lord give ye.

PSALM CV.

The firſt part of this Pſalm was ſung at the carrying up of the ark of God to the city of David, 1. Chron. xvi. 8. The whole Pſalm containeth an exhortation to the Church of Iſrael to praiſe God for his mercies ſhewn towards them, with reaſons ſerving to preſs the duty. The exhortation is ſet down, ver. 1, 2, 3, 4, 5, 6. The reaſons are more particularly expreſſed in the reſt of the Pſalm; the firſt rank whereof is taken from the Lord's covenanting with Abraham, Iſaac, and Jacob, and the care which the Lord had of their perſons, ver. 7, 8, 9, 10, 11, 12, 13, 14, 15. The ſecond rank is taken from the care the Lord had of their poſterity, when he sent them down from Egypt, and all the while they were there, ver. 16, 17, 18, 19, 20, 21, 22, 23, 24, 25. The third rank is taken from the manner of their delivery out of Egypt, when they were oppressed, and from the plaguing of the Egyptians for their sake, ver. 26, 27, 28, to 37. The fourth rank is taken from the Lord's care in leading them thro' the wilderness, from ver. 37. to 43. And the last rank of reasons is taken from the Lord's placing of them in Canaan, where they might serve God according to his law, ver. 44, 45.

1 GIVE thanks to God; call on his name;
    to men his deeds make known.
2 Sing ye to him, sing psalms: proclaim
    his wond'rous works each one.
3 See that ye in his holy name
    to glory do accord:
And let the heart of ev'ry one
    rejoice that seeks the Lord.

4 The Lord almighty, and his strength,
    with stedfast hearts seek ye:
His blessed and his gracious face
    seek ye continually.
5 Think on the works that he hath done,
    which admiration breed;
His wonders, and the judgments all,
    which from his mouth proceed.

6 O ye that are of Ab'ram's race,
    his servant well approv'n;
And ye that Jacob's children are,
    whom he chus'd for his own.
7 Because he, and he only, is
    the mighty Lord our God;
And his most righteous judgments are
    in all the earth abroad.

8 His cov'nant he rememb'red hath,
    that it may ever ſtand;
  To thouſand generations
    the word he did command.
9 Which covenant he firmly made
    with faithful Abraham,
  And unto Iſaac, by his oath,
    he did renew the ſame.
10 And unto Jacob for a law,
    he made it firm and ſure,
  A covenant to Iſrael,
    which ever ſhould endure.
11 He ſaid, I'll give Canaan's land
    for heritage to you:
12 While they were ſtrangers there, and few,
    in number very few.
13 While yet they went from land to land
    without a ſure abode,
  And while thro' ſundry kingdoms they
    did wander far abroad:
14 Yet notwithſtanding ſuff'red he
    no man to do them wrong:
  Yea, for their ſakes, he did reprove
    Kings, who were great and ſtrong.
15 Thus did he ſay, Touch ye not thoſe
    that mine anointed be,
  Nor do the prophets any harm
    that do pertain to me.
16 He call'd for famine on the land;
    he brake the ſtaff of bread.
17 But yet he ſent a man before,
    by whom they ſhould be fed;

    Ev'n Joseph, whom unnat'rally
      fell for a slave did they;
18 Whose feet with fetters they did hurt,
      and he in irons lay:
19 Until the time that his word came
      to give him liberty:
    The word and purpose of the Lord
      did him in prison try.
20 Then sent the King and did command
      that he enlarg'd should be:
    He that the people's ruler was,
      did send to set him free.
21 A lord, to rule his family,
      he rais'd him, as most fit:
    To him, of all that he possest,
      he did the charge commit;
22 That he might at his pleasure bind
      the princes of the land;
    And he might teach his senators
      wisdom to understand.
23 The people then of Israel
      down into Egypt came:
    And Jacob also sojourned
      within the land of Ham.
24 And he did greatly by his pow'r
      increase his people there:
    And stronger than their enemies
      they by his blessing were.
25 Their heart he turned to envy
      his folk maliciously,
    With those that his own servants were
      to deal in subtilty.

26 His servant Moses he did send,
    Aaron his chosen one:
27 By these his signs and wonders great
    in Ham's land were made known.
28 Darkness he sent, and made it dark;
    his word they did obey.
29 He turn'd their waters into blood,
    and he their fish did slay.
30 The land in plenty brought forth frogs,
    in chambers of their Kings.
31 His word all sorts of flies and lice
    in all their borders brings.
32 He hail for rain and flaming fire
    into their land he sent:
33 And he their vines and fig-trees smote;
    trees of their coasts he rent.
34 He spake, and caterpillars came:
    locusts did much abound,
35 Which in their land all herbs consum'd
    and all fruits of their ground.
36 He smote all first-born in their land;
    chief of their strength each one.
37 With gold and silver brought them forth;
    weak in their tribes were none.
38 Egypt was glad when forth they went:
    their fear on them did light.
39 He spread a cloud for covering,
    and fire to shine by night.
40 They ask'd, and he brought quails; with
    of Heav'n he filled them.   [bread
41 He op'ned rocks, floods gush'd and ran
    in desarts like a stream.

42 For on his holy promise he
  and servant Ab'ram thought.
43 With joy his people, his elect
  with gladness, forth he brought:
44 And unto them the pleasant lands
  he of the heathen gave;
 That of the people's labour they
  inheritance might have:
45 That they his statutes might observe
  according to his word;
 And that they might his laws obey.
  Give praise unto the Lord.

PSALM CVI.

The sum of this Psalm is to teach the Godly in the time of calamity, lying upon the Church, or upon themselves. First, To glorify God by faith in him. Secondly, To reckon up, for their encouragement, the frequent forgiveness of grievous sins to his people in former times. And thirdly, To pray for the like favour to themselves, and in hope to have their prayer granted to give thanks to God. There are three parts of the Psalm answerable thereunto. The first part, is the Prophet's strengthening of his own faith, ver. 1, 2, 3, 4, 5. The second part, is the confession of our sins in general, ver. 6. and in special, of eight or nine gross provocations which the Lord after correction did pardon, and gave comfort to his people, to ver. 46. which are so many arguments of hope, to find the like mercy to the Church in this time. The first sin, with the forgiveness of it, is set down from ver. 7. to ver 13. The second sin, ver. 13, 14, 15. The third sin, ver. 16, 17, 18. The fourth sin, ver. 19, 20, 21, 22, 23. The fifth sin, ver. 24, 25, 26, 27. The sixth sin, ver. 28, 29, 30, 31. The seventh sin, ver. 32, 33. The eighth sin, from ver. 34, to 43. The ninth point of confession is, of a general heap of sins, oft-times repeated, and all pardoned, with pity manifested to God's people, ver. 43, 44, 45, 46. The third part of the Psalm, is a Prayer for new experience of like mercy, and a close of the Psalm with praise and thanksgiving, ver. 47, 48.

1 GIVE praise and thanks unto the Lord,
   for bountiful is he,
 His tender mercy doth endure
  unto eternity.

2 God's mighty works, who can exprefs?
　　or fhew forth all his praife?
3 Bleffed are they that judgment keep,
　　and juftly do always.
4 Remember me, Lord, with that love
　　which thou to thine doft bear:
　With thy falvation, O my God,
　　to vifit me draw near:
5 That I thy chofen's good may fee,
　　and in their joy rejoice:
　And may, with thine inheritance,
　　triumph with cheerful voice.
6 We with our fathers finned have,
　　and of iniquity
　Too long we have the workers been,
　　we have done wickedly.
7 The wonders great, which thou, O Lord,
　　didft work in Egypt land,
　Our fathers, tho' they faw, yet them
　　they did not underftand;
　And they thy mercies' multitude
　　kept not in memory;
　But at the fea, ev'n the Red Sea,
　　provok'd him grievoufly.
8. Neverthelefs he faved them,
　　ev'n for his own name's fake:
　That fo he might to be well known
　　his mighty pow'r make.
9 When he the Red Sea did rebuke,
　　then dried up it was:
　Thro' depths, as thro' the wildernefs,
　　he fafely made them pafs.

10 From hands of thofe that hated them
    he did his people fave;
  And from the en'my's cruel hand
    to them redemption gave.
11 The waters overwhelm'd their foes,
    not one was left alive.
12 Then they believ'd his word, and praife
    to him in fongs did give.
13 But foon did they his mighty works
    forget unthankfully:
  And on his counfel and his will
    did not wait patiently:
14 But much did luft in wildernefs,
    and God in defert tempt.
15 He gave them what they fought, but to
    their foul he leannefs fent.
16 And againft Mofes in the camp,
    their envy did appear:
  At Aaron they, the Saint of God,
    envious alfo were.
17 Therefore the earth did open wide,
    and Dathan did devour,
  And all Abiram's company
    did cover in that hour.
18 Likewife among their company
    a fire was kindled then;
  And fo the hot confuming flame
    burnt up thefe wicked men.
19 Upon the hill of Horeb they
    an idol calf did frame,
  A molten image they did make,
    and worfhipped the fame.

20 And thus their glory, and their God,
   moſt vainly changed they
 Into the likeneſs of an ox
   that eateth graſs or hay.
21 They did forget the mighty God,
   that had their Saviour been,
 By whom ſuch great things brought t(
   they had in Egypt ſeen.   [paſs
22 In Ham's land he did wond'rous works
   things terrible did he,
 When he his mighty hand and arm
   ſtretch'd out at the Red Sea.
23 Then ſaid he, He would them deſtroy
   had not, his wrath to ſtay,
 His choſen Moſes ſtood in breach,
   that them he ſhould not ſlay.
24 Yea, they deſpis'd the pleaſant land,
   believed not his word:
25 But in their tents they murmured,
   not heark'ning to the Lord.
26 Therefore in deſert, them to ſlay,
   he lifted up his hand:
27 'Mong nations to o'erthrow their ſeed,
   and ſcatter in each land.
28 They unto Bael-peor did
   themſelves aſſociate;
 The ſacrifices of the dead
   they did profanely eat.
29 Thus by their lewd inventions,
   they did provoke his ire:
 And then upon them ſuddenly
   the plague brake in as fire.

30 Then Phineas rose, and justice did:
    and so the plague did cease.
31 That, to all ages, counted was
    to him for righteousness.
32 And at the waters where they strove,
    they did him angry make,
  In such sort, that it fared ill
    with Moses for their sake:
33 Because they there his spirit meek
    provoked bitterly,
  So that he utter'd with his lips
    words unadvisedly.
34 Nor, as the Lord commanded them,
    did they the nations slay:
35 But with the heathen mingled were,
    and learn'd of them their way.
36 And they their idols serv'd; which did
    a snare unto them turn.
37 Their sons and daughters they to dev'ls
    in sacrifice did burn.
38 In their own children's guiltless blood
    their hands they did imbrue,
  Whom to Canaan's idols they
    for sacrifices slew:
  So was the land defil'd with blood:
    They stain'd with their own way,
£6 And with their own inventions
    a whoring they did stray.
40 Against his people kindled was
    the wrath of God therefore,
  Insomuch, that he did his own
    inheritance abhor.

41 He gave them to the heathen's hand;
 their foes did them command.
42 Their en'mies them oppreſt, they were
 made ſubject to their hand.
43 He many times deliv'red them,
 but with their counſel ſo
 They him provok'd, that for their ſin
 they were brought very low.
44 Yet their affliction he beheld,
 when he did hear their cry.
45 And he for them his covenant
 did call to memory.
 After his mercies' multitude
46 he did repent: And made
 Them to be pity'd of all thoſe
 who did them captive lead.
47 O Lord, our God, us ſave, and gather
 the heathen from among,
 That we thy holy Name may praiſe
 in a triumphant ſong.
48 Bleſt be JEHOVAH, Iſra'l's God,
 to all eternity:
 Let all the people ſay, Amen.
 Praiſe to the Lord give ye.

PSALM CVII.

This Pſa'm is praiſe for God's gracious and wiſe diſpenſations towards men. In the former part whereof, the Pſalmiſt, reckoneth four exerciſes of God's people, by God's juſtice bringing them to ſtraits, and by his mercy delivering them again. The firſt exerciſe is, By baniſhment, and by the Lord's bringing them back from it, to ver. 10. The ſecond is, by captivity and impriſonment, and delivery out of it, to ver. 17. The third is, By bodily ſickneſs, and recovery from it, to ver. 23. The fourth is, By danger by ſea, and the delivery out of it, to ver 33.

In the latter part of the Psalm he praiseth God for his wise dealing with people and nations, in changes made among them, in their lands, persons, goods and estates, for the good of his own, and overthrow of the proud. One change is, Of a fertile into a barren wilderness, for the inhabitants' sins, ver. 33, 34. Another change is, Of a barren land into a fertile and plentiful soil, well peopled, to ver. 38. A third change is, Wasting and spoiling of a well-peopled and fertile country, ver. 39. A fourth change is, Pulling down princes and statesmen, and confounding of them, so that they knew not what to do, or whither to go, ver. 40. The fifth change is, The lifting up of the poor and desolate, and enlarging of them in all respects, ver. 41. The best witnesses of which changes, are the Godly and wise observers of God's Providence, who, for a reward of their observation, shall have comfortable use and benefit of all God's dispensations, ver. 42, 43.

1 PRAISE God, for he is good : for still
   his mercies lasting be.
2 Let God's redeem'd say so, whom he
   from th' en'mies hand did free :
3 And gather'd them out of the lands
   from north, south, east and west.
4 They stray'd in desarts pathless way,
   no city found to rest.
5 For thirst and hunger, in them faints
6   their soul. When straits them press,
They cry unto the Lord, and he
   them frees from their distress.
7 Them also in a way to walk,
   that right is, he did guide,
That they might to a city go
   wherein they might abide.
8 O that men to the Lord would give
   praise, for his goodness then,
And for his works of wonders done
   unto the sons of men !

9 For he the soul that longing is
     doth fully satisfy,
  With goodness he the hungry soul
     doth fill abundantly.
10 Such as shut up in darkness deep,
     and in death's shade abide,
  Whom strongly hath affliction bound,
     and irons fast have ty'd:
11 (Because against the words of God
     they wrought rebelliously,
  And they the counsel did contemn
     of him that is most high):
12 Their heart he did bring down with grief,
     they fell, no help could have.
13 In trouble then they cry'd to God,
     he them from straits did save.
14 He out of darkness did them bring,
     and from death's shade them take;
  These bands wherewith they had been
     asunder quite he brake.   [bound,
15 O that men to the Lord would give
     praise, for his goodness then,
  And for his works of wonder done
     unto the sons of men!
16 Because the mighty gates of brass
     in pieces he did tear,
  By him in sunder also cut
     the bars of iron were.
17 Fools, for their sin, and their offence,
     do sore affliction bear.
18 All kind of meat their soul abhors,
     they to death's gates draw near.

19 In grief they cry to God, he saves
 them from their miseries.
20 He sends his word, them heals, and them
 from their destructions frees.
21 O that men to the Lord would give
 praise, for his goodness then,
 And for his works of wonder done
 unto the sons of men!
22 And let them sacrifice to him
 off'rings of thankfulness,
 And let them shew abroad his works
 in songs of joyfulness.
23 Who go to sea in ships, and in
 great waters trading be:
24 Within the deep, these men God's works
 and his great wonders see.
25 For he commands, and forth in haste
 the stormy tempest flies,
 Which makes the sea with rolling waves
 aloft to swell and rise.
26 They mount to Heav'n, then to the depths
 they do go down again;
 Their soul doth faint, and melt away
 with trouble and with pain.
27 They reel and stagger like one drunk,
 at their wits end they be:
28 Then they to God in trouble cry,
 who them from straits doth free.
29 The storm is chang'd into a calm,
 at his command and will;
 So that the waves, which rag'd before,
 now quiet are and still.

30 Then are they glad, becauſe at reſt
 and quiet now they be;
So to the haven he them brings,
 which they deſire to ſee.
31 O that men to the Lord would give
 praiſe, for his goodneſs then,
And for his works of wonder done
 unto the ſons of men!
32 Among the people gathered,
 let them exalt his Name;
Among aſſembled elders ſpread
 his moſt renowned fame.
33 He to dry-land turns water-ſprings,
 and floods to wilderneſs:
34 For ſins of thoſe that dwell therein,
 fat land to barrenneſs.
35 The burnt and parched wilderneſs
 to water-pools he brings;
The ground that was dry'd up before,
 he turns to water-ſprings.
36 And there, for dwelling, he a place
 doth to the hungry give,
That they a city may prepare
 commodiouſly to live.
37 There ſow the fields, and vineyards [plant,
 to yield fruits of increaſe.
38 His bleſſing makes them multiply,
 lets not their beaſts decreaſe.
39 Again they are diminiſhed,
 and very low brought down,
Through ſorrow and affliction,
 and great oppreſſion.

40 He upon princes pours contempt,
 and causeth them to stray,
And wander in a wilderness
 wherein there is no way.
41 Yet setteth he the poor on high
 from all his miseries,
And he, much like unto a flock,
 doth make him families.
42 They that are right'ous shall rejoice
 when they the same shall see;
And, as ashamed, stop her mouth
 shall all iniquity.
43 Whoso is wise, and will these things
 observe, and them record,
Ev'n they shall understand the love
 and kindness of the Lord.

PSALM CVIII.
A Song or Psalm of David.

This Psalm is composed of part of the 57th Psalm, from ver. 7. to the end, and of a part of the 60th Psalm, from ver 5. to the end, but in a dive se notion; for in the 57th and 60th Psalms, David is praying for experience of the truth of the promise made to him, concerning the kingdom of Israel, and victory over his enemies on all sides, being now in hazard by them; but here he is making use of the experience received, and of victory obtained over enemies within and without the kingdom of Israel, for the encouragement of the Church militant to the end of the world, against intestine and foreign enemies whatsoever. Again, in these two former Psalms, whence he doth repeat the words of this Psalm, he had his own interest to plead, beside what was typical in his exercise: Here, his own interest being settled, and the promise made to himself performed, he recommendeth this experience of his in a more abstract notion from his own particular, and in a more typical way of a pledge of the victory of the true Church militant, under her head and Lord, over all her enemies both intestine and foreign, without the verge of the visible profession, that is the faith of Christ, and hope of his prevailing in the work of enlarging and reforming of the visible Catholic Church, and overthrowing of the open enemies of Christ's kingdom, typified under the exercise of David, the true subjects of Christ might go on in their warfare with the greater confidence.

This Psalm hath two parts: In the former is the thanksgiving of faith, and promise of praise, in hope of obtaining all which the Church is here to pray for, ver. 1, 2, 3, 4, 5. In the latter part is the prayer for preservation of the Church, ver. 6. with confidence to be heard and helped, whatsoever impediment appear, against all who stand out against Christ's kingdom, whether within the visible Church, ver. 7, 8. or whether without, such as are professed enemies unto it, ver. 9, 10, 11, which prayer is followed forth, ver. 12. and comfortably closed with assurance of the Church's victory by the assistance of God, ver. 13.

1 MY heart is fix'd, Lord: I will sing,
   and with my glory praise.
2 Awake up psaltery and harp,
   myself I'll early raise.
3 I'll praise thee 'mong the people, Lord,
   'mong nations sing will I.
4 For above Heav'n thy mercy's great,
   thy truth doth reach the sky.
5 Be thou above the Heavens, Lord,
   exalted gloriously;
   Thy glory all the earth above
   be lifted up on high.
6 That those who thy beloved are
   delivered may be;
   O do thou save with thy right hand,
   and answer give to me.
7 God in his holiness hath said,
   Herein I will take pleasure,
   Shechem I will divide, and forth
   will Succoth's valley measure.
8 Gilead I claim as mine by right,
   Manasseh mine shall be;
   Ephraim is of my head the strength,
   Judah gives laws for me.

9 Moab's my washing-pot, my shoe
    I'll over Edom throw,
  Over the land of Palestine
    I will in triumph go.
10 O who is he will bring me to
    the city fortify'd ?
  O who is he that to the land
    of Edom will me guide ?
11 O God, thou who hadst cast us off,
    this thing wilt thou not do ?
  And wilt not thou, ev'n thou, O God,
    forth with our armies go ?
12 Do thou from trouble give us help,
    for helpless is man's aid.
13 Through God we shall do valiantly,
    our foes he shall down tread.

PSALM CIX.

To the chief Musician, a Psalm of David.

David, as a type of Christ, hath here to do with his and the Lord's desperate enemies. The Psalm hath three parts. In the first part, he complaineth against them unto God, ver. 1, 2, 3, 4, 5. In the second, he pronounceth the fearful vengeance of God against them, by way of imprecation in the spirit of prophecy, unto ver. 21. In the third part, he putteth up a prayer to God for himself, and is comforted. In all which he is a type of Christ, and hath an eye unto Christ's kingdom, and to the desperate enemies thereof, as the apostle Peter doth teach us in his application of what is here spoken, as a Prophecy to be in part completed in Judas, Acts i. 20. And so David is not here satisfying his own private revenge against Achitophel, or any other such like traitor, but as a Prophet foretelling what judgment was to fall on the desperate enemies of God, and as a Saint subscribing to God's righteous judgments, for the terror of all opposers of Christ's kingdom.

1 O Thou the God of all my praise,
    do thou not hold thy peace:
2 For mouths of wicked men to speak
    against me do not cease;

The mouths of vile deceitful men
  againſt me op'ned be;
And with a falſe and lying tongue
  they have accuſed me.
3 They did beſet me round about
  with words of hateful ſpite:
And, tho' to them no cauſe I gave,
  againſt me they did fight.
4 They for my love became my foes:
  but I me ſet to pray.
5 Evil for good, hatred for love,
  to me they did repay.
6 Set thou the wicked over him,
  and upon his right hand
Give thou his greateſt enemy,
  ev'n Satan, leave to ſtand.
7 And when by thee he ſhall be judg'd,
  let him condemned be;
And let his pray'r be turn'd to ſin,
  when he ſhall call on thee.
8 Few be his days, and in his room
  his charge another take.
9 His children let be fatherleſs,
  his wife a widow make.
10 His children let be vagabonds,
  and beg continually:
And from their places deſolate,
  ſeek bread for their ſupply.
11 Let covetous extortioners
  catch all he hath away:
Of all for which he labour'd hath
  let ſtrangers make a prey.

12 Let there be none to pity him,
    let there be none at all
  That on his children fatherlefs
    will let his mercy fall.
13 Let his pofterity from earth
    cut off for ever be,
  And in the following age their name
    be blotted out by thee.
14 Let God his father's wickednefs
    ftill to rememb'rance call;
  And never let his mother's fin
    be blotted out at all.
15 But let them all before the Lord
    appear continually,
  That he may wholly from the earth
    cut off their memory.
16 Becaufe he mercy minded not,
    but perfecuted ftill
  The poor and needy, that he might
    the broken hearted kill.
17 As he in curfing pleafure took,
    fo let it fo him fall;
  And as he delighted not to blefs,
    fo blefs him not at all.
18 As curfing he like clothes put on,
    into his bowels fo,
  Like water, and into his bones,
    like oil, down let it go.
19 Like to the garment let it be
    which doth himfelf array,
  And for a girdle, wherewith he
    is girt about alway.

20 From God let this be their reward
      that en'mies are to me ;
   And their reward, that speak against
      my soul maliciously.
21 But do thou, for thine own name's sake,
      O God, the Lord, for me ;
   Sith good and sweet thy mercy is
      from trouble set me free.
22 For I am poor and indigent,
      afflicted sore am I ;
   My heart within me also is
      wounded exceedingly.
23 I pass like a declining shade,
      am like the locust tost :
24 My knees thro' fasting weak'ned are,
      my flesh hath fatness lost.
25 I also am a vile reproach
      unto them made to be ;
   And they that did upon me look,
      did shake their heads at me.
26 O do thou help and succour me,
      who art my God and Lord :
   And. for thy tender mercies' sake,
      safety to me afford :
27 That thereby they may know, that this
      is thy almighty hand :
   And that thou, Lord, hast done the same
      they may well understand.
28 Altho' they curse with spite, yet, Lord,
      bless thou with loving voice :
   Let them asham'd be when they rise :
      thy servant let rejoice.

29 Let thou mine adversaries all
      with shame be cloathed over :
   And let their own confusion
      them, as a mantle, cover.
30 But as for me, I with my mouth
      will greatly praise the Lord :
   And I among the multitude
      his praises will record.
31 For he shall stand at his right hand
      who is in poverty,
   To save him from all those that would
      condemn his soul to die.

PSALM CX.
A Psalm of David.

This Psalm containeth the doctrine of Christ, God and Man in one person, concerning his everlasting kingdom and Priesthood, whose kingdom albeit begun to be manifested among the Jews, yet was to be extended unto the Gentiles with great success, ver. 1, 2, 3. As for his priesthood, he is settled therein for ever by an oath, ver. 4. and that with the overthrow of his enemies, how great or many soever, ver. 5, 6. yet not without Christ's sufferings, by which he was first to be humbled, and then to be exalted, ver. 7.

1 THE Lord did say unto my Lord,
      Sit thou on my right-hand,
   Until I make thy foes a stool
      whereon thy feet may stand.
2 The Lord shall out of Sion send
      the rod of thy great pow'r :
   In midst of all thine enemies
      be thou the governor.
3 A willing people in thy day
      of pow'r, shall come to thee,
   In holy beauties from morn's womb :
      thy youth like dew shall be.

4 The Lord himself hath made an oath,
    and will repent him never,
 Of th' order of Melchisedeck
    thou art a priest for ever.
5 The glorious and mighty Lord,
    that sits at thy right hand,
 Shall, in his day of wrath, strike through
    Kings that do him withstand.
6 He shall among the heathen judge,
    he shall with bodies dead
 The places fill: o'er many lands
    he wound shall ev'ry head.
7 The brook that runneth in the way
    with drink shall him supply,
 And, for this cause, in triumph he
    shall lift his head on high.

PSALM CXI.

The scope of this Psalm is to stir up all to praise God, and that for so many reasons as there are verses in the Psalm. The exhortation is in the first words, Praise ye the Lord. The reasons follow in order. The Psalm is composed so after the order of the Hebrew alphabet, as every sentence or half verse beginneth with a several letter of the A B C in order, and all the Psalm is of praise only.

1 PRaise ye the Lord. With my whole heart
    I will God's praise declare,
 Where the assemblies of the just
    and congregations are.
2 The whole works of the Lord our God,
    are great above all measure;
 Sought out they are of ev'ry one
    that doth therein take pleasure.
3 His work most honourable is,
    most glorious and pure:
 And his untainted righteousness,
    for ever doth endure.

4 His works moſt wonderful he hath
    made to be thought upon :
  The Lord is gracious, and he is
    full of compaſſion.
5 He giveth meat unto all thoſe
    that truly do him fear :
  And evermore his covenant
    he in his mind will bear.
6 He did the power of his works
    unto his people ſhow,
  When he the heathen's heritage
    upon them did beſtow.
7 His handy-works are truth and right :
    all his commands are ſure ;
8 And, done in truth and uprightneſs,
    they evermore endure.
9 He ſent redemption to his folk,
    his covenant for ay
  He did command : holy his name,
    and rev'rend is alway.
10 Wiſdom's beginning is God's fear :
    good underſtanding they
  Have all, that his commands fulfil :
    his praiſe endures for ay.

PSALM CXII.

This Pſalm is a praiſing of God for bleſſing of the believers, and the whole Pſalm doth prove that the believer is bleſſed; which propoſition is ſet down, ver. 1. and confirmed with ſo many reaſons as there are verſes following

1 PRaiſe ye the Lord. The man is bleſt
    that fears the Lord aright,
  He who in his commandements
    doth greatly take delight.

2 His feed and offspring powerful
  shall be the earth upon :
Of upright men blessed shall be
  the generation.
3 Riches and wealth shall ever be
  within his house in store :
And his unspotted righteousness
  endures for evermore.
4 Unto the upright light doth rise,
  though he in darkness be :
Compassionate and merciful,
  and righteous is he.
5 A good man doth his favour shew,
  and doth to others lend :
He with discretion his affairs
  will guide unto the end.
6 Surely, there is not any thing
  that ever shall him move ;
The righteous man's memorial
  shall everlasting prove.
7 When he shall evil tidings hear,
  she shall not be afraid ;
His heart is fix'd, his confidence
  upon the Lord is stay'd.
8 His heart is firmly 'stablished,
  afraid he shall not be,
Until upon his enemies
  he his desire shall see.
9 He hath dispers'd ; giv'n to the poor
  his righteousness shall be
To ages all ; with honour shall
  his horn be raised high.

10 The wicked shall it see, and fret,
   his teeth gnash, melt away:
What wicked men do most desire,
   shall utterly decay.

PSALM CXIII.

This also is a Psalm of praise, wherein, first, The proposition, that God is to be praised by all, is set down, ver. 1, 2, 3. In the next place, are the reasons taken from his incomparable Majesty, ver. 4, 5. In the third place, are the reasons of his praise, taken from his bounty towards men, in raising the afflicted unto an honourable condition, ver. 6, 7, 8. and enlarging of desolate families, ver. 9.

1 PRaise God: ye servants of the Lord;
   O praise, the Lord's name praise.
2 Yea, blessed be the name of God
   from this time forth always.
3 From rising sun, to where it sets,
   God's name is to be prais'd.
4 Above all nations God is high,
   'bove heav'ns his glory rais'd.
5 Unto the Lord our God, that dwells
   on high, who can compare?
6 Himself that humbleth things to see
   in heav'n and earth that are.
7 He from the dust doth raise the poor
   that very low doth lie,
And from the dunghill lifts the man
   opprefs'd with poverty:
8 That he may highly him advance
   and with the princes set,
With those that of his people are
   the chief, ev'n princes great.
9 The barren woman, house to keep
   he maketh, and to be
Of sons a mother full of joy.
   Praise to the Lord give ye.

PSALM CXIV.

This Pſalm is a praiſing of God, for the gracious and glorious work of delivering of his people out of Egypt, and bringing them into Canaan, and that for ſix reaſons. The firſt whereof, ver. 1. The next, ver. 2. The third, ver. 3. The fourth, ver. 4. The fifth, with the ſpecial uſe thereof, ver. 5, 6, 7. The ſixth, ver. 8.

1 WHEN Iſra'l out of Egypt went,
    and did his dwelling change;
When Jacob's houſe went out from thoſe
    that were of language ſtrange:
2 He Judah did his ſanctuary,
    his kingdom Iſra'l make:
The ſea it ſaw, and quickly fled,
    Jordan was driven back.
4 Like rams the mountains, and like lambs
    the hills ſkipp'd to and fro.
5 O ſea, why fledd'ſt thou? Jordan back
    why waſt thou driven ſo?
6 Ye mountains great, wherefore was it
    that ye did ſkip like rams?
And wherefore was it, little hills,
    that ye did leap like lambs?
7 O at the preſence of the Lord,
    earth, tremble thou for fear,
While as the preſence of the God
    of Jacob doth appear.
8 Who from the hard and ſtony rock
    did ſtanding water bring;
And, by his pow'r, did turn the flint
    into a water-ſpring!

PSALM CXV.

The Church of Iſrael being under the power of the heathen, and unable to help themſelves, do flee to God for relief; and in the former part of the Pſalm they pray for delivery, strengthening their hope to be heard by four arguments, unto ver. 9. In the latter part, the Church is encouraged to trust in God, and to expect deliverance in due time, by several reasons, all serving to confirm their faith, unto the end of the Psalm.

1 NOT unto us, Lord, not to us,
　　but do thou glory take
Unto thy name, ev'n for thy truth
　　and for thy mercies' sake.
2 O wherefore should the heathen say,
　　Where is their God now gone?
3 But our God in the heavens is,
　　what pleas'd him he hath done.
4 Their idols silver are and gold,
　　work of men's hands they be:
5 Mouths have they, but they do not speak;
　　and eyes, but do not see.
6 Ears have they, but they do not hear;
　　noses, but favour not:
7 Hands, feet, but handle not, nor walk,
　　nor speak they through their throat.
8 Like them their makers are, and all
　　on them their trust that build.
9 O Isra'l, trust thou in the Lord:
　　he is their help and shield.
10 O Aaron's house, trust in the Lord,
　　their help and shield is he.
11 Ye that fear God, trust in the Lord,
　　their help and shield he'll be.
12 The Lord of us hath mindful been,
　　and he will bless us still;
He will the house of Isra'l bless,
　　bless Aaron's house he will.

13 Both small and great that fear the Lord,
   he will them surely bless.
14 The Lord will you, you and your seed,
   ay more and more increase.
15 O blessed are ye of the Lord,
   who made the earth and heav'n.
16 The heav'n, ev'n heav'ns are God's; but
   earth to men's sons hath giv'n. [he
17 The dead, nor who to silence go,
   God's praise do not record.
18 But henceforth we for ever will
   bless God.   Praise ye the Lord.

PSALM CXVI.

This Psalm is a threefold engagement of the Psalmist unto thanksgiving unto God for his mercy unto him, and in particular, for some notable delivery from death, both bodily and spiritual. The first engagement is, that he shall out of love have his recourse unto God always by prayer, ver. 1, 2. the reasons and motives whereof are set down, because of his delivery out of a great strait, ver. 3, 4, 5, 6, 7, 8. The second engagement is to a holy conversation, ver. 9. the motives and reasons whereof are set down, ver. 10, 11, 12. The third engagement is, unto promised praises, or paying of praises and vows before the Church, with the reasons thereof, ver. 13, 14, 15, 16, 17, 18, 19.

1 I Love the Lord, because my voice
    and prayers he did hear.
2 I, while I live, will call on him,
    who bow'd to me his ear.
3 Of death the cords and sorrows did
    about me compass round;
  The pains of hell took hold on me:
    I grief and trouble found.
4 Upon the name of God the Lord,
    then did I call, and say,
  Deliver thou my soul, O Lord,
    I do thee humbly pray.

5 God merciful and righteous is,
    yea, gracious is our Lord.
6 God saves the meek, I was brought low,
    he did me help afford.
7 O thou, my soul, do thou return
    unto thy quiet rest;
  For largely, lo, the Lord to me
    his bounty hath exprest.
8 For my distressed soul from death
    deliver'd was by thee;
  Thou didst my mourning eyes from tears,
    my feet from falling, free.
9 I in the land of those that live
    will walk the Lord before.
10 I did believe, therefore I spake
    I was afflicted sore.
11 I said, when I was in my haste,
    that all men liars be.
12 What shall I render to the Lord,
    for all his gifts to me?
13 I'll of salvation take the cup,
    on God's name will I call:
14 I'll pay my vows now to the Lord,
    before his people all.
15. Dear in God's sight is his Saints' death.
16   Thy servant, Lord, am I;
  Thy servant sure, thine hand-maid's son:
    my bands thou didst unite.
17 Thank-off'rings I to thee will give,
    and on God's name will call.
18 I'll pay my vows now to the Lord,
    before his people all:

19 Within the courts of God's own house,
　　within the midst of thee,
　O city of Jerusalem.
　Praise to the Lord give ye.

PSALM CXVII.

This Psalm is an exhortation to the Gentiles to praise God, ver. 1. for his mercy and truth towards his people, ver. 2.

1 O Give ye praise unto the Lord,
　　　all nations that be:
　Likewise, ye people all, accord
　　　his name to magnify.
2 For great to us-ward ever are
　　　his loving kindnesses;
　His truth endures for evermore.
　　　The Lord, O do ye bless.

PSALM CXVIII.

The Psalmist in his thanksgiving for bringing him so wonderfully to the kingdom, prophesieth in this Psalm of Christ's troubles by his enemies, and of his victories over them, both in his own person, and in his mystical body. This Psalm hath such an eye and respect unto Christ and his Church, that whatsoever shadow of these things may be found in David, the main substance and accomplishment of all things herein contained, are to be found most clearly and fully in Christ's wrestling with his enemies, and his triumphing over them for the comfort of the Church, and glory of the Father: and this the Church of Israel did perceive and acknowledge, as appeareth by their acclamation taken out of this Psalm, and made to Christ at his coming into Jerusalem, as King riding, and by Christ's interpretation, and appropriating of it unto himself, Matth. xxi. 9, 15, 42. For this cause also the Psalmist doth not prefix his name unto this Psalm, whatsoever might be fit for his particular experience in it, but leaveth it to run the more clearly and directly towards the Messiah, or Christ, who is here mainly intended.

This Psalm may be divided into three parts. In the first, The Psalmist, and Christ represented by him, exhorteth the Church to praise God, and giveth sundry reasons for it, to ver. 14. In the second, He reneweth the song of God's praise, and giveth new reasons for the same, to ver. 19. In the third, Christ's triumph is set down, wherein he goeth into the

Temple and solemn assembly of the Church; and here Christ by his rejoicing stirreth up the Church to rejoice, and the Church giveth acclamation to him as their Lord and King, and all the company do rejoice together, and priests and people stir up one another to praise the Lord, unto the end of the Psalm.

1 O Praise the Lord, for he is good:
    his mercy lasteth ever.
2 Let those of Israel now say,
    his mercy faileth never.
3 Now let the house of Aaron say,
    his mercy lasteth ever.
4 Let those that fear the Lord now say,
    his mercy faileth never.
5 I in distress call'd on the Lord;
    the Lord did answer me:
  He in a large place did me set,
    from trouble made me free.
6 The mighty Lord is on my side,
    I will not be afraid:
  For any thing that man can do
    I shall not be dismay'd.
7 The Lord doth take my part with them
    that help to succour me:
  Therefore on those that do me hate
    I my desire shall see.
8 Better it is to trust in God,
    than trust in man's defence:
9 Better to trust in God, than make
    Princes our confidence.
10 The nations, joining all in one,
    did compass me about:
  But in the Lord's most holy name
    I shall them all root out.

11 They compafs'd me about, I fay,
    they compafs'd me about:
  But in the Lord's moft holy name
    I fhall them all root out.
12 Like bees they compafs'd me about;
    like unto thorns that flame
  They quenched are: for them fhall I
    deftroy in God's own name.
13 Thou fore haft thruft, that I might fall;
    but my Lord helped me.
14 God my falvation is become,
    my ftrength and fong is he.
15 In dwellings of the righteous
    is heard the melody
  Of joy and health: the Lord's right hand
    doth ever valiantly.
16 The right hand of the mighty Lord
    exalted is on high:
  The right-hand of the mighty Lord
    doth ever valiantly.
17 I fhall not die, but live, and fhall
    the works of God difcover.
18 The Lord hath me chaftifed fore,
    but not to death giv'n over.
19 O fet ye open unto me
    the gates of righteoufnefs:
  Then will I enter into them,
    and I the Lord will blefs.
20 This is the gate of God, by it
    the juft fhall enter in.
21 Thee will I praife, for thou me heard'ft,
    and haft my fafety been.

22 That stone is made head corner-stone,
   which builders did despise:
23 This is the doing of the Lord,
   and wond'rous in our eyes.
24 This is the day God made, in it
   we'll joy triumphantly.
25 Save now, I pray thee, Lord, I pray,
   send now prosperity.
26 Blessed is he in God's great name
   that cometh us to save;
   We, from the house which to the Lord
   pertains, you blessed have.
27 God is the Lord, who unto us
   hath made light to arise;
   Bind ye unto the altar's horns
   with cords the sacrifice.
28 Thou art my God, I'll thee exalt:
   my God, I will thee praise.
29 Give thanks to God, for he is good;
   his mercy lasts always.

PSALM CXIX.

We read of no man who had more troubles and exercises of conscience, or greater vissicitude of changes, outward and inward, or more frequent experience of his own weakness, witlessness and sinfulness, or of God's merciful direction, consolation and deliverance, than David. This man did the Lord fit, by the immediate inspiration of the Holy Ghost, for the edification of the Church, to express his exercises, and good deliverances from them all: And in this Psalm as in a bundle, he hath collected the sum of his holy meditations, and of the profitable uses which he made of the revealed will of God in Scripture, in all the conditions wherein he was, to teach all the faithful after him, to have the word of God in special regard, and to have respect unto it, as the only rule whereby they might find direction, consolation and salvation, however matters went. To this end, for memory's sake, he hath filled the Hebrew alphabet with 22 meditations, every one of them beginning with a several letter of the alphabet, and every section having eight verses, beginning with the same letter, and every verse almost of every section under some expression, making mention of the Scripture.

The words wherein the Scripture, or revealed will of God in Scripture, here is expressed, is one of these ten. 1. The law or doctrine, which signifieth the Lord's will to be taught of God that all men should learn it. 2. Statutes, which signifieth that this revealed will of God containeth the duties which God hath appointed and prescribed for our rule. 3. Precepts, which signify that this will of God is imposed by the authority of our sovereign law-giver. 4. Commands, which signifieth that this revealed will is committed unto our trust to be kept. 5. Testimonies, which signifieth that this revealed will of God doth testify of our duty and of our doings, whether conform or not to the rule, and testifieth also what event maybe expected by our believing or misbelieving, by our obedience or disobedience thereof. 6. Judgments, which signifieth the Scripture to be God's judicial decree, ordaining how our words, deeds and thoughts shall be ordered, and what shall be the execution of his will answerable thereto. 7. Oracle, or speech, because the Scripture proceedeth, as it were, from the mouth of God. 8. The word, which signifieth God's expounding his mind to us, as if he were speaking unto us. 9. The way of God, which signifieth the Lord's giving direction for our several actions how we should walk, as by so many steps into the kingdom of Heaven. 10. Righteousness, which signifieth that the word of God hath in it the way how a man shall be justified, to wit, by faith, and how a justified man should approve himself to God and man, as justified by faith; and that every son of wisdom, must and will justify the word of God, as the perfect rule of righteousness.

ALEPH.—*The 1st Part.*

In this first section he describeth the blessed men, to be only they who walk in the obedience of faith, as God's word prescribeth, ver. 1, 2, 3. Then he maketh application of this doctrine to himself: and first acknowledgeth this obligation to follow the direction of the Lord in the obedience of faith, ver. 4. and then he wisheth to have grace to obey, ver. 5. because so he should not be ashamed nor disappointed of his hope, ver. 6. and also, so he should be enabled to glorify and praise God more perfectly, ver. 7. And thirdly, engageth himself to follow this course by promise and prayer, ver. 8.

1 BLESSED are they that undefil'd,
  and straight are in the way;
Who in the Lord's most holy law
 do walk, and do not stray.

2 Bleſſed are they who to obſerve
    his ſtatutes are inclin'd;
  And who do ſeek the living God
    with their whole heart and mind.
3 Such in his ways do walk, and they
    do no iniquity.
4 Thou haſt commanded us to keep
    thy precepts carefully.
5 O that thy ſtatutes to obſerve
    thou would'ſt my ways direct!
6 Then ſhall I not be ſham'd, when I
    thy precepts all reſpect.
7 Then with integrity of heart
    thee will I praiſe and bleſs,
  When I the judgments all have learn'd
    of thy pure righteouſneſs.
8 That I will keep thy ſtatutes all
    firmly reſolv'd have I:
  O do not then, moſt gracious God,
    forſake me utterly.

BETH.—*The 2d Part.*

In this ſection, firſt, he propounds this doctrine, The word of God is the only rule and effectual inſtrument of renewing and ſanctifying of an unrenewed man; and the only way to find the efficacy of the word, is to ſtudy to comfo:m a man's mind, will and actions thereunto, ver. 9. And then in the next place, to the end he may teach men to make uſe of this doctrine by his example, he ſheweth the ſincerity of his own endeavour by ſeven evidences; the firſt and ſecond is, ver. 10. The third is, ver. 11. The fourth is, ver. 12. The fith is, ver. 13. The ſixth is, ver. 14. The ſeventh is, ver. 15, 16.

9 By what means ſhall a young man learn
    his way to purify;
  If he according to thy word
    thereunto attentive be.

10 Unfeignedly thee have I fought
   with all my foul and heart :
   O let me not from the right path
   of thy commands depart.
11 Thy word I in my heart have hid,
   that I offend not thee.
12 O Lord, thou ever bleffed art :
   thy ftatutes teach thou me.
13 The judgments of thy mouth each one
   my lips declared have :
14 More joy thy teftimonies' way
   than riches all me gave.
15 I will thy holy precepts make
   my meditation :
   And carefully I'll have refpect
   unto thy ways each one.
16 Upon thy ftatutes my delight
   fhall conftantly be fet,
   And by thy grace I never will
   thy holy word forget.

GIMEL.—*The 3d Part.*

In this fection he prayeth the Lord for continuance of his life, that he may have occafion for further fervice, which he defireth may be done by him, and for this end alfo he prayeth, that he may have a deeper infight in the myfteries of God's word, ver. 17, 18. And thefe two petitions he preffeth by three reafons, ver. 19, 20, 21. He prayeth alfo for clearing of his innocency, and for removing reproach from him, for other three reafons, ver. 22, 23, 24.

17 With me thy fervant, in thy grace,
   deal bountifully, Lord :
   That by thy favour I may live
   and duly keep thy word.

18 Open mine eyes, that of thy law
    the wonders I may see.
19 I am a stranger on this earth,
    hide not thy laws from me.
20 My soul within me breaks, and doth
    much fainting still endure,
  Through longing that it hath all times
    unto thy judgment pure.
21 Thou hast rebuk'd the cursed proud,
    who from thy precepts swerve.
22 Reproach and shame remove from me,
    for I thy laws observe.
23 Against me princes speak with spite,
    while they in council sat:
  But I, thy servant, did upon
    thy statutes meditate.
24 My comfort and my heart's delight,
    thy testimonies be,
  And they, in all my doubts and fears,
    are counsellors to me.

DALETH — *The 4th Part.*

In this section, there are six petitions, with their several reasons annexed unto them, some of them set down before, some of them set down after the petition. The first is, ver. 25. The second is, ver. 26. The third is, ver. 27. The fourth is, ver. 28. The fifth is, ver. 29. The sixth is, ver. 30, 31, 32.

25 My soul to dust cleaves: quicken me
    according to thy word.
26 My ways I shew'd, and me thou heard'st:
    teach me thy statutes, Lord.
27 The way of thy commandements
    make me aright to know;
  So all thy works that wond'rous are,
    I shall to others show.

28 My soul doth melt, and drop away,
    for heaviness and grief:
  To me, according to thy word,
    give strength, and send relief.
29 From me the wicked way of lies
    let far removed be:
  And graciously thy holy law
    do thou grant unto me.
30 I chosen have the perfect way
    of truth and verity:
  Thy judgments that most righteous are
    before me laid have I.
31 I to thy testimonies cleave:
    shame do not on me cast.
32 I'll run thy precepts' way, when thou
    my heart enlarged hast.

HE. — *The 5th Part.*
In this section there are eight petitions according to the number of the verses.

33 Teach me, O Lord, the perfect way
    of thy precepts divine,
  And to observe it to the end
    I shall my heart incline.
34 Give understanding unto me,
    so keep thy law shall I;
  Yea, ev'n with my whole heart I shall
    observe it carefully.
35 In thy law's path make me to go,
    for I delight therein.
36 My heart unto thy testimonies,
    and not to greed, incline.

37 Turn thou away my sight and eyes
   from viewing vanity:
And in thy good and holy way
   be pleas'd to quicken me.
38 Confirm to me thy gracious word,
   which I did gladly hear,
Ev'n to thy servant, Lord, who is
   devoted to thy fear.
39 Turn thou away my fear'd reproach:
   for good thy judgments be.
40 Lo, for thy precepts I have long'd:
   in thy truth quicken me.

VAU. — *The 6th Part.*

In this section, he prayeth, first, For deliverance out of his hard condition, and giveth reasons for strengthening his hope in this prayer, ver. 41, 42. And next, He prayeth for grace to confess God's truth openly, till the deliverance came, and he strengthens his hope by six or seven reasons, in the rest of the section.

41 Let thy sweet mercies also come,
   and visit me, O Lord;
Ev'n thy benign salvation,
   according to thy word.
42 So shall I have wherewith I may
   give him an answer just,
Who spitefully reproacheth me:
   for in thy word I trust.
43 The word of truth out of my mouth
   take thou not utterly;
For on thy judgments righteous
   my hope doth still rely.
44 So shall I keep for evermore
   thy law continually.
45 And sith that I thy precepts seek,
   I'll walk at liberty.

46 I'll fpeak thy word to kings, and I
 with fhame fhall not be mov'd:
47 And will delight myfelf always
 in thy laws which I lov'd.
48 To thy commandments which I lov'd,
 my hands lift up I will:
 And I will alfo meditate
 upon thy ftatutes ftill.

ZAIN. — *The 7th Part.*

In this fection, he prayeth for the performance of the promife, which he hath believed, and whereof he hath found the fruits already in a good meafure, ver. 49. The fruits which he hath found already by his faith in the word, are feven, all in order fet down in the reft of the verfes of this fection.

49 Remember, Lord, thy gracious word
 thou to thy fervant fpake,
 Which for a ground of my fure hope
 thou caufedft me to take.
50 This word of thine my comfort is
 in mine affliction:
 For in my ftraits I am reviv'd
 by this thy word alone.
51 The men whofe hearts with pride are [ftuff'd,
 did greatly me deride:
 Yet from thy ftraight commandements
 I have not turn'd afide.
52 Thy judgments righteous, O Lord,
 which thou of old forth gave,
 I did remember; and myfelf
 by them comforted have.
53 Horror took hold on me, becaufe
 ill men thy law forfake.
54 I in my houfe of pilgrimage
 thy laws my fongs do make.

55 Thy name by night, Lord, I did mind
 and I have kept thy law.
56 And this I had, because thy word
 I kept, and stood in awe.

CHETH.—*The 8th Part.*

In this section he laboureth to confirm his faith, and to comfort himself in the certainty of his regeneration, by eight properties of a found believer, or eight marks of a new creature. The first and second whereof is, ver. 57. The third is, ver. 58. The fourth is, ver. 59, 60. The fifth is, ver. 61. The sixth is, ver. 62. The seventh is, ver. 63. The eighth is, ver. 64.

57 Thou my sure portion art alone,
 which I did chuse, O Lord:
 I have resolv'd, and said, that I
 would keep thy holy word.
58 With my whole heart I did intreat
 thy face and favour free:
 According to thy gracious word
 be merciful to me.
59 I thought upon my former ways,
 and did my life well try,
 And to thy testimonies pure
 my feet them turned I.
60 I did not stay, nor linger long
 as those that slothful are,
 But hastily thy laws to keep
 myself I did prepare.
61 Bands of ill men me robb'd; yet I
 thy precepts did not slight.
62 I'll rise at midnight thee to praise,
 ev'n for thy judgments right.
63 I am companion to all those
 who fear, and thee obey.
64 O Lord, thy mercy fills the earth:
 teach me thy laws, I pray.

TETH. — *The 9th Part.*

In this section he gives eight marks of a thankful soul, delivered from heavy trouble for a time, all in order set down in the eight following verses.

65 Well hast thou with thy servant dealt,
    as thou didst promise give.
66 Good judgment me, and knowledge
    for I thy word believe. [teach;
67 Ere I afflicted was, I stray'd:
    but now I keep thy word.
68 Both good thou art, and good thou dost:
    teach me thy statutes, Lord.
69 The men that are puft up with pride,
    against me forg'd a lie:
  Yet thy commandements observe
    with my whole heart will I.
70 Their hearts through worldly ease and
    as fat as grease they be, [wealth,
  But in thy holy law I take
    delight continually.
71 It hath been very good for me
    that I afflicted was:
  That I might well instructed be,
    and learn thy holy laws.
72 The word that cometh from thy mouth
    is better unto me,
  Than many thousands, and great sums
    of gold and silver be.

JOB. — *The 10th Part.*

In this section is set down the example of the right carriage of a believer, brought out of one calamity, and cast into another. His good behaviour, consisting in these six duties. The first is, ver. 73, 74. The second is, ver. 75. The third is, ver. 76, 77. The fourth is, ver 78. The fifth is, ver. 79. The sixth is, ver. 80.

73 Thou mad'st and fashion'dst me: thy [laws
 to know, give wisdom, Lord.
74 So who thee fear, shall joy to see
 me trusting in thy word.
75 That very right thy judgments are
 I know and do confess,
And that thou hast afflicted me
 in truth and faithfulness.
76 O let thy kindness merciful,
 I pray thee, comfort me,
As to thy servant faithfully
 was promised by thee.
77 And let thy tender mercies come
 to me, that I may live:
Because thy holy laws to me
 sweet delectation give.
78 Lord, let the proud ashamed be:
 for they without a cause,
With me perversely dealt; but I
 will muse upon thy laws.
79 Let such as fear thee, and have known
 thy statutes, turn to me.
80 My heart let in thy laws be found,
 that sham'd I never be.

CAPH.—*The* 11*th Part.*

In this section is shewn how deep the persecuted servant of God may draw in his affliction before God give him comfort. There are four degrees of his deepness in distress; to wit, fainting of faith, ver. 81. almost failing of hope, ver. 82. failing of the body, ver. 83. and longing for death, ver. 84. Then he sheweth how he behaved himself in this sad condition: He layeth out his enemies carriage before God, ver. 85, 86. and his own stedfastness in extreme danger, ver. 87. and prayeth for comfort, that he may in his trial bear out, ver. 88.

81 My foul for thy falvation faints :
 yet I thy word believe.
82 Mine eyes fail for thy word ; I fay
 when wilt thou comfort give ?
83 For like a bottle I'm become,
 that in the fmoke is fet :
 I'm black and parch'd with grief, yet I
 thy ftatutes not forget.
84 How many are thy fervant's days ?
 when wilt thou execute
 Juft judgment on thefe wicked men
 that do me perfecute :
85 The proud have digged pits for me,
 which is againft thy laws.
86 Thy words all faithful are : help me,
 purfu'd without a caufe.
87 They fo confum'd me, that on earth
 my life they fcarce did leave :
 Thy precepts yet forfook I not,
 but clofe to them did cleave.
88 After thy loving-kindnefs, Lord,
 me quicken and preferve ;
 The teftimony of thy mouth
 fo fhall I ftill obferve.

LAMED. — *The 12th Part.*

In this fection, he fheweth, firft, How he was comforted under perfecution, by faith in God's word ; and to this end he commends the worth of the word of God, or of the Scripture, for four reafons ; the firft is, Becaufe of the ftability of it in Heaven, ve.. 89. The next, For the durable ufefulnefs of it in every age of the Church, ver. 90. The third is, Becaufe by God's word the earth is eftablifhed, ver. 90 91. The fourth is, Becaufe of his own experience of comfort and ftrength by it in his affliction, ver. 92. And in the next part, he expreffeth his thankfulnefs ; firft, By engaging his heart to the faith and obedience of the word, ver. 93. Then, By dedication of himfelf unto God, as his fervant, to be saved by him, ver. 94. Thirdly, By engagement of his heart to continue against all persecution in the obedience of the word, ver. 95. And fourthly, By commendation of the word above all things in the world, ver. 96.

89 Thy word for ever is, O Lord,
    in Heav'n settled fast:
90 Unto all generations
    thy faithfulness doth last:
  The earth thou hast established,
    and it abides by thee.
91 This day they stand, as thou ordain'dst:
    for all thy servants be.
92 Unless in thy most perfect law
    my soul delights hath found,
  I should have perished, when as
    my troubles did abound.
93 Thy precepts I will ne'er forget;
    they quick'ning to me brought.
94 Lord, I am thine, O save thou me;
    thy precepts I have sought.
95 For me the wicked have laid wait,
    me seeking to destroy;
  But I thy testimonies true
    consider will with joy.
96 An end of all perfection
    here I have seen, O God;
  But as for thy commandement,
    it is exceeding broad.

MEM. — *The 13th Part.*

He goeth on in this section, to commend the word of God, and to shew his estimation of it for eight reasons, all in order set down in the eight following verses.

97 O how love I thy law! it is
    my study all the day.
98 It makes me wiser than my foes;
    for it doth with me stay.

99 Than all my teachers, now I have
  more underſtanding far :
Becauſe my meditation
  thy teſtimonies are.
100 In underſtanding I excel
  thoſe that are ancients ;
For I endeavoured to keep
  all thy commandements.
101 My feet from each ill way I ſtay'd,
  that I may keep thy word.
102 I from thy judgments have not ſwerv'd,
  for thou haſt taught me, Lord.
103 How ſweet unto my taſte, O Lord,
  are all thy words of truth !
Yea, I do find them ſweeter far
  than honey to my mouth.
104 I thro' thy precepts, that are pure,
  do underſtanding get :
I therefore ev'ry way that's falſe
  with all my heart do hate.

NUN. — *The 14th Part.*

As in the former ſection he gave evidence of his love and reſpect to the word of God ; ſo in this ſection he giveth eight evidences of his ſincere purpoſe to make uſe of it in his practice for time to come ; all in order ſet down in the eight following verſes.

105 Thy word is to my feet a lamp,
  and to my path a light.
106 I ſworn have, and I will perform,
  to keep thy judgments right.
107 I am with ſore affliction
  ev'n overwhelm'd, O Lord :
In mercy raiſe and quicken me,
  according to thy word.

108 The free-will off'rings of my mouth
    accept, I thee befeech;
And unto me, thy fervant, Lord,
    thy judgments clearly teach.
109 Tho' ftill my foul be in my hand,
    thy laws I'll not forget.
110 I err'd not from them, tho' for me
    the wicked fnares did fet.
111 I of thy teftimonies have
    above all things made choice,
To be my heritage for ay:
    for they my heart rejoice.
112 I carefully inclined have
    my heart, ftill to attend,
That I thy ftatutes may perform
    alway unto the end.

SAMECH.—*The 15th Part.*

As he gave before evidences of his affection to the Scripture, and of his purpofe to obey it in his practice; fo in this lection he giveth fix evidences of his hatred of the evil, which is contrary to the good which is promifed and commanded in the fcripture. The firft is, ver. 113, 114. The fecond is, ver. 115. The third is, ver. 116. The fourth is, ver. 117. The fifth is, ver. 118, 119. The fixth is, ver. 120.

113 I hate the thoughts of vanity;
    but love thy law do I.
114 My fhield and hiding-place thou art:
    I on thy word rely.
115 All ye that evil-doers are,
    from me depart away;
For the commandments of my God
    I purpofe to obey.
116 According to thy faithful word
    uphold and 'ftablifh me,
That I may live, and of my hope
    afhamed never be.

117 Hold thou me up, so shall I be
   in peace and safety still ;
And to thy statutes have respect
   continually I will.
118 Thou tread'st down all that love to stray;
   false their deceit doth prove.
119 Lewd men, like dross, away thou put'st,
   therefore thy law I love.
120 For fear of thee my very flesh
   doth tremble, all dismay'd ;
And of thy righteous judgments, Lord
   my soul is much afraid.

AIN. — *The 16th Part.*

In this section he prayeth to be directed, comforted and helped against his oppressors, for six reasons. The first is, ver. 121. The second is, ver. 122. The third is, ver. 123. The fourth is, ver. 124, 125. The fifth is, ver. 126. The sixth is, ver. 127, 128.

121 To all men I have judgment done,
   performing justice right :
Then let me not be left unto
   my fierce oppressors' might.
122 For good unto thy servant, Lord,
   thy servant's surety be:
From the oppression of the proud
   do thou deliver me.
123 Mine eyes do fail with looking long
   for thy salvation,
The word of thy pure righteousness
   while I do wait upon.
124 In mercy with thy servant deal,
   thy laws me teach and shew.
125 I am thy servant, wisdom give,
   that I thy laws may know.

126 'Tis time thou work, Lord; for they
    made void thy law divine.   [have
127 Therefore thy precepts more I love
    than gold, yea, gold moſt fine.
128 Concerning all things, thy commands
    all right I judge therefore;
And ev'ry falſe and wicked way
    I perfectly abhor.

P E. — *The* 17*th Part.*

In this ſection he profeſſeth his high eſtimation of, and affection to the word of God, ver. 129, 130, 131. And unto this profeſſion of his eſtimation and affection unto the Scripture, he ſubjoineth four petitions for the right uſe and benefit thereof. The firſt is, ver. 132. The ſecond is, ver. 133. The third is, ver. 134. The fourth is, ver. 135. And then he addeth a reaſon to this laſt petition, ver. 136.

129 Thy ſtatutes, Lord, are wonderful:
    my ſoul them keeps with care.
130 The entrance of thy words gives light,
    makes wiſe who ſimple are.
131 My mouth I have wide opened,
    and panted earneſtly:
While after thy commandements
    I long'd exceedingly.
132 Look on me, Lord, and merciful
    do thou unto me prove,
As thou art wont to do to thoſe
    thy name who truly love.
133 O let my footſteps in thy word
    aright ſtill order'd be:
Let no iniquity obtain
    dominion over me.
134 From man's oppreſſion ſave thou me:
    ſo keep thy laws I will.
135 Thy face make on thy ſervant ſhine:
    teach me thy ſtatutes ſtill.

136 Rivers of waters from mine eyes
 did run down, when I saw
How wicked men run on in sin,
 and do not keep thy law.

TSADDI.—*The* 18*th Part.*

In the last verse of this section, he prayeth for a greater measure of the saving knowledge of the Scripture, most ardently, and premiseth eight reasons before the prayer, from which he doth infer his petition as a conclusion: the reasons of his petition are all set down in order in the eight following verses.

137 O Lord thou art most righteous,
 thy judgments are upright.
138 Thy testimonies thou command'st,
 most faithful are and right.
139 My zeal hath even consumed me;
 because mine enemies
Thy holy words forgotten have,
 and do thy laws despise.
140 Thy word's most pure; therefore on it
 thy servant's love is set.
141 Small and despis'd I am; yet I
 thy precepts not forget.
142 Thy righteousness is righteousness,
 which ever doth endure;
Thy holy law, Lord, also is
 the very truth most pure.
143 Trouble and anguish have me found,
 and taken hold on me;
Yet in my trouble my delight
 thy just commandments be.
144 Eternal righteousness is in
 thy testimonies all:
Lord to me understanding give,
 and ever live I shall.

KOPH.—*The 19th Part.*

In this section he falleth on another main petition unto God, for restoring unto him, and increasing in him the vigour of spiritual life by his word, 'O Lord quicken me according to thy judgment,' ver. 149. And to press this petition he useth four arguments, some going before, some following after it. The first argument hath four branches. The first branch is, ver. 145. The second is, ver. 146. The third is, ver. 147. The fourth is, ver. 148. The second argument of this his prayer is, Hear my voice according to thy loving-kindness, ver. 149. The third is, ver. 150, 151. The fourth is, ver. 152.

145 With my whole heart I cry'd ; Lord, [hear :
    I will thy word obey.
146 I cry'd to thee, save me, and I
    will keep thy laws alway.
147 I of the morning did prevent
    the dawning, and did cry :
  For all mine expectation
    did on thy word rely.
148 Mine eyes did timeously prevent
    the watches of the night,
  That in thy word, with careful mind,
    then meditate I might.
149 After thy loving-kindness hear
    my voice that calls on thee :
  According to thy judgment, Lord,
    revive and quicken me.
150 Who follow mischief, they draw nigh :
    they from thy law are far.
151 But thou art near, Lord : most firm truth
    all thy commandments are.
152 As for thy testimonies, all,
    of old this have I try'd,
  That thou hast surely founded them
    for ever to abide.

ESH.—The 20th Part.

…on he prayeth for delivery out of his affliction, and quickening of him, by confolation and fpiritual ability, …erve God till the delivery came; and to ftrengthen himfelf in the hope of obtaining this, he bringeth forth eight reafons of his petition: all in order fet down in the eight following verfes.

153 Confider mine affliction,
   in fafety do me fet:
Deliver me, O Lord, for I
   thy law do not forget.
154 After thy word revive thou me:
   fave me, and plead my caufe.
155 Salvation is from finners far;
   for they feek not thy laws.
156 O Lord, both great and manifold
   thy tender mercies be:
According to thy judgments juft,
   revive and quicken me.
157 My perfecutors many are,
   and foes that do combine;
Yet from thy teftimonies pure
   my heart doth not decline.
158 I faw tranfgreffors, and was griev'd;
   for they keep not thy word.
159 See how I love thy law! as thou
   art kind, me quicken, Lord.
160 From the beginning, all thy word
   hath been moft true and fure:
Thy righteous judgments ev'ry one
   for evermore endure.

SCHIN.— *The 21st Part.*

In this section he taketh comfort by six approved evidences of saving grace felt in himself, which he presenteth unto God to be sealed by him. The first evidence of saving grace in the Psalmist is, ver. 161. The second is, ver. 162. The third is, ver. 163. The fourth is, ver. 164. And for the confirmation of the former marks of saving grace, he commendeth the love of God's word, by two notable effects. One is, that it bringeth a glorious peace with it. Another is, that it maketh a man hold on in the way of God's obedience, whatsoever impediments or stumbling blocks shall be cast in his way, ver. 165. The fifth evidence of saving grace in the Psalmist is, ver. 166. The sixth is, ver. 167, 168.

161 Princes have persecuted me,
 although no cause they saw;
But still of thy most holy word
 my heart doth stand in awe.
162 I at thy word rejoice, as one
 of spoil that finds great store.
163 Thy law I love, but lying all
 I hate and do abhor.
164 Sev'n times a day it is my care
 to give due praise to thee:
Because of all thy judgments, Lord,
 which righteous ever be.
165 Great peace have they who love thy
 offence they shall have none. [law:
166 I hop'd for thy salvation, Lord,
 and thy commands have done.
167 My soul thy testimonies pure
 observed carefully:
On them my heart is set, and them
 I love exceedingly.
168 Thy testimonies and thy laws
 I kept with special care;
For all my works and ways each one
 before thee open are.

TAU. — *The 22d Part.*

In this laſt ſection, he cloſeth all the former ſweet meditations, and comfortable expreſſions concerning his faith and love, and the fruits thereof, with five petitions. The firſt is, ver. 169. The ſecond is, ver. 170. And then he ſtrengthens his hope in theſe two prayers, by a promiſe of thankfulneſs for any meaſure of a gracious anſwer, ver. 171, 172 The third petition is, ver. 173, 174. The fourth is, ver. 175. The fifth and laſt is, ver. 176.

169 O let my earneſt pray'r and cry
    come near before thee, Lord:
Give underſtanding unto me,
    according to thy word.
170 Let my requeſt before thee come;
    after thy word me free.
171 My lips ſhall utter praiſe, when thou
    haſt taught thy laws to me.
172 My tongue of thy moſt bleſſed word
    ſhall ſpeak, and it confeſs:
Becauſe all thy commandements
    are perfect righteouſneſs.
173 Let thy ſtrong hand make help to me:
    thy precepts are my choice.
174 I long'd for thy ſalvation, Lord,
    and in thy law rejoice.
175 O let my ſoul live, and it ſhall
    give praiſes unto thee:
And let thy judgments gracious
    be helpful unto me.
176 I, like a loſt ſheep, went aſtray;
    thy ſervant ſeek and find:
For thy commands I ſuff'red not
    to ſlip out of my mind.

PSALM CXX.
A Song of Degrees.

The scope of this Psalm is, by the experience of the Psalmist, to teach and comfort such as shall be traduced, and falsly slandered. His exercise and deliverance is set down summarily, ver. 1. And then in the rest of the Psalm, he first puts up his petition to be saved from the bloody tongue of the calumniator, ver. 2. and then denounceth God's judgment against him, ver. 3, 4. and closeth with a lamentation, ver. 5, 6, 7.

1 IN my distress to God I cry'd,
    and he gave ear to me.
2 From lying lips, and guileful tongue,
    O Lord, my soul set free.
3 What shall be giv'n thee? or what shall
    be done to thee, false tongue?
4 Ev'n burning coals of juniper,
    sharp arrows of the strong.
5 Wo's me, that I in Meshech am
    a sojourner so long;
  That I in tabernacles dwell
    to Kedar that belong.
6 My soul with him that hateth peace
    hath long a dweller been.
7 I am for peace: but when I speak,
    for battle they are keen.

PSALM CXXI.
A Song of Degrees.

The scope of this Psalm is to shew, that howsoever we are ready to seek help any where else, rather than in God, yet no help is to be had, except from God; perfect help, and full delivery is to be had in him undoubtedly, as the Psalmist's experience and example of faith doth teach; wherein, the Psalmist leaving all other confidences beside God, betaketh him to God Almighty only, ver. 1, 2. And from his own experience, giveth encouragement to all God's people to place their confidence in God alone, by six promises, in the six verses following, to the end of the Psalm.

1 I To the hills will lift mine eyes,
    from whence doth come mine aid.
2 My safety cometh from the Lord,
    who heav'n and earth hath made.
3 Thy foot he'll not let slide : nor will
    he slumber that thee keeps.
4 Behold, he that keeps Israel,
    he slumbers not, nor sleeps.
5 The Lord thee keeps : the Lord thy shade
    on thy right hand doth stay.
6 The moon by night thee shall not smite,
    nor yet the sun by day.
7 The Lord shall keep thy soul : he shall
    preserve thee from all ill.
8 Henceforth thy going out and in
    God keep for ever will.

PSALM CXXII.

A Song of Degrees of David.

The ark of God had for a long time moved from place to place; at length the Lord revealeth unto David the place whereof Moses hath spoken, to be Sion where the ark should rest, and there David set up the ark, having revealed unto the people the oracle; whereupon the people did heartily embrace the will of God, and came to that place appointed for public worship, and did invite one another to go up to worship. In this Psalm, we have first, David's joy for the people's willingness to assemble unto the Lord's house, ver. 1, 2. In the next place, he praises Jerusalem, ver. 3, 4, 5. In the third place, he exhorteth all to pray for the peace of Jerusalem, representing the universal Church, and useth some reasons to set them forward on the duty, ver. 6, 7, 8, 9.

1 I Joy'd, when to the house of God,
    go up, they said to me.
2 Jerusalem, within thy gates
    our feet shall standing be.

3 Jerus'lem as a city is
	compactly built together:
4 Unto that place the tribes go up,
	the tribes of God go thither:

To Ifra'l's teſtimony, there
	to God's name thanks to pay.
5 For thrones of judgment, ev'n the thrones
	of David's houſe, there ſtay.
6 Pray that Jeruſalem may have
	peace and felicity:
Let them that love thee, and thy peace,
	have ſtill proſperity.
7 Therefore I wiſh that peace may ſtill
	within thy walls remain,
And ever may thy palaces
	proſperity retain.
8 Now, for my friend's and brethren's ſakes,
	peace be in thee, I'll ſay.
9 And for the houſe of God our Lord,
	I'll ſeek thy good alway.

PSALM CXXIII.
A Song of Degrees.

he ſcope of this Pſalm is to teach the Lord's people, how to carry themſelves when they are oppreſſed by the tyranny of their proud adverſaries, and are deſtitute of all help under Heaven; wherein the Pſalmiſt maketh his addreſs to God, in patience, humility, and hope, ver. 1, 2 and prayeth for comfort under, and relief from the contempt of the proud adverſaries, ver. 3, 4

O Thou that dwelleſt in the heav'ns,
	I lift mine eyes to thee.
Behold, as ſervants' eyes do look
	their maſter's hand to ſee;

As hand-maid's eyes her miſtreſs' hand,
  ſo do our eyes attend
Upon the Lord our God, until
  to us he mercy ſend.
3 O Lord, be gracious to us,
  unto us gracious be :
Becauſe repleniſh'd with contempt
  exceedingly are we.
4 Our ſoul is fill'd with ſcorn of thoſe
  that at their eaſe abide,
And with the inſolent contempt
  of thoſe that ſwell in pride.

PSALM CXXIV.
A Song of Degrees of David.

The ſcope of this Pſalm is, firſt, to acknowledge the delivery of the Church to be evidently the Lord's own work, the danger being ſo great out of which they were lately delivered, ver. 1, 2, 3, 4, 5. And next, to bleſs the Lord for their preſervation, ver. 6, 7, 8.

1 HAD not the Lord been on our ſide,
    may Iſrael now ſay :
2 Had not the Lord been on our ſide,
    when men roſe us to ſlay,
3 They had us ſwallow'd quick, when as
    their wrath 'gainſt us did flame.
4 Waters had cov'red us, our ſoul
    had ſunk beneath the ſtream.
5 Then had the waters ſwelling high,
    over our ſoul made way.
6 Bleſt be the Lord, who to their teeth
    us gave not for a prey.
7 Our ſoul's eſcaped, as a bird
    out of the fowler's ſnare ;
The ſnare aſunder broken is,
    and we eſcaped are.

8 Our sure and all-sufficient help
    is in JEHOVAH's name:
  His name who did the heav'n create,
    and who the earth did frame.

Another of the same.

1 NOW Israel
    may say, and that truly,
  If that the Lord
    had not our cause maintain'd:
2 If that the Lord
    had not our right sustain'd,
  When cruel men
    against us furiously
  Rose up in wrath,
    to make of us their prey.
3 Then certainly
    they had devour'd us all,
  And swallow'd quick,
    for ought that we could deem:
  Such was their rage,
    as we might well esteem.
4 And as fierce floods
    before them all things drown,
  So had they brought
    our soul to death quite down.
5 The raging streams,
    with their proud swelling waves,
  Had then our soul
    o'erwhelmed in the deep:
6 But blest be God,
    who doth us safely keep,

And hath not giv'n
 us for a living prey
Unto their teeth,
 and bloody cruelty.

7 Ev'n as a bird
 out of the fowler's snare
Escapes away,
 so is our soul set free:
Broke are their nets,
 and thus escaped we.
8 Therefore our help
 is in the Lord's great name,
Who heav'n and earth
 by his great pow'r did frame.

PSALM CXXV.
A Song of Degrees.

The scope of this Psalm is to confirm the faith of the Believer, persecuted and oppressed by the wicked, that he may hold out walking in the right way of God's obedience; and to this end, the Psalmist useth four arguments. The first is, from the stability of the Believer's felicity, ver. 1, 2. The second, is from the short time of his trouble, which he shall suffer by persecutors, ver. 3. The third, is from the goodness which God will manifest toward him, set down in the Psalmist's prayer, ver. 4. The fourth, is from the Lord's judgments upon back-sliding Hypocrites, who make shift for themselves to be freed from trouble by unlawful means, ver. 5.

1 THEY in the Lord that firmly trust,
 shall be like Sion hill,·
Which at no time can be remov'd,
 but standeth ever still.
2 As round about Jerusalem
 the mountains stand alway,
The Lord his folk doth compass so
 from henceforth and for ay.

3 For ill men's rod upon the lot
    of juſt men ſhall not lie :
  Leſt righteous men ſtretch forth their
    unto iniquity. [hands
4 Do thou to all thoſe that be good,
    thy goodneſs, Lord, impart;
  And do thou good to thoſe that are
    upright within their heart.
5 But as for ſuch as turn aſide
    after their crooked way,
  God ſhall lead forth with wicked men :
    on Iſra'l peace ſhall ſtay.

PSALM CXXVI.
A Song of Degrees.

This is the Church's ſong o thankſgiving foꞏ her delivery from the captivity of Babylon, wherein, fiꞏſt, the gꞏeatneſs of the mercy is ſet down, verꞏ 1, 2, 3 Then a prayer to God for enlarging of the benefit, by making many tꞏ embrace the offer of delivery, ver. 4. And thirdly, an encouraging conſolation to ſuch as had returꞏned or ſhould return from Babylon to their own land, ver. 5, 6.

1 WHen Sion's bondage God turn'd back,
    as men that dream'd, were we.
2 Then fill'd with laughter was our mouth,
    our tongue with melody :
  They 'mong the heathen ſaid, The Lord
    great things for them hath wrought.
3 The Lord hath done great things for us ;
    whence joy to us is brought.
4 As ſtreams of water in the ſouth,
    our bondage, Lord, recall.
5 Who ſow in tears, a reaping time
    of joy enjoy they ſhall.

6 That man, who, bearing precious seed,
    in going forth doth mourn,
  He doubtless, bringing back his sheaves,
    rejoicing shall return.

PSALM CXXVII.
A Song of Degrees for Solomon.

The scope of this Psalm is to shew, first, That the defence of our persons, and success in our affairs, do depend upon God's blessing upon the means used, ver. 1, 2. Next, To shew that multitudes of God's children, is God's blessing also, ver. 3, 4, 5. The Psalm is intituled for Solomon, who was to build the house of God, and to enlarge the kingdom of Israel.

1 EXCEPT the Lord do build the house,
    the builders lose their pain;
  Except the Lord the city keep,
    the watchman watch in vain.
2 'Tis vain for you to rise betimes,
    or late from rest to keep,
  To feed on sorrow's bread: so gives
    he his beloved sleep.
3 Lo, children are God's heritage,
    the womb's fruit his reward.
4 The sons of youth as arrows are,
    for strong men's hands prepar'd.
5 O happy is the man that hath
    his quiver fill'd with those:
  They, unashamed, in the gate
    shall speak unto their foes.

PSALM CXXVIII.
A Song of Degrees.

The scope of this Psalm is to shew the blessedness of the man that feareth God, which doth appear, first, In temporal blessing of him in his calling, ver. 1, 2. Secondly, In his family, ver. 3, 4. Thirdly, in pouring spiritual blessings upon him, ver. 5, 6.

1 BLEST is each one that fears the Lord,
    and walketh in his ways.
2 For of thy labour thou shalt eat,
    and happy be always.
3 Thy wife shall as a fruitful vine
    by thy house sides be found;
Thy children like to olive plants
    about thy table round.
4 Behold, the man that fears the Lord,
    thus blessed shall he be.
5 The Lord shall out of Sion give
    his blessing unto thee;
Thou shalt Jerus'lem's good behold
    whilst thou on earth dost dwell.
6 Thou shalt thy children's children see,
    and peace on Israel.

PSALM CXXIX.

A Song of Degrees.

The scope of this Psalm is, to confirm the faith of God's people against persecution. The parts thereof are two. The former is, Praise to God for delivering many times his Church from the oppression of persecutors, ver. 1, 2, 3, 4. The other hath a prophetical curse against the enemies of the Church, ver. 5, 6, 7, 8.

1 OFT did they vex me from my youth,
    may Isra'l now declare:
2 Oft did they vex me from my youth;
    yet not victorious were.
3 The plowers plow'd upon my back:
    they long their furrows drew.
4 The righteous Lord did cut the cords
    of the ungodly crew.

5 Let Sion's haters all be turn'd
    back with confusion.
6 As grass on houses tops be they,
    which fades e'er it be grown :
7 Whereof enough to fill his hand
    the mower cannot find ;
  Nor can the man his bosom fill,
    whose work is sheaves to bind.
8 Neither say they who do go by,
    God's blessing on you rest :
  We, in the name of God the Lord,
    do with you to be blest.

PSALM CXXX.
A Song of Degrees.

This Psalm containeth the exercise of the Psalmist, wrestling under the sense of sin with fearful temptations, which were like to overcome him, wherein he prayeth for relief, ver. 1, 2. opposeth God's mercy to his justice, ver. 3, 4. and waiteth for comfort, ver. 5, 6 then he bringeth forth the use which he maketh of the relief and comfort which God gave unto him, by encouraging the Church to trust in God's mercy, because he will deliver his people from all trouble and sin, ver. 7, 8.

1 LORD, from the depths to thee I cry'd.
2   My voice, Lord, do thou hear :
  Unto my supplication's voice
    give an attentive ear.
3 Lord, who shall stand, if thou, O Lord,
    should'st mark iniquity ?
4 But yet with thee forgiveness is,
    that fear'd thou mayest be.
5 I wait for God, my soul doth wait,
    my hope is in his word.
6 More than they that for morning watch,
    my soul waits for the Lord :

I say, more than they that do watch
    the morning light to see.
7 Let Israel hope in the Lord,
    for with him mercies be;

And plenteous redemption
    is ever found with him.
8 And from all his iniquities
    he Isra'l shall redeem.

PSALM CXXXI.

A Song of Degrees of David.

In this Psalm, the Prophet minding to teach the Godly to be humble before God, however matters go with them, doth propound his own example, ver. 1, 2. that so the Believer may persevere in hope, ver. 3. He proveth his humility by the lowliness of his heart, sobriety of carriage, and keeping himself within his vocation, ver. 1. and by the submission of his will unto God's dispensation, ver. 2. The use and profit whereof, as he had found in his own experience, so he recommendeth the following of his example unto all God's people, as the way to be constant in their hope, ver. 3.

1 MY heart not haughty is, O Lord;
    mine eyes not lofty be:
Nor do I deal in matters great,
    or things too high for me.

2 I surely have myself behav'd
    with quiet sp'rit and mild,
As child of mother wean'd: my soul
    is like a weaned child.

3 Upon the Lord let all the hope
    of Israel rely,
Ev'n from the time that present is
    unto eternity.

PSALM CXXXII.

A Song of Degrees.

In this Psalm the Church is taught to pray, according to the covenant made with David, representing Christ. First, For the maintainance of true religion, to ver. 10. Next, For the continuing of the kingdom in his race, and preservation of the Church of Israel, and so of the kingdom and Church of Christ figured by it. In the first petition, He prayeth for the Lord's affectionate and effectual remembrance of David, and of the sufferings undergone by David, for maintaining his covenant with God, ver. 1. And then, calleth to mind the care which David had in settling of the place of God's worship, ver. 2, 3, 4. 5. Thirdly, He sheweth, how after the Lord's departing from Shiloh, his ark was found in Kirjath-jearim, and thence brought up the city of David, ver. 6. Fourthly, The Church professeth her willingness and purpose to worship the Lord, now ascended unto mount Sion, ver. 7, 8. And fifthly, He prayeth for holiness of doctrine in the Lord's Ministers, and joy to the Godly in obeying them, ver. 9. In the next petition, first, The Church prayeth for the covenant's sake made with David, that the Lord would not withdraw countenance from his offspring, ver. 10. Then, to strengthen their faith in the petition, they repeat the covenant of God made with David, as we have it, Psalm lxxxix. concerning his offspring, and mainly concerning Christ, ver. 11, 12. Then, they pray concerning the temple and city of Jerusalem, representing the universal Church, ver. 13, 14. and concerning his ministry, ver. 15, 16. and concerning the increase of Christ's kingdom, and for confusion of his enemies, ver. 17, 18. for we must not conceive this prayer delivered to the Church for the use of all ages, to have the full accomplishment, except Christ and his Church and kingdom be mainly comprehended and aimed at in it.

1 DAVID, and his afflictions all,
    Lord, do thou think upon:
2 How unto God he sware, and vow'd
    to Jacob's Mighty One.
3 I will not come within my house,
    nor rest in bed at all:
4 Nor shall mine eyes take any sleep,
    nor eye-lids slumber shall.

5 Till for the Lord a place I find,
    where he may make abode :
A place of habitation
    for Jacob's mighty God.
6 Lo, at the place of Ephratah
    of it we underſtood,
And wé did find it in the fields
    and city of the wood.
7 We'll go into his tabernacles,
    and at his footſtool bow :
8 Ariſe, O Lord, into thy reſt,
    th' ark of thy ſtrength and thou.
9 O let thy prieſts be cloathed, Lord,
    with truth and righteouſneſs :
And let all thoſe that are thy Saints,
    ſhout loud for joyfulneſs.
10 For thine own ſervant David's ſake,
    do not deny thy grace,
Nor of thine own anointed One
    turn thou away the face.
11 The Lord in truth to David ſware,
    he will not turn from it,
I of thy body's fruit will make
    upon thy throne to ſit.
12 My cov'nant if thy ſons will keep,
    and laws to them made known ;
Their children then ſhall alſo ſit
    for ever on thy throne.
13 For God of Sion hath made choice,
    there he deſires to dwell.
14 This is my reſt : here ſtill I'll ſtay,
    for I do like it well.

15 Her food I'll greatly bless : her poor
    with bread will satisfy.
16 Her Priests I'll clothe with health : her
    shall shout forth joyfully.   [Saints
17 And there will I make David's horn
    to bud forth pleasantly :
For Him that mine Anointed is,
    a lamp ordain'd have I.
18 As with a garment I will clothe
    with shame his en'mies all :
But yet the crown that he doth wear
    upon him flourish shall.

PSALM CXXXIII.

A Song of Degrees of David.

This Psalm doth fit the condition of God's people, in David's time, when after their civil wars they were brought to a happy unity in religion, and civil government. This sort of concord and communion of Saints is here commended to the Church as both pleasant and profitable. The goodness of it is spoken of, ver. 1. The pleasantness of it, ver. 2. The profitableness of it, ver. 3.

1 BEHOLD, how good a thing it is,
    and how becoming well,
Together such as brethren are
    in unity to dwell.
2 Like precious ointment on the head,
    that down the beard did flow,
Ev'n Aaron's beard, and to the skirts
    did of his garments go
3 As Hermon's dew, the dew that doth
    on Sion hills descend :
For there the blessing God commands,
    life that shall never end.

PSALM CXXXIV.

A Song of Degrees.

In this short Psalm, the spirit of the Lord, by the mouth of the Psalmist, exhorteth the Lord's Ministers to go about the exercise of their public Ministry, in praying, preaching, and praising God, ver. 1, 2. and blessing the congregation met together.

1 BEHOLD, bless ye the Lord, all ye
   that his attendants are,
 Ev'n you that in God's temple be,
   and praise him nightly there.
2 Your hands within God's holy place
   lift up and praise his name.
3 From Sion hill the Lord thee bless,
   that heaven and earth did frame.

PSALM CXXXV.

The scope of this Psalm, is to set forth the praises of the Lord; wherein there is an earnest exhortation of all the Church, and of all the Lord's Ministers to praise God, ver. 1, 2, 3. whereunto are added seven motives or reasons, from ver. 3. to ver. 12. In the next place, the Psalmist turneth his speech towards the Lord, and praiseth him, and giveth two reasons more for the praising of God, ver. 13, 14, 15, 16, 17, 18. In the third place, more specially he exhorteth the Ministers, and every particular Member of the Church, to praise God, and so closeth with blessing of him.

1 PRAISE ye the Lord, the Lord's name
   his servants praise ye God.   [praise;
2 Who stand in God's house, in the courts
   of our God make abode.
3 Praise ye the Lord, for he is good,
   unto him praises sing:
 Sing praises to his name, because
   it is a pleasant thing.
4 For Jacob to himself the Lord
   did choose of his good pleasure,
 And he hath chosen Israel
   for his peculiar treasure.

5 Becaufe I know affuredly
   the Lord is very great,
 And that our Lord above all Gods
   in glory hath his feat.
6 What things foever pleas'd the Lord,
   that in the heav'n did he,
 And in the earth, the feas, and all
   the places deep that be.
7 He from the ends of earth doth make
   the vapours to afcend,
 With rain he lightnings makes, and wind
   doth from his treafures fend.
8 Egypt's firft-born from man to beaft
9 who fmote. Strange tokens he
 On Pharaoh and his fervants fent,
   Egypt, in midft of thee.
10 He fmote great nations, flew great kings;
11 Sihon of Hefhbon king;
 And Og of Bafhan, and to nought
   did Canaan's kingdoms bring.
12 And for a wealthy heritage
   their pleafant land he gave,
 An heritage which Ifrael
   his chofen folk fhould have.
13 Thy name, O Lord, fhall ftill endure,
   and thy memorial
 With honour fhall continu'd be
   to generations all.
14 For why, the righteous God will judge
   his people righteoufly,
 Concerning thofe that do him ferve,
   himfelf repent will he.

15 The idols of the nations
    of silver are and gold,
And by the hands of men is made
    their fashion and mould.
16 Mouths have they, but they do not
    eyes, but they do not see :   [speak;
17 Ears have they, but hear not, and in
    their mouths no breathing be.
18 Their makers are like them, so are
    all that on them rely.
19 O Isra'l's house, bless God : bless God,
    O Aaron's family.
20 O bless the Lord, of Levi's house
    ye who his servant's are ;
And bless the holy name of God,
    all ye the Lord that fear.
21 And blessed be the Lord our God,
    from Sion's holy hill.
Who dwelleth at Jerusalem.
    The Lord, O praise ye still.

PSALM CXXXVI.

This Psalm is an exhortation to confess God's goodness and mercy, and to praise and thank him for the manifestation thereof, in so many sundry works of his ; up in this ground, because the fountain of his mercy, whence his works did flow, doth run still, and endure for ever, to the benefit of his own people in special. The reasons of the exhortation unto thanks and praise are set down in order, so many in number as the verses are, unto every one whereof is added one common reason, from the everlasting endurance of his mercy. In the first place, the exhortation is thrice propounded, with reasons taken from the Lord's attributes or names, ver. 1, 2, 3. In the second place, reasons are given from his works, and in special from the work of Creation, ver. 4. to ver. 10. In the third place, reasons are given from the work of Redemption of Israel, and bringing them forth out of Egypt, and planting them in Canaan, from ver. 10. to ver. 23. In the fourth place, reasons of thanks are given, from his late mercy to the Church in the Pſalmiſt's time, ver. 23, 24. And laſt of all, a reaſon is given from his goodneſs to all living creatures, ver. 25. whereupon he cloſeth with an exhortation unto thankſgiving to the God of Heaven, ver. 26.

1 GIVE thanks to God, for good is he:
    for mercy hath he ever.
2 Thanks to the God of Gods give ye:
    for his grace faileth never.
3 Thanks give the Lord of Lords unto:
    for mercy hath he ever.
4 Who only wonders great can do:
    for his grace faileth never.
5 Who by his wiſdom made heav'ns high:
    for mercy hath he ever.
6 Who ſtretch'd the earth above the ſea,
    for his grace faileth never.
7 To him that made the great lights ſhine:
    for mercy hath he ever.
8 The ſun to rule till day decline:
    for his grace faileth never.
9 The moon and ſtars to rule by night:
    for mercy hath he ever.
10 Who Egypt's firſt-born kill'd outright:
    for his grace faileth never.
11 And Iſra'l brought from Egypt land:
    for mercy hath he ever.
12 With ſtretch'd out arm, and with ſtrong
    for his grace faileth never.   [hand:
13 By whom the Red Sea parted was:
    for mercy hath he ever.
14 And through its midſt made Iſra'l paſs:
    for his grace faileth never.

15 But Pharaoh and his hoſt did drown :
    for mercy hath he ever.
16 Who through the deſert led his own :
    for his grace faileth never.
17 To him great kings who overthrew :
    for he hath mercy ever.
18 Yea, famous kings in battle ſlew :
    for his grace faileth never.
19 Ev'n Sihon, King of Amorites :
    for he hath mercy ever
20 And Og, the King of Baſhanites :
    for his grace faileth never.
21 Their land in heritage to have :
    (for mercy hath he ever.)
22 His ſervant Iſra'l right he gave :
    for his grace faileth never.
23 In our low ſtate who on us thought :
    for he hath mercy ever.
24 And from our foes our freedom wrought:
    for his grace faileth never.
25 Who doth all fleſh with food relieve :
    for he hath mercy ever.
26 Thanks to the God of heaven give :
    for his grace faileth never.

Another of the ſame.

1 PRAISE God, for he is kind :
    His mercy laſts for ay.
2 Give thanks with heart and mind
    To God of Gods alway :
        For certainly
        His mercies dure
        . Moſt firm and ſure
        Eternally.

3 The Lord of Lords praife ye,
  Whofe mercies ftill endure.
4 Great wonders only he
  Doth work by his great pow'r:
      For certainly, &c.

5 Which God omnipotent,
  By might and wifdom high,
  The heav'n and firmanent
  Did frame, as we may fee:
      For certainly, &c.

6 To him who did out-ftretch
  This earth fo great and wide,
  Above the waters reach,
  Making it to abide:
      For certainly, &c.

7 Great lights he made to be;
  For his grace lafteth ay.
8 Such as the fun we fee,
  To rule the lightfome day:
      For certainly, &c.

9 Alfo the moon fo clear,
  Which fhineth in our fight;
  The ftars that do appear,
  To guide the darkfome night;
      For certainly, &c.

10 To him that Egypt fmote,
   Who did his meffage fcorn;
   And in his anger hot
   Did kill all their firft-born:
      For certainly, &c.
11 Thence Ifra'l out he brought:
   For his grace lafteth ever.

12 With a strong hand he wrought,
 And stretch'd-out arm deliver:
  For certainly, &c.
13 The sea he cut in two:
 For his grace lasteth still.
14 And through its midst to go
 Made his own Israel:
  For certainly, &c.
15 But overwhelm'd and lost
 Was proud King Pharaoh,
 With all his mighty host,
 And chariots there also:
  For certainly, &c.
16 To him who powerfully
 His chosen people led,
 Ev'n through the desart dry,
 And in that place them fed:
  For certainly, &c.
17 To him great Kings who smote:
 For his grace hath no bound.
18 Who flew, and spared not
 Kings famous and renown'd:
  For certainly, &c.
19 Sihon, th' Amorite's King:
 For his grace lasteth ever.
20 Og, also who did reign
 The land of Bashan over;
  For certainly, &c.
21 Their land by lot he gave:
 For his grace faileth never.
22 That Isra'l might it have
 In heritage for ever:
  For certainly, &c.

23 Who hath remembered
 Us in our low estate;
24 And us delivered
 From foes which did us hate:
  For certainly, &c.
25 Who to all flesh gives food:
 For his grace faileth never.
26 Give thanks to God most good,
 The God of heav'n for ever:
  For certainly, &c.

PSALM CXXXVII.

This Psalm may be divided into three parts. In the first, is set down the lamentable condition wherein the Lord's people were in their captivity in Babylon, ver. 1, 2, 3. In the next, is their constancy in religion, ver. 4, 5, 6. In the third, is their denouncing of judgment by way of imprecation against the instruments and chief authors of their calamity, ver. 7, 8, 9.

1 BY Babel's stream we sat and wept,
   when Sion we thought on:
2 In midst thereof we hang'd our harps
   the willow-trees upon.
3 For there a song required they,
   who did us captive bring;
  Our spoiler's call'd for mirth, and said,
   A song of Sion sing.
4 O how the Lord's song shall we sing
   within a foreign land?
5 If thee, Jerus'lem, I forget,
   skill part from my right-hand.
6 My tongue to my mouth's roof let cleave,
   if I do thee forget,
  Jerusalem, and thee above
   my chief joy do not set.

7 Remember Edom's children, Lord,
    who, in Jerus'lem's day,
  Ev'n unto its foundation
    raze, raze it quite, did say.
8 O daughter thou of Babylon,
    near to destruction:
  Blest shall he be that thee rewards,
    as thou to us hast done.
9 Yea, happy surely shall he be,
    thy tender little ones
  Who shall lay hold upon, and them
    shall dash against the stones.

PSALM CXXXVIII.
A Psalm of David.

This Psalm is David's thanksgiving unto God, and praising of him for the experience he had of his love and faithfulness. The promise of praise or thanksgiving is set down, ver. 1. and six reasons are to be subjoined in the verses following, which are closed with a prayer in the end of the Psalm.

1 THEE will I praise with all my heart,
    I will sing praise to thee
2 Before the gods: and worship will
    toward thy sanctuary.
  I'll praise thy name, ev'n for thy truth,
    and kindness of thy love:
  For thou thy word hast magnify'd
    all thy great name above.
3 Thou didst me answer in the day
    when I to thee did cry:
  And thou my fainting soul with strength
    didst strengthen inwardly.
         O

4 All Kings upon the earth that are,
    shall give thee praise, O Lord :
  When as they from thy mouth shall hear
    thy true and faithful word.
5 Yea, in the righteous ways of God
    with gladness they shall sing :
  For great's the glory of the Lord,
    who doth for ever reign.
6 Though God be high, yet he respects
    all those that lowly be :
  Whereas the proud and lofty ones
    afar off knoweth he.
7 Though I in midst of trouble walk,
    I life from thee shall have ;
  'Gainst my foes' wrath thou'lt stretch thine
    thy right hand shall me save.   [hand,
8 Surely, that which concerneth me,
    the Lord will perfect make :
  Lord, still thy mercy lasts, do not
    thine own hand's works forsake.

PSALM CXXXIX.

To the chief Musician, a Psalm of David.

David being wickedly slandered and persecuted by his adversaries, findeth his zeal kindled against them ; and least his own heart's corruption should deceive him, as being carnal in this matter, he presenteth his heart unto God, the all-seeing and every-where present Judge of the secrets of all hearts, and he presenteth also his adversaries both persons and cause, with his own carriage toward them, to be tried by God, praying that himself may be directed toward life everlasting.

In the first place, the omniscience of God is declared, ver. 1. 2, 3, 4, 5, 6. In the next, the omnipresence of God, with his omniscience is set forth, ver. 7, 8, 9, 10, 11, 12. In the third place, the reason is given of God's so exact knowledge of all the secrets of his heart, because the Lord did form and fashion him, in so wonderfully wise and powerful a way, as he could neither express nor comprehend, ver. 13, 14, 15, 16, 17, 18. In the fourth place, he confesseth to

God his judgment of wicked men, and his hatred of their ways, making God, who is the searcher of hearts, witness and judge of his sincerity, corrector and director of his course toward everlasting life, ver. 19, 20, 21, 22, 23, 24.

1 O Lord, thou hast me search'd and known.
2   Thou know'st my sitting down
   And rising up; yea, all my thoughts
     afar to thee are known.
3 My footsteps, and my lying down,
     thou compassest always:
   Thou also most entirely art
     acquaint with all my ways.
4 For in my tongue, before I speak,
     not any word can be,
   But altogether, lo, O Lord,
     it is well known to thee.
5 Behind, before, thou hast beset,
     and laid on me thine hand.
6 Such knowledge is too strange for me,
     too high to understand.
7 From thy Sp'rit whither shall I go?
     or from thy presence fly?
8 Ascend I heav'n, lo! thou art there:
     there, if in hell, I lie.
9 Take I the morning's wings, and dwell
     in utmost parts of sea:
10 Ev'n there, Lord, shall thy hand me lead,
     thy right hand hold shall me.
11 If I do say, that darkness shall
     me cover from thy sight;
   Then surely shall the very night
     about me be as light.

12 Yea, darkneſs hideth not from thee,
   but night doth ſhine as day :
 To thee the darkneſs and the light
   are both alike alway.
13 For thou poſſeſſed haſt my reins,
   and thou haſt cov'red me,
 When I within my mother's womb
   incloſed was by thee.
14 Thee will I praiſe, for fearfully
   and ſtrangely made I am :
 Thy works are marv'llous, and right well
   my ſoul doth know the ſame.
15 My ſubſtance was not hid from thee,
   when as in ſecret I
 Was made ; and in earth's loweſt parts
   was wrought moſt curiouſly.
16 Thine eyes my ſubſtance did behold,
   yet being unperfect :
 And in the volume of thy book
   my members all were writ ;

 Which after in continuance
   were faſhion'd ev'ry one,
 When as they yet all ſhapeleſs were,
   and of them there was none.
17 How precious alſo are thy thoughts,
   O gracious God, to me !
 And in their ſum how paſſing great,
   and numberleſs they be !
18 If I ſhould count them, than the ſand
   they more in number be :
 What time ſoever I awake,
   I ever am with thee.

19 Thou, Lord, wilt sure the wicked slay:
   hence from me bloody men.
20 Thy foes against thee loudly speak,
   and take thy name in vain.
21 Do not I hate all those, O Lord,
   that hatred bear to thee?
   With those that up against thee rise
   can I but grieved be?
22 With perfect hatred them I hate:
   my foes I them do hold.
23 Search me, O God, and know my heart;
   try me, my thoughts unfold.
24 And see if any wicked way
   there be at all in me,
   And in thine everlasting way
   to me a leader be.

PSALM CXL.

To the chief Musician, a Psalm of David.

David, being pursued for his life, and loaded with false calumnies of wicked men, prayeth, first, for deliverance from them, ver. 1, 2, 3, 4, 5, 6, 7. Secondly, prayeth against them, ver. 8, 9, 10, 11. Thirdly, declareth the Lord's gracious answer, ver. 12, 13.

1 LORD, from the ill and froward man
   give me deliverance:
   And do thou safe preserve me from
   the man of violence.
2 Who in their heart mischievous things
   are meditating ever;
   And they for war assembled are
   continually together.

3 Much like unto a ſerpent's tongue,
    their tongues they ſharp do make;
And underneath their lips there lies
    the poiſon of a ſnake.
4 Lord, keep me from the wicked's hands,
    from vi'lent men me ſave,
Who utterly to overthrow
    my goings purpos'd have.
5 The proud for me a ſnare have hid,
    and cords, yea, they a net
Have by the way-ſide for me ſpread:
    they gins for me have ſet.
6 I ſaid unto the Lord, Thou art
    my God: unto the cry
Of all my ſupplications,
    Lord, do thine ear apply.
7 O God the Lord, who art the ſtrength
    of my ſalvation:
A cov'ring, in the day of war,
    my head thou haſt put on.
8 Unto the wicked man, O Lord,
    his wiſhes do not grant:
Nor further thou his ill device,
    leaſt they themſelves ſhould vaunt.
9 As for the head and chief of thoſe
    about that compaſs me,
Ev'n by the miſchief of their lips
    let thou them cov'red be.
10 Let burning coals upon them fall
    them throw in firey flame;
And in deep pits, that they no more,
    may riſe out of the ſame.

11 Let not an evil speaker be
 on earth established:
Mischief shall hunt the vi'lent man
 till he be ruined.
12 I know God will th' afflicted's cause
 maintain, and poor men's right.
13 Surely the just shall praise thy name,
 th' upright dwell in thy sight.

PSALM CXLI.

A Psalm of David.

The Psalmist being in distress by the malicious persecution of his adversaries, prayeth for relief, and for a holy carriage under his trouble, till his own full delivery, and till his enemies destruction should come. The petitions are seven. The first is general, for acceptation of his person, and granting of his prayer, ver. 1, 2. The next is, for direction of his speeches, ver. 3. The third is, for guiding of his heart and actions, ver. 4. The fourth is, for the benefit of the fellowship of the Saints, by their wholsome counsel and admonition, ver. 5. with the reasons thereof, ver. 6, 7. The fifth is, for the comfort of spiritual communion with God, ver. 8. The sixth is, for preservation from the plots of the enemies, ver. 6 The seventh is, for the overthrow of his enemies, ver 10.

1 O Lord, I unto thee do cry,
 do thou make haste to me;
And give an ear unto my voice,
 when I cry unto thee.
2 As incense let my prayer be
 directed in thine eyes;
And the uplifting of my hands
 as th' ev'ning sacrifice.
3 Set, Lord, a watch before my mouth,
 keep of my lips the door.
4 My heart incline thou not unto
 the ills I should abhor,

To practife wicked works wjth men
　　　that work iniquity :
　And with their delicates, my tafte
　　　let me not fatisfy.
5 Let him that right'ous is, me fmite,
　　　it fhall a kindnefs be ;
　Let him reprove, I fhall it count
　　　a precious oil to me :
　Such fmiting fhall not break my head :
　　　for yet the time fhall fall,
　When I in their calamities
　　　to God pray for them fhall.
6 When as their judges down fhall be
　　　in ftony places caft :
　Then fhall they hear my words, for they
　　　fhall fweet be to their tafte.
7 About the grave's devouring mouth
　　　our bones are fcatt'red round,
　As wood which men do cut and cleave,
　　　lies fcatt'red on the ground.
8 But unto thee, O God the Lord,
　　　mine eyes uplifted be :
　My foul do not leave deftitute,
　　　my truft is fet on thee.
9 Lord, keep me fafely from the fnares
　　　which they for me prepare,
　And from the fubtile gins of them
　　　that wicked workers are.
10 Let workers of iniquity
　　　into their own nets fall,
　Whilft I do by thine help, efcape
　　　the danger of them all.

PSALM CXLII.

Maschil of David; a Prayer when he was in the Cave.

This Psalm doth shew what was David's exercise, when he was in the cave of one of the mountains of En-gedi, (1. Sam. xxiv.) flying from Saul; wherein he first setteth down his betaking of himself to prayer in general, ver. 1, 2. Secondly, the straits wherein he was for the time, ver. 3, 4. Thirdly, what were the special petitions of his prayer, with the reasons thereof, ver. 5, 6, 7.

1 I With my voice cry'd to the Lord,
    with it made my request:
2 Pour'd out to him my plaint; to him
    my trouble I exprest.
3 When in me was o'erwhelm'd my sp'rit,
    then well thou knew'st my way:
Where I did walk, a snare for me
    they privily did lay.
4 I look'd on my right hand, and view'd,
    but none to know me were;
All refuge failed me; no man
    did for my soul take care.
5 I cry'd to thee, I said, Thou art
    my refuge, Lord, alone;
And, in the land of those that live,
    thou art my portion.
6 Because I am brought very low,
    attend unto my cry:
Me from my persecutors save,
    who stronger are than I.
7 From prison bring my soul, that I
    thy name may glorify:
The just shall compass me, when thou
    with me deal'st bounteously.

PSALM CXLIII.
A Psalm of David.

David being in great trouble of mind, for the long continuance of his persecution by his enemies, and also under some exercise of conscience, thro' the sense of his sin, prayeth in this Psalm for deliverance in general, from the two-fold trouble, ver. 1, 2. and then he giveth two reasons of his prayer; the first is taken from the miserable condition, wherein the violence and oppression of the enemy hath driven him, ver 3, 4. The other is from his careful use of the means for finding grace, ver. 5, 6. Then he presseth his prayer in nine more special petitions in the rest of the Psalm.

1 Lord, hear my pray'r, attend my suits;
  and in thy faithfulness
Give thou an answer unto me,
  and in thy righteousness.

2 Thy servant also bring thou not
  in judgment to be try'd:
Because no living man can be
  in thy sight justify'd.

3 For th' en'my hath pursu'd my soul,
  my life to ground down tread:
In darkness he hath made me dwell,
  as who have long been dead.

4 My sp'rit is therefore overwhelm'd
  in me perplexedly:
Within me is my very heart
  amazed wond'rously.

5 I call to mind the days of old,
  to meditate I use
On all thy works: upon the deeds
  I of thy hands do muse.

6 My hands to thee I stretch; my soul
  thirsts as dry land for thee.

7 Haste, Lord, to hear, my spirit fails,
  hide not thy face from me;

Left like to them I do become
    that go down to the duft.
8 At morn let me thy kindnefs hear,
    for in thee do I truft:
  Teach me the way that I fhould walk;
    I lift my foul to thee.
9 Lord, free me from my foes: I flee
    to thee to cover me.
10 Becaufe thou art my God, to do
    thy will do me inftruct:
  Thy fp'rit is good, me to the land
    of uprightnefs conduct.
11 Revive and quicken me, O Lord,
    ev'n for thine own name's fake;
  And do thou, for thy righteoufnefs,
    my foul from trouble take.
12 And of thy mercy flay my foes;
    let all deftroyed be
  That do afflict my foul: for I
    a fervant am to thee.

Another of the fame.

1 OH, hear my pray'r, Lord,
    And unto my defire
  To bow thine ear accord,
    I humbly thee require:
  And, in thy faithfulnefs,
    Unto me anfwer make,
  And, in thy righteoufnefs,
    Upon me pity take.
2 In judgment enter not
    With me thy fervant poor:
  For why, this well I wot,
    No finner can endure

The fight of thee, O God,
If thou his deeds shalt try,
He dare make none abode
Himself to justify.

3 Behold, the cruel foe
Me persecutes with spite,
My soul to overthrow:
Yea, he my life down quite
Unto the ground hath smote:
And made me dwell full low
In darkness, as forgot,
Or men dead long ago.

4 Therefore, my sp'rit much vex'd,
O'erwhelm'd is me within:
My heart right sore perplex'd,
And desolate hath been.

5 Yet I do call to mind
What ancient days record;
Thy works of ev'ry kind
I think upon, O Lord.

6 Lo, I do stretch my hands
To thee my help alone,
For thou well understands
All my complaint and moan:
My thirsting soul desires,
And longeth after thee,
As thirsty ground requires
With rain refresh'd to be.

7 Lord, let my pray'r prevail,
To answer it make speed,
For lo, my sp'rit doth fail:
Hide not thy face in need,

Lest I be like to those
That do in darkness sit,
Or him that downward goes
Into the dreadful pit.
8 Because I trust in thee,
O Lord, cause me to hear
Thy loving-kindness free,
When morning doth appear:
Cause me to know the way
Wherein my path should be;
For why, my soul on high
I do lift up to thee.
9 From my fierce enemy,
In safety do me guide,
Because I flee to thee,
Lord, that thou may'st me hide.
10 My God alone art thou,
Teach me thy righteousness:
Thy sp'rit's good, lead me to
The land of uprightness.
11 O Lord, for thy name's sake,
Be pleas'd to quicken me:
And, for thy truth, forth take
My soul from misery.
12 And of thy grace destroy
My foes, and put to shame
All who my soul annoy:
For I thy servant am.

PSALM CXLIV.

A Psalm of David.

David being now King, but yet not fully settled on his throne, in this Psalm giveth thanks to God for the work already wrought, ver. 1, 2, 3, 4. and prayeth for compleating the deliverance, and settling of him in his kingdom, ver. 5, 6, 7, 8. And in hope to be heard, promiseth praise to God, ver. 9, 10. And in the last place, repeateth his petition, with reasons taken from the benefit which should redound unto the Lord's people, by settling of him in his kingdom, ver. 11, 12, 13 14.

1 O Blessed ever be the Lord,
 Who is my strength and might;
Who doth instruct my hands to war,
 my fingers teach to fight.

2 My goodness, fortress, my high tow'r,
 deliverer, and shield,
In whom I trust: who under me
 my people makes to yield.

3 Lord, what is man, that thou of him
 dost so much knowledge take?
Or son of man, that thou of him
 so great account dost make?

4 Man is like vanity: his days
 as shadows pass away.

5 Lord, bow thy heav'ns; come down; touch
 the hills, and smoke shall they. [thou

6 Cast forth thy light'nings; scatter them:
 thine arrows shoot; them rout.

7 Thine hand send from above, me save;
 from great depths draw me out;
And from the hand of children strange:

8 Whose mouth speaks vanity;
And their right hand is a right hand
 that works deceitfully.

9 A new song I to thee will sing,
 Lord, on a psaltery:
I on a ten-string'd instrument,
 will praises sing to thee.

10 Ev'n he it is, that unto Kings
   salvation doth send:
 Who his own servant David doth
   from hurtful sword defend.
11 O free me from strange children's hand,
   whose mouth speaks vanity;
 And their right hand a right hand is
   that works deceitfully.
12 That as the plants our sons may be
   in youth grown up that are;
 Our daughters like to corner-stones,
   carv'd like a palace fair.
13 That to afford all kind of store,
   our garners may be fill'd:
 That our sheep thousands, in our streets
   ten thousands they may yield:
14 That strong our oxen be for work,
   that no in-breaking be,
 Nor going out; and that our streets
   may from complaints be free.
15 Those people blessed are, who be
   in such a case as this:
 Yea, blessed all those people are,
   whose God JEHOVAH is.

PSALM CXLV.

David's Psalm of Praise.

This Psalm is altogether of praises, every verse beginning with a several lette. of the Hebrew, A, B, C. from the first to the last; wherein David engageth himself unto the work of praising of God twice. In the former part of the Psalm once, ver. 1, 2. and of this he giveth a reason, and prophesieth that the praises of the Lord shall be perpetuated throughout all ages, ver. 3, 4. Then he engageth himself the second time, and prophesies of the Church's holding up this song, ver. 5, 6, 7. And from the eighth verse, he praiseth

God more particularly, giving ten arguments of praise unto the last verse; and closeth the Psalm with engaging of himself anew again, and exhortation of others to follow the song for ever.

1 I'LL thee extol, my God, O King,
    I'll bless thy name always.
2 Thee will I bless each day, and will
    thy name for ever praise.
3 Great is the Lord, much to be prais'd,
    his greatness search exceeds.
4 Race unto race shall praise thy works,
    and show thy mighty deeds.

5 I of thy glorious Majesty
    the honour will record;
  I'll speak of all thy mighty works
    which wond'rous are, O Lord.
6 Men of thine acts the might shall show,
    thine acts that dreadful are;
  And I, thy glory to advance,
    thy greatness will declare.

7 The mem'ry of thy goodness great
    they largely shall express;
  With songs of praise they shall extol
    thy perfect righteousness.
8 The Lord is very gracious,
    in him compassions flow;
  In mercy he is very great,
    and is to anger slow.

9 The Lord JEHOVAH unto all
    his goodness doth declare;
  And over all his other works
    his tender mercies are.

10 Thee all thy works shall praise, O Lord,
    and thee thy Saints shall bless.
11 They shall thy kingdom's glory show,
    thy pow'r by speech express.
12 To make the sons of men to know
    his acts done mightily,
  And of his kingdom th' excellent
    and glorious majesty.
13 Thy kingdom shall for ever stand,
    thy reign through ages all.
14 God raiseth all that are bow'd down,
    upholdeth all that fall.
15 The eyes of all things wait on thee,
    the giver of all good;
  And thou, in time convenient,
    bestows on them their food.
16 Thine hand thou op'nest lib'rally,
    and of thy bounty gives
  Enough to satisfy the need
    of ev'ry thing that lives.
17 The Lord is just in all his ways,
    holy in his works all.
18 God's near to all that call on him,
    in truth that on him call.
19 He will accomplish the desire
    of those that do him fear:
  He also will deliver them,
    and he their cry will hear.
20 The Lord preserves all who him love,
    that nought can them annoy;
  But he all those that wicked are
    will utterly destroy.

21 My mouth the praises of the Lord,
    to publish cease shall never:
  Let all flesh bless his holy name
    for ever and for ever.

Another of the same.

1 O Lord, thou art my God and King,
    Thee will I magnify and praise:
  I will thee bless, and gladly sing
    Unto thy holy name always.
2 Each day I rise, I will thee bless,
  And praise thy name time without end.
3 Much to be prais'd, and great God is,
  His greatness none can comprehend.
4 Race shall thy works praise unto race,
  The mighty acts show done by thee.
5 I will speak of the glorious grace,
  And honour of thy Majesty:
  Thy wond'rous works I will record.
6 By men the might shall be extol'd,
  Of all thy dreadful acts, O Lord:
  And I thy greatness will unfold.
7 They utter shall abundantly,
  The mem'ry of thy goodness great,
  And shall sing praises chearfully
  Whilst they thy righteousness relate.
  8 The Lord our God is gracious,
  Compassionate is he also;
  In mercy he is plenteous,
  But unto wrath and anger flow.
  9 Good unto all men is the Lord:
  O'er all his works his mercy is.
10 Thy works all praise to thee afford;
  Thy Saints, O Lord, thy name shall bless.

11 The glory of thy kingdom shew
  Shall they, and of thy pow'r tell.
12 That so mens' sons his deeds may know,
  His kingdom's grace that doth excel.
13 Thy kingdom hath none end at all,
  It doth through ages all remain.
14 The Lord upholdeth all that fall,
  The cast-down raiseth up again.
15 The eyes of all things, Lord, attend,
  And on thee wait, that here do live :
  And thou in season due dost send
  Sufficient food them to relieve.
16 Yea, thou thine hand dost open wide,
  And ev'ry thing dost satisfy
  That lives, and doth on earth abide,
  Of thy great liberality.
17 The Lord is just in his ways all,
  And holy in his works each one.
18 He's near to all that on him call,
  Who call in truth on him alone.
19 God will the just desire fulfil
  Of such as do him fear and dread :
  Their cry regard, and hear he will,
  And save them in the time of need.
20 The Lord preserves all, more and less,
  That bear to him a loving heart :
  But workers all of wickedness
  Destroy will he, and clean subvert.
21 Therefore my mouth and lips I'll frame
  To speak the praises of the Lord :
  To magnify his holy name
  For ever let all flesh accord.

PSALM CXLVI.

This Psalm is a Psalm of praise wholly, wherein, when the Psalmist hath exhorted all men to praise the Lord, he engageth himself to the work, ver. 1, 2. Then he teacheth the way how to praise God in effect, to wit, by renouncing all carnal confidence, and trusting only in the Lord, ver. 3, 4, 5. Thirdly, he giveth ten reasons, both of trusting in God, and praising of God. The first and second reasons are, ver. 6. The third, fourth and fifth are, ver. 7. The sixth, seventh and eighth are, ver. 8. The ninth is, ver. 9. The tenth is, ver. 10. and closeth as he began, with the same exhortation to praise God.

1 PRAISE God. The Lord praise, O my
2 I'll praise God while I live; [soul.
   While I have being, to my God
     in songs I'll praises give.
3 Trust not in princes, nor man's son,
     in whom there is no stay.
4 His breath departs, to's earth he turns:
     that day his thoughts decay.

5 O happy is that man, and blest,
     whom Jacob's God doth aid;
   Whose hope upon the Lord doth rest,
     and on his God is stay'd:
6 Who made the earth, and heav'ns high,
     who made the swelling deep,
   And all that is within the same:
     who truth doth ever keep:
7 Who righteous judgment executes
     for those opprest that be,
   Who to the hungry giveth food:
     God sets the pris'ners free.
8 The Lord doth give the blind their sight,
     the bowed down doth raise:
   The Lord doth dearly love all those
     that walk in upright ways.

9 The stranger's shield, the widow's stay,
   the orphan's help is he:
But yet by him the wicked's way
   turn'd upside down shall be.
10 The Lord shall reign for evermore;
   thy God, O Sion, he
Reigns to all generations.
   Praise to the Lord give ye.

PSALM CXLVII.

This Psalm is for stirring up of the Church to praise and thanksgiving. The exhortation is threefold. The first is, ver. 1. and six reasons for it, or motives unto it are set down, ver. 2, 3, 4, 5, 6. The second exhortation is, ver. 7. and three reasons for it, ver. 8, 9, 10, 11. The third is, ver. 12. and six reasons for it, unto the end.

1 PRAISE ye the Lord: for it is good
      praise to our God to sing:
   For it is pleasant, and to praise
      it is a comely thing.
2 God doth build up Jerusalem:
      and he it is alone
   That the dispers'd of Israel
      doth gather into one.
3 Those that are broken in their hearts,
      and grieved in their minds,
   He healeth, and their painful wounds
      he tenderly upbinds.
4 He counts the number of the stars:
      he names them ev'ry one.
5 Great is our Lord, and of great pow'r:
      his wisdom search can none.
6 The Lord lifts up the meek: and casts
      the wicked to the ground.
7 Sing to the Lord, and give him thanks,
      on harp his praises sound.

8 Who covereth the heav'n with clouds,
    who for the earth below
  Prepareth rain, who maketh grafs
    upon the mountains grow.
9 He gives the beaſt his food, he feeds
    the ravens young that cry.
10 His pleaſure not in horſe's ſtrength,
    nor in man's legs, doth lie.
11 But in all thoſe that do him fear,
    the Lord doth pleaſure take,
  In thoſe that to his mercy do
    by hope themſelves betake.
12 The Lord praiſe, O Jeruſalem:
    Sion, thy God confeſs.
13 For thy gates' bars he maketh ſtrong:
    thy ſons in thee doth bleſs.
14 He in thy borders maketh peace,
    with fine wheat filleth thee.
15 He ſends forth his command on earth:
    his word runs ſpeedily.
16 Hoar froſt, like aſhes, ſcatt'reth he:
    like wool he ſnow doth give.
17 Like morſels caſteth forth his ice:
    who in its cold can live?
18 He ſendeth forth his mighty word,
    and melteth them again:
  His wind he makes to blow, and then
    the waters flow amain.
19 The doctrine of his holy word
    to Jacob he doth ſhow;
  His ſtatutes and his judgments he
    gives Iſrael to know.

20 To any nation never he
    such favour did afford :
For they his judgments have not known.
    O do ye praise the Lord.

PSALM CXLVIII.

In this Psalm, the Church is stirred up to praise God, because of the incomparable excellency of his glory and Majesty, appearing first in the Heavens above, ver. 1, 2, 3, 4, 5, 6. Secondly, in the earth and sea beneath, and lower parts under the Heaven, ver. 7, 8, 9, 10. Thirdly, in the governing of men, and of all sorts and ranks of men, but especially in doing for his Church, ver. 11, 12, 13, 14. In all which, as he sheweth how the world is full of God's glory, so he pointeth at it as a matter of his praise, whithersoever we turn our eyes.

1 PRAISE God. From heavens praise the
    in heights praise to him be.   [Lord,
2 All ye his angels, praise ye him :
    his hosts all, praise him ye.
3 O praise ye him, both sun and moon ;
    praise him, all stars of light.
4 Ye heav'ns of heav'ns him praise, and
    above the heav'ns height.   [floods

5 Let all the creatures praise the name
    of our almighty Lord :
For he commanded, and they were
    created by his word.
6 He also for all times to come,
    hath them establish'd sure :
He hath appointed them a law,
    which ever shall endure.

7 Praise ye JEHOVAH from the earth,
    dragons, and ev'ry deep.
8 Fire, hail, snow, vapour, stormy wind,
    his word that fully keep.

9 All hills and mountains, fruitful trees,
    and all ye cedars high.
10 Beasts, and all cattle, creeping things,
    and all ye birds that fly.
11 Kings of the earth, all nations,
    princes, earth's judges all:
12 Both young men, yea, and maidens too,
    old men, and children small.
13 Let them God's name praise; for his
    alone is excellent: [name
His glory reacheth far above
    the earth and firmament.
14 His people's horn, the praise of all
    his Saints exalteth he;
Ev'n Isra'l's seed, a people near
    to him. The Lord praise ye.

Another of the same.

1 THE Lord of heav'n confess,
    On high his glory raise.
2 Him let all angels bless,
  Him all his armies praise.
3   Him glorify
    Sun, moon, and stars;
4   Ye higher spheres,
    And cloudy sky.
5 From God your beings are,
  Him therefore famous make:
  You all created were,
  When he the word but spake.
6   And from that place,
    Where fix'd you be
    By his decree,
    You cannot pass.

7 Praise God from earth below,
   Ye dragons, and ye deeps:
8 Fire, hail, clouds, wind, and snow,
  Whom in command he keeps.
9   Praise ye his name,
    Hills great and small,
    Trees low and tall:
10   Beasts wild and tame,
  All things that creep or fly.
11 Ye kings, ye vulgar throng,
  All princes mean or high,
12 Both men and virgins young.
    Ev'n young and old
13   Exalt his name:
    For much his fame
    Should be extoll'd.

  O let God's name be prais'd
  Above both earth and sky:
14 For he his Saints hath rais'd,
  And set their horn on high;
    Ev'n those that be
    Of Isra'l's race,
    Near to his grace,
    The Lord praise ye.

PSALM CXLIX.

The foregoing Psalm was a hymn of praise to the Creator; this to the Redeemer. It is a psalm of triumph in the God of Israel, and over the enemies of Israel. Probably it was penned upon occasion of some victory which Israel was blessed and honoured with. Some conjecture that it was penned when David had taken the strong hold of Zion, and settled his government there; but it looks further to the kingdom of the Messiah, who, in the chariot of the everlasting Gospel, goes forth conquering and to conquer. To him, and his graces and glories, we must have an eye in singing this psalm, which speaks, (1) Abundance of joy to all the people of God, ver. 1, 5 (2) Abundance of terror to the proudest of their enemies, ver. 6, 9.

1 PRAISE ye the Lord: unto him sing
    a new song, and his praise
In the assembly of his Saints
    in sweet psalms do ye raise.

2 Let Isra'l in his Maker joy,
    and to him praises sing:
Let all that Sion's children are,
    be joyful in their king.

3 O let them unto his great Name
    give praises in the dance:
Let them, with timbrel and with harp,
    in songs his praise advance.

4 For God doth pleasure take in those
    that his own people be:
And he, with his salvation,
    the meek will beautify.

5 And in his glory excellent,
    let all his Saints rejoice:
Let them, to him, upon their beds,
    aloud lift up their voice.

6 Let, in their mouth aloft, be rais'd
    the high praise of the Lord;
And let them have in their right hand,
    a sharp two-edged sword:

7 To execute the vengeance due
    upon the heathen all,
And make deserved punishment
    upon the people fall:

8 And ev'n with chains, as pris'ners, bind
  their kings that them command;
Yea, and with iron fetters strong,
  the nobles of their land.

9 On them the judgement to perform
  found written in his word:
This honour is to all his Saints:
  O, do ye praise the Lord.

PSALM CL.

The first and last of the Psalms have both the same number of verses, are both short, and very memorable; but the scope of hem is very different. The first psalm is an elaborate instruction in our duty, to prepare us for the comforts of devotion; this is all rapture and transport, and perhaps was penned on purpose to be the conclusion of those sacred songs, to shew what is the design of them all, and that is, to assist us in praising God. The Psalmist had been himself full of the praises of God, and here he would fain fill all the world with them; again and again he calls, "praise the Lord, praise him, praise him," no less than 13 times in these six short verses! — He shews, (1) For what, and upon what account God is to be praised, ver. 1, 2. (2) How, and with what expressions of joy God is to be praised, ver. 3, 4, 5. (3) Who must praise the Lord; it is every one's business, ver. 6. — In singing this psalm, we should endeavour to get our hearts much affected with the perfections of God, and the praises with which he is, and shall be, for ever attended throughout all ages, world without end.

1 PRAISE ye the Lord. God's praise
    his sanctuary raise: [within
  And to him in the firmament
    of his pow'r give ye praise.

2 Becaufe of all his mighty acts,
    with praife him magnify:
  O praife him, as he doth excel
    in glorious majefty.
3 Praife him with trumpets' found: his praife
    with pfaltery advance.
4 With timbrel, harp, ftring'd inftrnments,
    and organs, in the dance
5 Praife him on cymba's loud, him praife
    on cymbals founding high.
6 Let each thing breathing praife the Lord:
    praife to the Lord give ye.

FINIS.

www.ingramcontent.com/pod-product-compliance
Lightning Source LLC
Chambersburg PA
CBHW031853220426
43663CB00006B/611